DOWN UNDER DREAMING:

TRAVELS IN AUSTRALIA

© Terry Marsh 2017
All rights reserved

ISBN: 978 1521010068

Cover picture: Photograph of Aboriginal painting by unknown artist, Darwin railway station, Northern Territory (© Terry Marsh)

CONTENTS

CHAPTER ONE:
Is this place weird...or simply wonderful?................................. 4

CHAPTER TWO:
In the beginning and afterwards................................. 12

CHAPTER THREE:
Things that go bite in the night and other beasties................................. 24

CHAPTER FOUR
Perth and some of the west coast................................. 34

CHAPTER FIVE
Sydney................................. 70

CHAPTER SIX
Canberra................................. 86

CHAPTER SEVEN
Adelaide and the Great Ocean Road................................. 107

CHAPTER EIGHT
Melbourne................................. 121

CHAPTER NINE
Tasmania................................. 136

CHAPTER TEN
Queensland................................. 171

CHAPTER ELEVEN
The Red Centre................................. 189

CHAPTER TWELVE
The north................................. 227

APPENDIX
A few words of Aussie slang................................. 241

CHAPTER ONE

IS THIS PLACE WEIRD...OR SIMPLY WONDERFUL?

Australia: the only place where Christ could never have been born because you can't find three wise men and a virgin. Anon

It's not often you turn up in a place you have avoided most of your life, but here I am coming in to land at Perth in Western Australia, following the longest flight I've ever made.

Come to think of it, I can't in all honesty say that I'd 'avoided' Australia, I just hadn't given the country much thought, not since my wife and I failed to follow through our investigation into the ten quid emigration deal back in 1968 - a political ploy that showed how adept the British government was at planning ahead by getting rid of people to Australia, especially now that it could no longer rely on convict transportation.

In fact, I'd given the country little or no thought at all, apart from the usual half-hearted protests of foul play whenever Australia won the Ashes, or an expression of mild but disaffected concern as British news reporting covered major bush fires or Aboriginal unrest. It was, quite simply, too far for regular holidays, and that ten quid had risen a fair bit, and then some. But the fact is that while the majority of flights from the UK to Australia, by whatever route, are often full, suggesting a healthy tourist trade if nothing else - Qantas have now introduced non-stop flights from London - daily life in the UK is generally too pre-occupied to pay much attention to what might be happening to our distant cousins 'Down Under'.

Do you know who the current prime minister of Australia is? In the time that it's taken to write this book, they've had five.

It's 1998, and I'm standing in line with a few hundred other weary long-distance fliers waiting to get in. I may even be suffering from deep-veined thrombosis, but I don't think it's been invented yet.

'Good eye.'

I'm not sure if it was some retinal scanning form of greeting peculiar to Australia, or some devious form of questioning intended to put me off my guard, but the immigration officer is appraising me in a way that sends a chill down my spine. His pale blue eyes - there were two, not just the one - search deep into mine as if trying to read my deepest thoughts. How can he know that 'deep' is not an adjective that best describes my thinking? Superficial; banal; incoherent; rambling, occasionally alcohol-induced - Yes. But not deep. Nope; my deepest thoughts are lying on the surface for all to see; it saves time trying to understand me.

A hand the size of a spade hovers menacingly close to a large red alarm button on the desk; the other reaches out and swallows my passport as if by sleight of hand. Does he know something I don't? Have I come all this way just to be sent back, humiliated? - 'Visa cancelled' stamped in my passport?

Do I look like someone with a secret compartment in their case concealing child pornography, drugs, an illegal immigrant, or something equally offensive - like an anthology of the sermons of the late Ian Paisley, or a CD of the 'Greatest Hits of the Singing Nun'?

What does someone with a secret compartment in their case look like, anyway?

Me, I guess.

Or you.

'Is this your first time in Australia?'

'Yeah.'

'Staying long?'
'About seven weeks.'
'Where're you planning on going?'
'Oh, looking round Western Australia, then heading for Sydney. Haven't decided after that.'

His face breaks into a massive grin as he stamps my passport with the large red button.

'Have a great time. Welcome to Australia.'

And I did have a great time, until I reached the queue for quarantine thirty seconds later, and ran afoul of a quarantine officer because I hadn't declared a packet of mints! Ho hum. Since then they've run endless repeats of 'Nothing to Declare' on British TV. If they'd started a few years earlier, I would have known that just about everything is prohibited.

Anyway...what was the question?

Is this place weird...or simply wonderful?

I must say at the outset that for me, it's both, which is why I've now been back numerous times, and on each visit finding endless reasons to make the stay last longer. On more than one visit I held to a simple guideline: I came home at the end of my money. There is something heart-warming about knowing that you've maxed-out all your credit cards, and couldn't have done any more without sowing the seeds of fiscal discontent for future harvesting.

What follows is a recounting of those experiences, in that memorable phrase: 'In no particular order'. Here are tales of kangaroos, potoroos, Tassie tigers, convicts, complicated time zones, a lost prime minister, outlaws, brave hearts, Aussie slang, and so much more.

For me, the sad thing is that although I've visited vast areas of Australia, I've yet to get to Kimberley, and the Bungle Bungles, and I'm now getting too old to withstand such a long flight. But, you never know.

The Kimberley plateau covers the top left bit of Australia, a rugged, wild and largely untouched region of plains and tidal rivers, mountains and dramatic, lush vegetated gorges, and all as far away from the major population centres as it could be. Moreover, there is just one sealed road, the Great Northern Highway, connecting Broome in the west with Kununurra in the east. But maybe little choice is a good thing.

That choice is further reduced by what the Australians call the 'Wet Season', also called the monsoon season. It lasts about six months, between November and March, and is hotter than the dry season, with temperatures between 30° and 50° Celsius. This is because of the high humidity during the wet, which is caused by large amounts of water in the air. During the wet there is a lot of rain, which frequently causes flooding. And that flooding means that whole areas, including parts of the Great Northern Highway, are under water, leaving visitors stranded for days at a time, if not longer. 'Be prepared' is very much the motto here.

The fact is, however, until you go and see for yourself, Australia is an enigma. Most of it is empty, its population for the most part clinging tenaciously to the edges and rarely more than 10 kilometres from it. In April 2017, this was estimated to be more than 24.4 million, a projection based on the estimated resident population at 30 June 2014 and assuming growth since then of one birth every 1 minute and 40 seconds; one death every 3 minutes and 18 seconds; a net gain of one international migration every 2 minutes and 18 seconds, leading to an overall total population increase of one person every 1 minute and 22 seconds, or 740 persons per day. If you look at the website for the Australian Bureau of Statistics (www.abs.gov.au), you can watch the population rise in accordance with that projection. In the time, it's taken me to write this, the population has risen by a net 4.

On the world population scale, Australia currently ranks 53rd (but gaining quickly on Madagascar), compared with the UK (21st,

65.1 million), the United States (324 million, 3rd) and China (1382 million, 1st). Yet by area, Australia (7.7million sq km/2.9 million sq miles) is the sixth largest country in the world, the largest in Oceania, the largest country in the world without a land border, the largest country wholly in the Southern Hemisphere and the only country that is coterminous with a continent, although this often results in heated debates among geographers about what is a continent. When I went to school, the continents were North America, South America, Africa, Europe, Asia, Antarctica, and Australia. But then, when I was at school, Pluto was still a planet. Anyway, you could fit the UK into Australia about 31 times over and still have space left over for a decent-sized town; yet Australia has only about one-third of the UK population.

So, roomy, then.

So roomy, in fact, that it crosses three time zones. You can take the 8am flight from Perth to Sydney, and arrive not in time for lunch four hours later, as you might expect, but in time for afternoon tea. So, you've flown for four hours, but you've aged seven; thankfully, when you fly back, you get back to Perth more youthful than when you left Sydney…somehow, they've contrived to shrink that four-hour flight to just one hour.

And, being a bit academic, I can't help advancing the thesis that if, as I have just demonstrated, by flying west you become younger, then by continuing to fly west you become ever and ever younger, and never die…except from boredom with in-flight movies.

Who says you can't time travel? But there is a flaw in that thesis; you figure it out.

But, back on theme, here is where it gets complicated because while, in general, Australia uses just three time zones - Australian Western Standard Time (AWST; UTC+08:00), Australian Central Standard Time (ACST; UTC+09:30), and Australian Eastern Standard Time (AEST; UTC+10:00) - time is regulated by the individual state governments, only some of which observe daylight saving time – South Australia, New South Wales, Victoria, Tasmania, and the Australian Capital Territory (ACT). Daylight saving time is not currently used in Western Australia, Queensland, or in the Northern Territory. Now if that seems confusing, imagine the situation before the switch to standard time zones, when each local city or town was free to determine its local time, called local mean time. Furthermore, imagine the problems facing a police officer investigating officer trying to determine where a suspect was at any given time.

Should you want to visit the legendary mining town of Broken Hill in far western New South Wales, you need to allow for the fact that Broken Hill unlike the rest of New South Wales, observes Australian Central Standard Time (UTC+9:30) a time zone it shares with South Australia and the Northern Territory. Throw daylight saving time into the equation and you get a slightly bizarre situation when the Northern Territory, immediately to the east of Western Australia is 1½ hours ahead, while Southern Australia, also to the east of Western Australia but due south of the Northern Territory is 2½ hours ahead yet only an hour ahead of the Northern Territory with which it is longitudinally parallel. Queensland in the east of Australia is just 2 hours ahead of Western Australia, but half an hour behind South Australia which is almost wholly to the west. And immediately due south of Queensland, New South Wales, Victoria and Tasmania are a further hour ahead of Queensland, but only half an hour ahead of South Australia, and three hours ahead of Western Australia.

To make matters worse, a compromise between Western and Central time (UTC+8:45, without DST), known as Central Western Standard Time, is used in just one area in the south-eastern corner of Western Australia and a solitary roadhouse in South Australia. Towns east of Caiguna on the Eyre Highway (including Border Village, just over the border into South Australia), follow Central Western Standard Time instead of Western Australian time. But,

I suppose, that doesn't matter, because CWST is not officially recognised.

Add to that the fact that the Indian Pacific train, which crosses Australia between Sydney and Perth has its own time zone - a so-called 'train time', but only when travelling between Kalgoorlie, Western Australia and Port Augusta, South Australia, east of Port Augusta it...I give up!

When I first visited Australia, I had only the key essentials of a plan - fly, land, eat, sleep. After that it was free range. Well, okay, I admit I did have other flights pre-booked that would whisk me to Sydney, Cairns and Darwin at some point. But in between it was a case of going where the wind blew me, or the vacuum of curiosity pulled me.

On that first visit, the common denominator was not to incur expenditure beyond the barest minimum, and that meant sleeping in some rather seedy backpacker hostels. I'm not going to pussyfoot; they were grim. Subsequently I've side-lined my fetish for unmade beds damp with the diverse bodily residues of last night's occupants, and opted for hotels - with air conditioning and bar room occupants that don't look as if they belong on another planet. But, I hasten to add, since then, many of the backpacker hostels have seriously improved their game: they now have mixed gender dorms, as I discovered when I overheard two young ladies asking for a room occupied by a couple of hunks...like they might be ordering a Big Mac, which, come to think of it, they may have been.

It certainly puts a new slant on 'Room service'.

Aeons after the Aboriginal people first arrived, Australia became a country that offered a bright new life, prosperity, healthy living and a comfortable wackiness with which everyone is at ease, and much in demand. So much so that in the mid-1960s, Australian athlete Reg Spiers finding himself stranded in London with no money and needing to buy a plane ticket back to Australia in time for his daughter's birthday, decided to post himself in a wooden crate. He succeeded, too, and made it to his daughter's birthday party. But then, with all the twists and turns you come to associate with the Aussie way of life, Reg Spiers disappeared from Adelaide in 1981 after he was charged with conspiracy to import cocaine. He was arrested in Sri Lanka in 1984 and sentenced to death for drugs offences, successfully appealed against the sentence but then spent five years in jail in Australia.

CHAPTER TWO

IN THE BEGINNING AND AFTERWARDS

An ancient place

Australia is old: it's about 40 million years since it broke off from Antarctica, give or take 20 million years, arguably the oldest continent in the world, and for most of that time it was stunningly, eerily silent. Nothing happened for millions of years; landscapes, rocks, fossils all remained untouched, unmoved and, as a result, today provide a fantastic record of Earth's early geology. It was the last continent to be settled.

Long before the arrival of humans in Europe, evidence of a quiet race of people, Aboriginals, begins to appear, a presence that can be explained only by recognising that they had somehow mastered the seas anything up to 45,000 years before anyone else... or they were aliens transported from some distant galaxy, although I think this must be side-lined as a plausible thesis. Then, having reached this new land, these erstwhile skilled - or very fortunate - mariners promptly ignored everything they knew about the sea and became part of the land.

This was their Dreamtime, when the Ancestors sang the world into existence. It heralded an outstandingly long period of habitation that is scarcely understood by modern historians, and even less frequently studied.

In his remarkable and satisfying book *The Songlines*, Bruce Chatwin explains that the Aboriginal people had '...an earthbound philosophy. The earth gave life to a man; gave him his food, language and intelligence; and the earth took him back when he died. A man's "own country", even an empty stretch of spinifex, was itself a sacred ikon (sic) that must remain unscarred.' Aboriginal Creation myths parallel the first two books of Christian Genesis (with a slight difference), and tell of totemic beings who wandered the continent in a period known to them as 'Dreamtime', singing out the name of everything they encountered – birds, plants, rock features, animals, waterholes – in essence, singing the world into existence, leaving a trail of words and musical notes along the line of his footprints; the paths they followed, the Aboriginals knew as the 'Footprints of the Ancestors', and Europeans came to call them 'Songlines'.

This is all rather esoteric, so it's not surprising that contemporary histories of Australia dwell on the chance, i.e. storm-blown, arrival, from a time spent surveying New Zealand, of Captain James Cook and his Ship HMS Endeavour in Botany Bay in 1770.

On a Point of Order, it's worth mentioning that at the time Cook was a Lieutenant, not a Captain, and that the first undisputed sighting of Australia by European explorers was in 1606, by a Dutch explorer named Willem Janszoon. In 1642, another Dutchman, Abel Tasman, sailed right round Australia and landed on the coast of Van Diemen's Land, which today we know as Tasmania. An English, Somerset-born explorer, William Dampier, landed on the north-western coast of Australia and spent three months of 1688 near King Sound. On another visit, he sailed from England in January 1699 in HMS Roebuck and on 6 August anchored at the entrance to the inlet he named Shark Bay. In his memoirs, he described the country as '...sandy and waterless, the natives the miserablest people in the world'. If you visit Shark Bay, you'll understand how he might arrive at this view.

Yet, even those accounts are in contention. In his book, *The Secret Discovery of Australia: Portuguese Ventures 200 Years before Captain Cook*, Kenneth Gordon McIntyre, an Australian lawyer, shows that

Australia was actually discovered and its coastline mapped by the Portuguese 200 years before Cook and 100 years before the Dutch. Not to be outdone, some of the evidence presented in this book for the Portuguese discovery of Australia has been used more recently by Gavin Menzies in *1421: The Year China Discovered the World* to support his argument that the Chinese discovered Australia prior to the Portuguese.

What they all seem to overlook is that the Aboriginals were there first...singing Songlines and inventing walkabout. And you must admire them. Just imagine – and given the way exploration of the world has developed since the Aboriginal people first arrived, imagine is all we can do these days – here they stood, arriving after what may well have been a perilous sea crossing, possibly from Indonesia, and stepping ashore on the coast of Arnhem Land or northern Queensland – no eagerly waiting family and friends waving silk handkerchiefs of welcome, no border control, no sniffer dogs checking for drugs, no quarantine officers waiting to riffle through your undies for an illicit apple or other prohibited fruit... just a huge, endless expanse of raw, virgin terrain, and whatever you brought with you, which was probably just a few spears and your birthday suit, no doubt in need of ironing by now.

'Hey, guys, this looks...yeah, ridgy didge desert; let's go, er... that way [Points to distant mountain on far horizon]. Let's all start dreaming. On the count of three...'.

I find it daunting enough just to launch myself into a French town centre market: setting out tens of thousands of years ago into the real unknown, no maps, no compass, just not knowing... anything...about it...well, respect, I say.

Regardless of who did what and when, Cook, son of a Scottish farm labourer, reported that a self-supporting settlement could be established in Australia. He'd only seen bits of the east coast, but he was in His Britannic Majesty's Royal Navy, so that gave him enough clout to convince everyone back home that he knew what he was talking about, although his gravitas didn't pull many punches when he later returned to Hawaii.

His evaluation of Australia coincided with a time when the British government were enthusiastically decanting convicts and settlers to America, which was fine, until the American Revolution compelled the government to turn their eyes elsewhere. They alighted on the Great South Land, Terra Australis.

On the 26th day of January 1788, having survived the vicissitudes and traumas of the sea journey, a fleet of eleven ships arrived off the coast of Australia, at the head of a deep-water bay, later named after the man in charge of colonial affairs, Lord Sydney. They carried 1,030 people, including 548 males and 188 female convicts. In the intervening years, since Cook's visit there had been nothing; no reconnaissance, no further exploration, just the largely silent immensity of heat, tropical forests, bush, sandstone and the constant crashing of Pacific waves.

Now, as Robert Hughes explains at the start of *The Fatal Shore*, came a new colonial experiment, founded on virtually complete ignorance of the land it was to occupy, and as far away from its parent state as might be imagined. This unexplored, unknown continent was to become a jail, with oceanic walls thousands of miles thick. Back in Britain, the madness that was, some say, King George III, still had thirty-two years to rule, through a period that abounded in schemes of social goodness that sought the wonders of Utopia. But for no fewer than 160,000 men, women and children, some innocent, some not, this was Dystopia, a place of exile, enchainment, deracination, and anything but imaginary. It represented the British government's hope to defend its country from the criminal classes, by removing them, and forgetting about them. It was the largest forced exile of citizens in pre-modern history.

A small colony was set up, but was dogged by bad luck as food supplies were lost at sea, while in contrast a steady flow of ships carrying convicts successfully completed the journey. To be fair, most these 'convicts' would today scarcely be brought to court; their offences were often petty - stealing a loaf of bread, poaching fish, or simply being in debt. Many of these earliest convicts went on to earn their freedom, and, since the British government had not seen fit to give them a return ticket, they settled in this new land, and became the founding fathers of the country, supplemented by shiploads of free immigrants who started to arrive from 1793, but in greater numbers from the early 1820s. To encourage emigration, the British government offered grants of land on condition that they took convicts to work for them, and were awarded 100 acres of land for every convict they accepted responsibility for.

First footfall

Before moving on from this introductory chapter, I'm drawn back to something my mind won't surrender - a bit like a dog with a bone. To make matters worse, it's something the nuances, complexities and implications of which I'm having trouble getting my head round, namely the subject of Man's first footfall on what even now is a strange and largely barren land.

In his *A Short History of Australia*, Manning Clarke writes 'Australia was probably first colonized by Homo sapiens, as distinct from his antecedents, during the last ice age'. He goes on to add that '...carbon tests have established the presence of...man on the mainland of Australia at least fifty thousand years ago'. And that's about it, so far as the Aboriginals are concerned. I accept the need for brevity in a 'short' history, but, come on. A few pages later, covering the arrival of Europeans he writes 'The Europeans offered the Aborigines the precious gift of their civilization in return for the right to use the wealth of their land'.

My jaw dropped when I first read that. How monumentally patronising. Firstly, the conceit that underpins the notion that

European civilisation was de rigueur, indispensable, crucial to survival, the only way. Secondly, that the Aboriginal people had no civilisation of their own. But even more importantly, if you hover over the words, those first settlers must have recognised that the '...wealth of their land', if it belonged to anyone, 'Belonga the Aboriginal people' in the first place. In *Down Home*, Peter Conrad underlines what I've come to understand is a primary Aboriginal concept, when he writes 'People are owned by their landscape, which outlasts them'. Aboriginal people, understanding their land from childhood, knew and respected it; it was their raison d'être, the source of their beliefs, their spirituality and their strength.

Aboriginal culture must rank as one of the world's most ancient. Their cave art pre-dates that at Lascaux in the Dordogne of France by almost 20,000 years; evidence suggests that they had developed burial practices based on some elemental form of religious belief more than 10,000 years earlier than in the western world, and they knew how to resolve the complexities of aerodynamics: just think about what you would have to do to a slender piece of wood to be able to throw it away and for it to come back to you...without the aid of a dog.

Now I have virtually no understanding of the many strata of issues that layer the subject of territorial conflict, and somewhat less when it comes to the profound issue of the Aboriginal people of Australia. But I just can't bring myself to comprehend the justice in arriving in a new land, seeing it occupied by what are evidently human beings, and then ignoring them, saying 'Right, we'll have this; you don't matter'. The Vikings did it in Britain; the British did it in America; the Brits and other Europeans did it in Australia. The Romans tried it on, too. But that's no excuse for perpetuating the technique.

But that isn't the fundamental issue over which I'm troubled. It's this: how did the Aboriginal people get here in the first place? This, I've found, is a question that seems to be either ignored or glossed over. In 2015, I visited the newest museum in Lyon, France, the Musée des Confluences. It purports, at a simplistic level, to portray the history of everything, a story of our origins. And while much relates to the importance of the Aboriginal people of Australia, which I found gratifying, no mention is made of how they got there; it's as if this either isn't important, or falls into the pending tray labelled 'TBD' – Too Bloody Difficult.

But think about it.

At no time, so the geologists tell us, within the timescale of Man, has Australia been anything other than an island. So, they could not have walked there. Wherever they came from, they couldn't see Australia; Cape Yorke, the northernmost point of Australia is some 150 kilometres (94 miles) from Papua New Guinea. At no time has Australia been occupied by the sort of ape-like creatures from which Man evolved. So, Man could not have evolved independently, as elsewhere in the world.

The only remaining possibility, given that Qantas hasn't been in operation quite that long, is that they came by sea. But, and here's the point, they must have come in sufficient numbers, and stayed for long enough, to colonise the country…make babies, wait for them to grow to hunting stature, make babies of their own. And, unless the first people were hermaphroditic, there must also have been women in the party.

Now, why would that be?

Why would a group of people, male and female, be out on the open seas in one or more sea-going vessels, heading south to a land they couldn't know existed? Moreover, if this is what they did, anything up to fifty thousand years ago, it occurred thousands of years before the so-called civilised people of Europe figured out how to do it. Admittedly, some of the European explorers went off not quite sure that they wouldn't fall of the edge of the world. But would prehistoric man have such a basic understanding? – that what they stood on was a world, and that it might have an edge.

And, if so, why did they set sail towards it?

Academics have demonstrated that as few as twenty-five people could produce a population of 300,000 within two millennia, but you must have the starting group of twenty-five. And if it was like that, and a brave band of two dozen or so souls set off to boldly go where no man had gone before, and didn't come back, how many would volunteer to follow them?

On the other hand...

...Australia sits on what geologists call the Sahul Shelf, a continental shelf that stretches north-west from Australia much of the way below the Timor Sea towards Timor. When sea levels fell during the Pleistocene ice age, including the last glacial maximum about 18,000 years ago, the Sahul Shelf was exposed as dry land, in much the same way that Britain was joined to the rest of Europe. Evidence of the shoreline of this time has been identified in locations which now lie 100-140 metres below sea level. This certainly puts a different perspective on things, because now, with much less sea-faring involved, the original visitors could have followed the line of island from Java, to Bali, Lombok and Timor, leading to a relatively short hop onto the Sahul Shelf, and, in time, onto what is the mainland of today.

Either way, the first Aboriginal people to reach Australia undoubtedly had sea-faring skills superior to those of the same era in Europe.

Did the Aboriginal people have a civilisation?

Well, they certainly had a descriptive language, many parts of which have travelled down the years into Australian nomenclature. Geelong, a swamp on a plain; Katoomba, a waterfall, and Turramurra, elevated land, are easy enough to get to grips with. But try your tongue on Roolcarirultaduannaaram, a tree on a hill, Taengarrahwarrawarildi, the place of the yellow-jacket trees, and the Gold Award-winning, Warrapanillamullolacoopalline, which apparently means 'the water hole with cane grass shaped like a man's leg, with trees growing around'.

I wonder what would happen if I put that in my SatNav.

As for the people, they must certainly have had some form of society to be able to expand across a hostile land, to populate it, to master the vagaries of the land and its climate, to find enough food to eat before you died of starvation, to develop a means of communicating sufficient to pass down to posterity the makings of their Dreamtime. It is an achievement that consensus decrees endows the Aboriginal people with the distinction of having the oldest, unbroken culture in the world, one with some fundamental hierarchy: a leader, a chief, someone who could direct and persuade others. That fact alone ought to be enough to draw me away from the tourist treadmill, and in time it did, but, sadly, in a sitting-on-the-fence kind of way.

Aboriginal people are synonymous with Australia, and extensively marketed as such through their art, music and culture, and while indigenous Australians represent about 2.5% of Australia's 24 million people the Australian constitution does not even recognise them as the country's first people. Yet it is clear that how they survived more than 40,000 years ago while having all the hallmarks of a miracle, is actually a reflection of an intimate relationship with their land.

Their story is complex, and while to a degree it appears that some came to be the authors of their own misfortune, equally there's no doubt that they were very badly treated; putting strychnine in a gift of oatmeal is not the best way to make friends and influence people; nor is driving them up trees and then using them for target practice, or hitching women to posts for communal sexual gratification.

Convicts deported from Britain saw the Aboriginals as sub-human, or at least certainly lower down the line of human development, and beat them up, massacring many of them without penalty or punishment.

In his book *Blood on the Wattle*, Bruce Elder sums up the story, which, because I'm many years and 18,000 miles removed from what happened, I can but summarise, rather than pretend that I have any place to comment or criticise. Elder says that the 'Aboriginal Australians had what we all now want', but that we, the European invaders, took it all away; we destroyed it; we took their land; killed native wildlife and '...replaced ecology with aggressive nineteenth-century exploitative capitalism.' We built roads across sacred sites; denied the land its spirituality – in the way I was to do when I climbed Uluru – killed the native people, and herded those who survived into reserves, taking away their reason to exist. Many more stories of massacres are contained in Geoffrey Blomfield's *Baal Belbora: The End of the Dancing*.

Of course, not everyone agrees that it was quite like that, and, as ever, history is seldom written by the vanquished. So, perhaps we will never know the full truth of the matter beyond the evidence we see with our own eyes. Bruce Elder acknowledges a weight of opinion that holds that this aspect of history is Aboriginal, and should therefore be written by Aboriginal historians. But he makes an equally valid point that the massacres of Aboriginal people were atrocities perpetrated by European settlers, and are, as such, part of contemporary white Australian history.

For me, there is something deeply unsettling about this aspect of Australia's history, and it makes me uneasy in the same way I feel ill at ease about the Highland Clearances of Scotland. Yet I feel no entitlement to comment without greater understanding. I can neither cast judgement nor grind a polemical axe.

A duck-filled fatty puss and Christmas turkey

Changing tack to an altogether different realm of accomplishment

– although I'll concede there must have been an element of derring-do about it – the first European people to arrive from the Northern Hemisphere must have felt bewildered, or at least aware that something wasn't quite right.

For a start, those heavenly configurations by which they'd recently navigated were noticeably upside down, and set above a quite different night sky most of which no-one had seen before. You can almost hear the astrologers queuing up to be the first to develop a whole new branch of this abstruse science based on southern constellations, rather than just the northern sky constellations in use since two millennia BCE...except, they didn't.

To make matters even more confusing, everything about the fauna they encountered was alien to them: birds squawked harshly, cackled, screeched, laughed and whistled, animals bounded across the land in an amazing form of propulsion, while the egg-laying duck-billed platypus living in a burrow like a rabbit must surely have freaked out its discoverer. The first scientists to encounter it believed someone had sewn together the body of a beaver with a duck's bill as a joke...they had yet to learn about the spurs on its hind feet connected to a gland that produces toxic venom. No joke.

A slower penny to drop, probably, was that the seasons were somehow out of sync with home; in fact, they were quite the opposite. But if you've been at sea for a few years, sometimes without knowing precisely where you were, going around in circles while the crew sobered up, and generally losing all track of time, it may not immediately register that the turkey on the barbie on Christmas Day was cooking itself under a blazing sun. And phoning home wasn't an option, until that other great explorer, the intergalactic botanist, ET, worked it out.

Today, flights to Australia from Britain invariably go via Dubai, or Singapore, where Changi Airport is so large it can take a day to walk across it. Losing a day in this manner is careless, but at least you had a choice in the matter. Pity anyone flying to Australia from the United States. They go the other way, across the Pacific, and, like it or not, contrive to lose a day just by breathing as they cross the international date line. Nod off and you wake up in yesterday...or is it tomorrow? Thankfully, they get it back when they return, although it must feel seriously weird to arrive home in California earlier than you left Sydney. I have yet to apply my mind to questioning what would happen in terms of temporal dislocation if they chose to fly back to the US, westwards, via Britain. Which way do you have to travel to arrive in tomorrow rather than yesterday?

You can work it out, if you like.

CHAPTER THREE

THINGS THAT GO BITE IN THE NIGHT... AND OTHER BEASTIES

The great attraction of Australia for me – apart from the fact that it was somewhere I'd never been, was on the other side of the world and somewhere that once I'd had a pen friend, had the most stunning scenery ranging from benign to downright hostile and temperatures that went from below zero to egg-frying levels – was its reputation for flora and fauna, although I did have some reservations.

One might be forgiven for assuming that Australia is a land overrun by dangerous, life-threatening creatures. Certainly, the country has more than its fair share of venomous animals, but they rarely present a danger to man. Moreover, some of the non-venomous creatures have an undeserved reputation and are shunned, swatted, trodden on or, as I witnessed in Kakadu, deliberately run over. Left to their own devices virtually many of Australia's beasties are adept (and happiest) at consuming unwanted pests.

Over the years, I have had close encounters, admittedly of an unintentional kind, with many of the land-based species from spiders to snakes with no ill effect for either of us. And I know many people who also have this experience. A bit of hype is always good for a story, apocryphal or otherwise, but the bad press isn't always justified.

As far as anyone knows – and the doubt is expressed because they are still finding new things, even in the 21st century –

Australia has more than 370 mammal species, 830 bird species, 4,000 fish species, 300 species of lizards, 140 snake species, two crocodile species and about 50 types of marine mammal. More than 80 per cent of the plants, mammals, reptiles and frogs found here are unique to Australia and are found nowhere else. Some of the best-known animals are the kangaroo, koala, echidna, dingo, platypus, wallaby and wombat.

The fauna of Australia consists of more than 200,000 animal species of which some 83% of mammals, 89% of reptiles, 24% of fish and insects and 93% of amphibians are endemic to Australia in the sense that they occur here and nowhere else in the world. It's a vast and impressive pedigree, yet 23 species of birds, 78 of frogs, and 27 mammal species including the paradise parrot, pig-footed bandicoot and the broad-faced potoroo, are believed to have become extinct since European settlement began in 1788.

Just as a taster, there are a few other things you might like to know about Australia, not least that if trying to understand the time zones doesn't see you off, then the country has more things that can kill you than anywhere else in the world: even trees can induce anaphylactic shock and death if not instantly dealt with. And that overlooks the presence of the deadliest snake in the world, the Inland Taipan (*Oxyuranus microlepidotus*), while its near cousin the Coastal Taipan (*O. scutellatus*) comes in at number two or three, depending on who you're asking...and does it matter, really? For good measure the eastern tiger snake (Notechis scutatus) comes in at number six. As if that isn't enough, Australian researchers have discovered another, the Central Ranges Taipan (*O. temporalis*).

Don't these guys know when to stop?

Spiders

Ever since Frodo Baggins did battle with Shelob in Lord of the Rings, and probably long before that, fear of spiders is high on many people's hate list. Spiders are the most widely distributed venomous creatures in Australia, with around 10,000 species within a variety of ecosystems. But even though spiders live around us, bites are infrequent. In fact, spiders are less life-threatening than bees.

I'd like to say that they are just cute and fluffy little creatures, but you won't believe me. Even so, they are unquestionably the most misrepresented of Australian beasties. Because of the notoriety of the funnel-web and redback spiders, all spiders are umbrella'd as 'nasty', when, in fact, most are harmless to man (and woman). Records show no deaths from spider bites have occurred in Australia since 1981, and fewer than 30 in the last 100 years. What you should keep in mind is that while spider venom contains a cocktail of chemicals, some of which can be harmful to humans, humans are not really the intended victims. Spider venom is designed for small prey and delivered in small quantities that, while often fatal to tiny creatures, can be handled by bigger organisms.

I still remember the shrieks of horror when a young girl walked straight into the six-foot diameter web of a golden orb spider in Daintree, carefully woven just outside the ladies' toilets. The spider wasn't going to do anything other than scuttle away – big as they are, they eat their mates, not humans – but it's very difficult with spider's web clinging to your face and clothing simply to stay rational and walk backwards out of it.

The most common spider encountered indoors is likely to be the huntsman, often described as a tarantula, even though scientifically there is no such thing as a tarantula. Huntsman spiders have been known to inflict defensive bites, but are not widely regarded as dangerous to healthy humans. What's more, they are widely considered beneficial because they feed on insect pests such as cockroaches, mosquitoes, moths and flies. That doesn't mean you have to be chummy with them, but if you don't want them around, put them outside alive rather than splatter them on your walls.

Crocodiles

Crocs have figured prominently in tropical Australia, and in Aboriginal culture, appearing frequently in stories, songs and artwork; it even appeared on a 1948 postage stamp. Yet I confess that I experience nothing but an inordinate fear whenever I see crocodiles. I suspect that I'm not alone in that. Nothing that has survived from prehistory, can grow to over six metres in length, weigh more than 1,000kg and call on awesome power to overcome its prey is ever likely to endear itself to humans. If you want to think differently, fine, but count me out.

In Australia, there are two types of croc: the freshwater and the salt water. Only the saltie deserves its reputation; the freshie settles for fish. Freshies aren't aggressive, so I'm reliably informed, but if disturbed during the breeding season or if they feel threatened they may attack. Their teeth are razor sharp and can inflict serious wounds. To make matters worse they are a protected species, and their numbers are estimated to be more than 100,000.

The diet of freshwater crocodiles includes the small animals normally found near and in rivers – insects, fish, frogs, turtles, water birds and snakes. What isn't on their diet are humans.

Saltwater crocodiles, on the other hand, are the largest terrestrial and riparian predator in the world, and have a strong tendency to treat humans in their territory as prey and have a long history of attacking humans who unknowingly stray into their territory. According to the mythology of the Aboriginal people, the saltwater crocodile was banished from the fresh water for becoming full of bad spirits and growing too large. For this reason, Aboriginal rock art depicting the saltwater crocodile is rare, although examples of up to 3,000 years old can be found in Kakadu and Arnhem land.

Kangaroos

The kangaroo is the very icon of Australia and appears as an emblem on the Australian coat of arms. on some currency, and is used by some of Australia's well known organisations, including Qantas and the Royal Australian Air Force, not that I've heard that kangaroos can fly, although I wouldn't be surprised given the many other bizarre things that happen in this wonderland. The kangaroo is important to both Australian culture and the national image, and consequently there are numerous popular culture references.

There are 55 different native species of kangaroos and wallabies alone, and these vary in size and weight from half a kilogram rock wallaby to the 90-kilogram red kangaroo (*Macropus rufus*). Estimates of Australia's kangaroo population vary between 30 and 60 million, and you would have to try hard (or spend your whole time in a city) not to encounter one or more on your travels.

Although the stereotypical image of a kangaroo is of it bounding across the ground, its usual posture is upright. According to new research, the extinct 'sthenurine' family of giant kangaroos, up to three times larger than living kangaroos, could walk on two feet. Today's kangaroos can only hop or use all fours, but analysis of the bones of extinct species suggest a two-legged gait. This extinct family ranged from small animals, under 1m tall, to the Procoptodon goliah, that reached 2m in height and weighed 240 kilograms, almost three times the weight of the largest red kangaroo today.

The word 'kangaroo' derives from the Guugu Yimithirr word gangurru, referring to grey kangaroos. The name was first recorded as 'kanguru' in 1770 in an entry in the diary of Sir Joseph Banks, at the site of modern Cooktown, where HMS *Endeavour* under the command of Lieutenant (yet-to-be Captain) James Cook was beached for seven weeks to repair damage sustained on the Great Barrier Reef. Cook first referred to kangaroos in his diary entry of 4 August. Guugu Yimithirr is the language of the people of the area.

A common myth about the English name is that 'kangaroo' was a Guugu Yimithirr phrase for 'I don't know'. According to this legend, Cook and Banks were exploring the area when they happened upon the animal. They asked a nearby native what the creatures were called. The local responded 'gangurru', which, for some reason, Cook took to mean that he didn't know. This myth was debunked in the 1970s by linguist John B. Haviland in his research with the Guugu Yimithirr people. But the explanations are unconvincing. Apart from anything else, how likely is it that a native, well-accustomed to life among kangaroos would not know what one was? Which begs the question: why would Cook, who didn't speak Guugu Yimithirr, assume that the native was saying anything other than the name of the animal? So, the story that the native is believed to have said that he didn't know what the animal was is pure bunkum, a myth invented to adorn a legend.

So, happy to have cleared that up.

Kangaroos are often colloquially referred to as 'roos'. Male kangaroos are called bucks, boomers, jacks, or old men; females are does, flyers, or jills, and the young ones are joeys. The collective noun for kangaroos is a mob, troop, or court.

There are four species that are commonly referred to as kangaroos:

- The red kangaroo (*Macropus rufus*) is the largest surviving marsupial anywhere in the world, and occupies the arid and semi-arid centre of Australia. The highest population densities occur in western New South Wales. A large male can be 2 metres (6ft 7in) tall and weigh 90 kg (200 lb).
- The eastern grey kangaroo (*M. giganteus*) is less well-known than the red, but the more often seen, as its range covers the fertile eastern part of the country, extending from the top of the Cape York Peninsula in north Queensland down

- to Victoria, as well as areas of south-eastern Australia and Tasmania.
- The western grey kangaroo (M. *fuliginosus*) is slightly smaller weighing in at about 54 kg (119 lb) for a large male. It is found in the southern part of Western Australia, South Australia near the coast, and the Darling River basin.
- The antilopine kangaroo (M. *antilopinus*) is, essentially, the far-northern equivalent of the eastern and western grey kangaroos. It is gregarious and a creature of the grassy plains and woodlands. Their name comes from their fur, which is similar in colour and texture to that of antelopes.

Kangaroos are by nature shy and retiring, and present little or no threat to humans. In fact, in 2003, a hand-reared Eastern Grey named Lulu, saved farmer Leonard Richards' life by alerting family members to his location when he was injured by a falling tree branch. She received the RSPCA Australia National Animal Valour Award on 19 May 2004.

In 2015, researchers discovered that most kangaroos are left-handed, making them the only other species apart from humans to show a 'handedness' on a large scale. But will they ever learn to play the piano.

Snakes

Snakes are found all over Australia, not only in the Outback. But, you will hardly ever see them, and only a fool would go looking for them.

There are roughly 50 different kinds of venomous snakes in Australia from a species list of 140 land and 32 sea snakes, of which about 100 are venomous, yet 80% of all snakebites in the country are from the Eastern Brown snake (*Pseudonaja textilis*), often referred to as the common brown snake. This is regarded as

Number Two on the deadliest snake list: thankfully, I didn't know that when I encountered one near Lake St Clair in Tasmania.

Toxicologists argue that lists or rankings of the world's most venomous snakes are tentative and differ greatly because of numerous factors, which must be a crumb of comfort to any mice unfortunate enough to be on the test panel. But a snake doesn't have to be venomous to cause a problem. At the beginning of 2014, reports came in of a snake, believed to be a python, which caught, killed and consumed a whole crocodile, at Lake Moondarra, near Mount Isa, in northern Queensland. Now that's just plain greedy, and doubly unfortunate for anything the croc may just have eaten. I was going to write 'Snakes usually won't attack anything that is too big to swallow', but I'm starting to rethink that theory not least because putting it to the test could be hazardous.

Not all the snakes considered poisonous have venom that is capable to kill humans, or even cause severe illness. It used to be the advice that if you see a snake, stamp your feet. But these days the contrary view is taken: Do not stamp your feet when a snake crosses your path, this will provoke the snake to bite. Just stay perfectly still and let the snake move along. Sudden movements could well cause a snake to panic, and there is profound wisdom in not wanting to be close to a panicking venomous animal. Of course, you should make extra noise as you travel on foot though grass and snake areas as this will warn the snake that something large is in its area and it will move away and try to avoid you.

In addition to my Lake St Clair encounter, I have experienced the presence of snakes on a few occasions from king and green pythons to the rather attractive bright-eyed brown tree snake. On Kangaroo Island I was out with a ranger watching yellow-tailed black cockatoos. A few minutes earlier he had checked out a fallen log on the edge of a forest clearing and pronounced it safe to sit on; so, we did, happy in the warm sun and especially pleased to see the cockatoos, which are quite rare. After about twenty minutes he touched my arm and pointed across the clearing to where a very big – even he said it was very big, it's not me being melodramatic – tiger snake was easing into view. It came, it turned and moved off beneath the canopy.

Later, as we prepared to move on, the ranger turned to me, putting a finger to his lips and whispered: 'Don't move', and pointed to my side. There, much to my sudden adrenalin-fuelled joy, another tiger snake was curled up only inches away sunning itself, as unaware of my presence as I had been of its. It must have been there for some time, and mistook me for a rock. Even more joy. Then, as if sensing something remiss, it slowly uncoiled and slithered off, thankfully away from me, into the bush.

The ranger smiled: 'Well done'.

Yeah. Right.

Where's the vodka?

More to the point: 'Where's the toilet?'

At the less robust end of the scale, this is a place where even a fluffy caterpillar can lay you out; where ants bite, jelly fish sting like blazes (and can cause death), and spiders lurk in the most unsuspected places. If that isn't bad enough, carelessness in deciding which cove to swim in, which beach to use for a picnic or billabong for a paddle can be interpreted as an open invitation to sharks or crocodiles to an al fresco party. Not without foundation are inexperienced surfers known as 'shark biscuits'. And if the cassowaries of Queensland don't like the look of you, they have a can-opener claw on each foot that can disembowel you in a trice... useless at opening tins of beans, but stomachs...wow! They even have a bat – the ghost bat (*Macroderma gigas*) – endemic to the Northern Pilbara and Kimberley in Western Australia, the top end of the Northern Territory, and throughout Queensland that is carnivorous, feeding on small mice, other bats, birds, lizards, geckos, snakes and insects. I thought it was daunting enough when I first encountered fruit bats flying over Sydney Opera House, not least because the sky darkened appreciably, but they never felt like much of a threat. Yet to find one shunning the conventional grabbed-on-the-wing insect diet of bats, and which opts for more substantial fare makes you think...what else have they got?

It doesn't take long to realise that the wildlife of Australia is different from what anyone from Europe will have been used to. But what takes longer to appreciate is that there is just so much wildlife that is unlike anything else, anywhere in the world: indigenous and endemic are adjectives that occur with unfailing regularity in describing Australian flora and fauna. It's here, and much of it is nowhere else. And there is a lot of it, and probably an awful lot we still don't know about.

By way of example, the UK has around 1,700 native plants of which just 15 are endemic. Australia, in contrast, has a staggering 27,000 species of which 90% are endemic. Even allowing for Australia being rather larger than the UK, that's a difference you can't help remarking upon.

CHAPTER FOUR

Perth and some of the west coast

Perth (Western Australia) – brief history – Kings Park – eucalyptus trees – a concert with the Treorchy Male Voice Choir – the Bell Tower

What little I'd read about the Australian weather did nothing to prepare me for the barbecue temperatures outside the air-conditioned terminal building in Perth. It's early March and a mere twenty-eight degrees, but I've come from the tail end of a bleak British winter, and instantly feel the difference.

Suddenly, having never been farther abroad than the French Alps, I was in the land of the sandgropers: I'd read that's what residents of Western Australia are called, but decide it might be safer to acclimatise to the local sense of humour before investigating that nugget of information...and probably be safely back home before even thinking of using it.

'Good eye, mate. Heading for town?'

He is short, fat like a pigeon ready for a pie, wearing shorts, knee-length white stocks – the stock-in-trade of gentlemen of a certain age, if you'll pardon the pun – and an open-necked shirt, and all the hair from his head has somehow retreated inwards and is now sprouting from his ears and nostrils like rampant caterpillars. I don't doubt that he has an armpit full, too, but I'm remarkably disinclined to investigate.

I nod; I haven't quite got my mouth to work yet.

'Jump in. Sling your sack in the back.'

Obediently, I throw my rucksack into the trailer and hop onto the Airport Shuttle, wide-eyed with wonder...me, not the bus.

After months of planning, bouts of umm-ing and ah-ing over which credit card to punish the most, and no amount of checking I had everything I needed – and I mean, no amount – I have survived the sixteen-hour flight, the interminable boredom of in-flight movies you can never quite see, nor hear without blasting your neighbour out of their seat, the endless banality of other people's conversation and the inhalation of recycled air and body gases, I couldn't believe this. I'm in Australia and thousands of miles from home; no big deal for you, maybe, but for a backwood's Johnny from industrial Lancashire like me, this was way off the scale. They drive on the left. They speak a language I understand, which is more than I can say for a sizeable chunk of the UK population. And everyone is so friendly – not at all what I'd been told to expect. And none of them looked even remotely like Edna Everidge, or Barry Humphries for that matter, although come to think of it perhaps the guy I bumped into at the airport did look at bit like Edna Everidge.

In *The First Book of Australia* Edna Mason Kaula described the average Australian as '...breezy in manner and casual in dress. He is possibly the most generous and hospitable person in the world. Usually, he is willing to trust a stranger at first sight, to the extent of lending him small change or even the keys to his car.' Some of those particular qualities I have yet to encounter, but in my experience the everyday Aussie is affable, friendly, welcoming, cheerful, massively extrovert, agreeable and possessed of a wicked sense of humour that they direct as much at themselves as at visitors...probably more so. For example, the beer known as XXXX comes from Queensland, and is so named because the Queenslanders (they call them Banana Benders) can't spell 'beer'... so I'm told. They are also very competitive...keep well away from drinking competitions if you value your liver.

But this was it. I was in Australia, and as excited as a child tackling a Christmas present. It's been like that every time I've returned: exciting, exhilarating, inviting, warm and welcoming. Even the fair lady doing a tittybong on the occasion I passed through Kalgoorlie some years later was expressing a welcome in her own sweet way, just like the guy next to her doing a Moonie.

The shuttle full, the driver starts collecting the fares. It was twelve dollars into Perth city. I offer a hundred dollar note.

'Sorry, I've nothing less.'

'No worries, mate. No worries.'

No worries, eh? Lucky man.

That just about sums up Australia and the egalitarian Australian way of life, and it's why I love the place. The food is excellent; the wine, out of this world, especially in my opinion that from McLaren Vale; the sun seems to shine endlessly; the cities are clean, bright, safe and often built to a grid iron street plan, so, if you get lost, just keep turning left; you'll find your way back to your friends eventually.

The trip into Perth slips by in a blur of motels, supermarkets, hotels, garages, advertisement hoardings urging me to visit the Red Centre – have the Russians discovered Australia? – or take out life insurance, traffic lights that all seem to be on green (which I take as having some kind of spiritual 'All systems go!' significance, as well as being very eco-friendly) and bronzed people. Sun-tanned, smiling, happy, be-shorted individuals; everywhere I look. I'm more than halfway certain it's not at all like that once you get to know it, but, for the moment, the imagery was well good.

Of course, I'm doing it on the cheap, as a backpacker. So, everyone else on the shuttle gets dropped off first. Interesting how you can so easily become stereotyped: here's me with millions in the bank, and just because I'm choosing to slum it in a backpackers' hostel, and dressed in my best scruff with the remains of yesterday's egg down the front, I'm bottom of the pile.

Actually, I'm lying about the millions in the bank.

But not about the egg.

An hour later, I check in at the backpackers' hostel in Northbridge, the centre of all after-dark action and the heart of Perth's café scene with more than forty eateries crammed into a single square kilometre – that's Northbridge, not the hostel. It's also the focal point of Perth's gay and lesbian scene, a robust, good-natured environment you either join in on, or stand on the touchline wondering what the hell's going on – that, too, is Northbridge and not the hostel, well, not necessarily the hostel.

The room is, well, a room, in the sense that it has walls and a door. And a bed, which looks only recently vacated by someone who left behind a virulent selection of body fluids. And a rotating, free-standing fan. But no window, even though it would have a lovely view over the bustling main street. Air conditioning this marginally over-sized broom cupboard does not possess; until you switch on the fan. Judging by the smell, the previous occupants died in there and lay undiscovered for a couple of weeks. That, or the room had been used for growing a variety of exotic mushrooms new to Man, by someone well up on the nouveau riche varieties of funny weed that people smoke in roll ups. It's the only room I've been in that has the sort of effect you might expect from a cocktail of Mogadon and Valium with vodka chasers.

Maybe that's all part of the plan.

It must have been thirty-five degrees in the room. And humid; the kind of place where you might want to spend a few minutes when you become bored with well-furnished en suite hotel rooms with clean bed linen and an ambient temperature that didn't roast turkeys, just to remind you what you're missing. But I don't want to knock the place: you get what you pay for, and Perth has some fabulous hotels; it's just that I chose to avail myself of the interesting possibilities – socially interactive, physical, scientific and economical – that a backpackers' hostel offered. I just didn't expect them to give me a taste of narcosis combined with an overwhelming urge to take up vomiting for Britain.

Anyway, seriously ripe from too much travelling, I head for the communal showers, a long concrete rectangle of washbasins, shower cubicles, sodden, raised wooden platforms you'd have to think twice about standing on, and pools of other people's water that had me wondering what was breeding in there; in fact, for a moment I wondered if it was all water, in the sense of $H2O$. The place was steaming, though I could see only one guy in there and he was wrestling with a snake, or at least I thought it was a snake until I realised he was unselfconsciously swabbing dry a penis that reached halfway to his knees.

Forty minutes later, clean but no cooler, I hit the streets, out on the frazzle – in this heat I can't do razzle.

'Good eye, mate; you from England?'

I figured something about the bewildered stare gave me away; that or the untanned skin.

'Yeah.'

'Went to England once. They show Neighbours twice a day over there. Know why?'

He didn't wait for me to answer.

'Because nobody believes it the first time! Have a good day.'

He moved on a few strides, then turned back.

'They do a decent meal for two dollars at the health food store across the road.'

'Right. Thanks.'

'Hey', he started again. 'They show Neighbours twice a day in England. Know why?'

I didn't want to tangle with his short-term transient global amnesia, or his short-term transient global amnesia.

'Because they don't believe it the first time.'

Goldfish ancestors. That's how I saw it. But he scuttles off happily with the 'lots-to-do-and-so-little-time' air of an inmate out for the weekend from some institution for the terminally bizarre.

But two dollars; that's about eighty-five pence – well, it was then. They do, too, if you don't mind something mushy that would be better on a landfill site or surfacing people's driveways. But I'm not yet feeling brave, and need more identifiable nourishment, and find a dimly lit Lebanese café sandwiched badly between a laundry and a newsagent, and lash out seven dollars on falafel with salad, humus, taboul and a 'Muguccino'.

I'm trying to stay awake long enough to slot into Western Australia's time pattern, and head towards the station. It isn't long before I meet another inmate from the local funny farm, proof, if proof were needed, that more than one had a weekend pass.

'They're giving away Zones down there. Hey, they're great. Only supposed to get one free, but I've been back a few times, and they haven't noticed yet. Want some?'

I hold out my hand, hoping a hand would be enough. They turn out to be mints, but something of a cross between a Treble X and a Fisherman's Friend. Good for clearing your sinuses, but lousy for close encounters of any kind.

Perth is the State capital of Western Australia, and has a reputation for enjoying more hours of sunshine than any other capital city in Australia. The size of the state is simply staggering: it is the largest state in Australia and covers nearly one-third of the entire continent (2,525,500 square kilometres, or about one million square miles), enough to accommodate the UK ten times over. Incredibly, Western Australia has a coastline of 12,500 kilometres (7,813 miles). From the northernmost part of the State at Cape Londonderry to the southernmost near Albany it is 2,400 kilometres (1,500 miles) by crow. That's one Hell of a journey, even assuming you could make it, and, if you could, most of it would be over desolate, inhospitable terrain.

Perth is the fourth most populous city in Australia, with an estimated population of two million living in Greater Perth. The city forms part of the South West Land Division of Western Australia, with the greater part of the metropolitan area of Perth located on the Swan Coastal Plain, a narrow strip between the Indian Ocean and the Darling Scarp. The first areas settled were on the Swan River, with the city's central business district and port (Fremantle) located on its shores.

Originally founded by Captain James Stirling in 1829 as the administrative centre of the Swan River Colony, Perth gained city status in 1856, and was named after Perth in Scotland, by Sir George Murray, then British Secretary of State for War and the Colonies. The city's population grew hugely at the time of the Western Australian gold rushes in the late 19th century, largely as a result of emigration from the eastern colonies of Australia.

Archaeological findings on the Upper Swan River reveal that before European colonisation, Western Australia had been inhabited by the Whadjuk Noongar people for over 40,000 years. These Aboriginal people lived as hunter-gatherers, and the wetlands on the Swan Coastal Plain were especially important to them, both spiritually – featuring in local mythology – and as a source of food. Rottnest, Carnac and Garden Islands were also important to the Noongar. About 5,000 years ago the sea levels were low enough that they could walk to these limestone outcrops.

Where Perth stands today was called Boorloo by the Aboriginals living there in 1827, at the time of their first contact with Europeans. Boorloo formed part of Mooro, the tribal lands of the Yellagonga, one of several groups based around the Swan River and known collectively as the Whadjuk. The Whadjuk were part of a larger group of thirteen or more tribes which formed the southwest socio-linguistic block known as the Noongar (meaning 'the people'), also sometimes called the Bibbulmun. On 19 September 2006, the Federal Court of Australia brought down a judgment recognising Noongar native title over the Perth metropolitan area. The judgment was overturned on appeal.

The nearest city to Perth with a population of more than 100,000 is Adelaide in South Australia, which is 2,692 kilometres (1,682.5 miles) away by car, a bit shorter if you're walking (like you would: 2,422 kilometres/1,513.75 miles) and a bit shorter still by rainbow lorikeet, assuming they fly over water. Author Bill Bryson claims, erroneously, that Perth is the 'most remote big city on earth'. However, Honolulu is 3,841 kilometres (2,387 miles) from San Francisco. But Perth is way out: geographically closer to parts of Indonesia, than Sydney, Brisbane, or Canberra. It's so way out that it never ceases to amaze me that we find it at all, but since I invariably arrive from Singapore I suppose the pilot always has the Plan B of simply following the coastline...and what a coastline; but I'll come to that later.

Perth is one of the most beautiful cities in the world; not that I've seen them all, but the view of the city from the south side of the Swan River or from the heights of Kings Park is stunning. The city is bright and cheerful, welcoming and friendly especially to anyone whose semi-comatose body is eight hours adrift of local time.

Kings Park is always the first place I head on arriving in Perth, and that, so far, has meant every time I've arrived in Australia because I always fly into Perth. There is something very relaxing about Perth in general, it's easy-going, unhurried, and I find it perfect for mooching around and letting my body clock adjust to the time change.

But Kings Park is one of the finest in Australia, and sets Perth apart. Here, greeted by the sound of galahs and rainbow lorikeets that zoom around the treetops like demented and vivid bats from Hell, there is everything an inner-city park should be, vibrant, colourful, and rich in Aboriginal and European history.

There is always a frisson of excitement as I cross the Mitchell

Freeway and climb up Mount Street into Bellevue Terrace to the Kings Park Lookout. And what a belle vue it is, truly breathtaking, although some of that I put down to the slopes of Mount Street.

After that, I wander into the park, yet despite numerous visits, each time extending my exploration, I never come away without feeling there's a great swathe of it that somehow, I've missed. Not only is it a place of recreation for walkers and cyclists alike, and conventional as city parks go, but two-thirds of the park is protected as bushland, providing an important haven for native biodiversity.

Elsewhere, in the south-east corner overlooking the Swan River, the Western Australian Botanic Garden showcases over 3,000 varieties of the State's unique flora, including many rare and threatened species. I'm not normally drawn to botanic gardens, but, coming in the first days of my visits to Australia, I'm prepared to make an exception for Kings Park Botanic Garden because it instantly reminds me what an exceptional and varied diversity of plants grow in Australia; I use the garden as a catalyst to switch from the familiar back home to the unfamiliar down under. And when I say 'unfamiliar' as like as not some of them are unfamiliar to Australian botanists, just as much as they are to me, with new species being identified on a regular basis: too big a country, too few botanists, that's the problem. Budding botanists note: the scope for identifying a new species and having your name attached to the scientific description must be incomparable, and tempting.

And that goes for birdlife, too, because Australia has over twice as many species as are recorded in Britain, and, like plants, many of them are only found here, and nowhere else in the world.

Why should that be?

Well, it's to do with isolation. For millions of years, Australia was an island that enabled indigenous life-forms to evolve free from competition or the risk of cross-fertilisation with species from other countries. But not only that, flora and fauna communities are isolated within Australia; comparatively small oases of species diversity separated by almost sterile gulfs of inhospitable harshness.

Wandering further into the park I come face-to-face with an unusual war memorial. All I can recall from my first visit is a long avenue of white eucalypts planted to commemorate the fallen of World War I. The planting of trees as a dedication to individual service personnel who gave their lives while serving their countries in time of war seems to be an Australian innovation. The idea was taken up in Kings Park in 1918 by Arthur Lovekin, an original member of the Kings Park Board. Dedication plaques sit at the base of each tree along May Drive, Lovekin Drive and Marri Walk, and this is where I found myself. Coming, as I had, from a recent visit to the war cemeteries of Picardy in France, I was moved to find that instead of regimented rows of headstones, in Kings Park they let the trees do the talking...or, at least, the remembering. This arboreal commemoration may have started at the end of World War I, but it now embraces the Second World War as well as the Korean and Malaysian conflicts of later years.

What is probably little known beyond Australia is that all the soldiers who fought in the First World War were volunteers, who simply didn't need to become involved in Europe's conflict. Sadly, many of them made the ultimate sacrifice. Estimates of how many died during the conflict vary and are imprecise, but the Statistics of the Military Effort of the British Empire during the Great War 1914-1920, produced by the War Office in 1922, suggest that 59,330 soldiers lost their lives, while the 2010-2011 Annual Report of the Commonwealth War Graves Commission puts the figure a little higher, at 62,081, in addition to which there were a further 152,171 who were wounded. That number of deaths represents between 1.32% and 1.38% of the population of Australia, a figure surpassed only by New Zealand (1.52-1.65%) and the United Kingdom (1.79-2.2%).

Whichever way you look at it, that's a huge sacrifice for a country that didn't have to get involved in the first place. Small wonder then that the country decided to commemorate their sacrifice, and to do so by planting trees that have a lifespan of over 400 years. It's a very moving place, perhaps not as in-your-face as the serried ranks of headstones in the Somme Battlefield cemeteries, but every bit as poignant.

Kings Park is usually my first encounter with eucalyptus trees, visually and olfactory. Soldiers returning by sea from European conflicts said that they could smell the eucalyptus, commonly known as gum trees, long before they saw land. These magnificent trees, introduced to the rest of the world following Cook's 1770 expedition when they were collected by Sir Joseph Banks, are an integral part of the Australian identity and a defining part of Australian life and culture. Given this immense significance, I make no apology for introducing a few interesting facts about the eucalyptus tree:

- The size of eucalyptus depends on the species, but they can reach 200 feet in height.
- The leaves of eucalyptus are lanceolate shaped and are positioned downwards to prevent direct exposure to the sunlight; they are also rich in oil widely used to alleviate symptoms of bronchitis, sore throat and nasal congestion
- The koala's diet is based on the leaves of eucalyptus, although only few species are on the koala's menu
- The bark of eucalyptus, shed once a year, is usually brown in colour, but the so-called rainbow eucalyptus sheds its bark several times per year to reveal an inner bark that is variously red, blue, yellow, purple
- Some insects lay eggs and feed on the bark of eucalyptus tree. They leave marks on the bark that look like man-made scribbles
- The eucalyptus has unique strategy to survive fires that are a frequent occurrence in the Australian forests: deep inside the tree and inside the roots, the tree has dormant shoots

that germinate only under the influence of hormones triggered by heat
- Eucalyptus is known as the gum tree because of a sticky rubbery substance that flows from the injured bark
- The lifespan of eucalyptus depends on the species. Most eucalyptus trees can survive more than 250 years and in excess of 400 years in the wild.

Later that day, still reflecting on the deeds of others, I sit at the edge of the Swan River, camera on its tripod, and shoot at one minute intervals picture after picture of the same city centre skyline as the sun goes down and the moon comes up, and the city puts on the display that greeted John Glenn, the American astronaut, as he flew over on his orbital flight in 1962. He called it 'The City of Lights', and I can see why, but I can't help wondering whether it ever occurred to Glenn what a humungous waste of electrical energy it was if he could see the street lights of Perth from the edge of space.

I have to run to catch the last ferry back across the river, or face a long walk round. The America's Cup skipper Dennis Connor described Perth as 'the most isolated city in the world'. Well, he's no more right than Bryson; but the sensation of remoteness is palpable, and the city is separated from everywhere else by thousands of miles of sand or ocean. But who needs neighbours? – after all, we get it on the television twice a day back home.

On the flight from Singapore to Perth I'd encountered members of the Treorchy Male Voice Choir, heading out for a three-week tour. They last did the same in 1999, and I just missed their appearance in Hobart, so was delighted to get a seat for their first Perth appearance. But it's somehow sadly ironic that I have to come this far to get to see a bunch of singers from the Rhondda. I was in the Rhondda only a few months ago!

It was a moving experience, and I soon realised that Australian audiences are clearly more relaxed about their concert going. No-one thinks anything of chatting during programme items: 'That was lovely, wasn't it?' 'Sure was, honey. D'y'wanna beer?"

Actually, I lie about that. It wasn't a beer he was offering. I distinctly heard reference to something far more vigorous and intimate, summed up in a four-letter word beginning with 'sh' and ending in 'g', and with a vowel in between that isn't 'e', 'i', 'o', or 'u'.

And you certainly need to learn how to whoop, whistle and stomp your feet; no polite British applause here. Let them know how you feel.

At the end of the concert we all stood up and sang Hen Wlad Fy Nhadau, the Welsh National Anthem...fortunate then that I'd lived in Wales for a time and could still manage the first verse, after which I hummed, and lah-lah'd...in Welsh, of course.

Well, I don't know; maybe it's all too informal. I mean, a typical Brit audience would do no more than cough, sneeze, snuffle and burp at inappropriate moments, rustle sweet papers, mark the hour on their digital wristwatches, forget to switch off mobile phones, fart, fall asleep and occasionally vomit. I've seen all of that in concert halls in England.

I know which I prefer.

On the northern shore of the Swan River, the Bell Tower is Perth's newest landmark, completed only in 2000.

When Captain Cook sailed into London in 1771 following his first voyage to the south seas, his return was celebrated by the ringing of the bells of St Martin-in-the-Fields church in Trafalgar Square. Today, those same bells, twelve in number, along with five modern bells cast in the 1980s, ring out across the city of Perth, presented to the University of Western Australia, the City of Perth and the people of Western Australia by the City of London in 1988 to commemorate Australia's bicentenary. To complete a ring of eighteen bells, as used in England over many centuries in the historic art of change-ringing, a sixth bell was commissioned by the West Australian Government to mark the second millennium.

Designed by William Hames, the six-storey, 82.5m-high glass-and-steel tower is clad in copper sails constructed from sixteen tons of recycled copper. With its full complement of bells, the tower, located on Riverside Drive in Barrack Square, the tower must be one of the world's largest musical instruments.

Later, as I prepare to leave Perth to head back home, I wander down to the quayside and sit outside the Lucky Shag Bar listening to the old St Martin's bells, sipping Chardonnay and eating fish and chips. The bells seem to be chiming a familiar peel, a call of home, a bit like the fish and chips.

It's time to go. I pick up my bits and head for the airport, but I'll be back, again.

North of Perth – road trains – Nambung National Park and the Pinnacles Desert – Shark Bay World Heritage Site (Monkey Mia, dugongs, turtles and feeding the dolphins) – Denham – Hamelin Pool and stromatolites – Shell Beach – Murchison Gorge and Kalbarri National Park

The sky is a 10/10 dome of cerulean blue as I leave Perth along the northbound freeway to the Reid Highway and then up the Great Northern and Brand highways heading for Cervantes and the Pinnacles Desert. Within minutes of leaving the centre of Perth the bush starts to appear as houses become fewer and are replaced by scattered farmsteads or roadside eateries offering chilled Crown lager, fresh melons, hydroponic tomatoes, badgie and dump burgers, and the finest barramundi and chips in Australia. They also offer free coffee for all drivers, which is a neat idea.

Bobtail skinks trundle optimistically across the road, hoping to make it to the other side unscathed; western red kangaroos that tried the same during the night weren't all so lucky. The red-sand roadside verges display the inevitable result of high-speed animal versus machine contacts ranging from still-twitching lumps of red meat to parched canvas bags of bleached bones. I keep encountering signs warning me that I'm approaching a floodway, but quite where the water comes from or goes to is anyone's guess. It's hard to imagine this place flooded...but it does.

From time to time there are signs warning drivers of the infamous road trains: Eddie Stobart on steroids. They don't mean to be infamous, it just works out that way, especially if you misjudge your overtaking manoeuvre. These four-trailer brutes are up to fifty-five metres in length, can weigh up to 200 tonnes and rage along at 100km/hour. The good news is that they are limited to 100kph, but it's still critically important to note that stopping takes them a long time, and changing direction even the slightest to avoid oncoming vehicles is not an option; or, at least, it doesn't seem to be an option the drivers comprehend. In other words: GET OUT OF THE WAY, DIPSTICK; it shouldn't be too difficult to figure out who would win in a head-to-head contest. To be fair, and I've tested this a few times in dusty road stops and bars, the drivers of the big trucks are the most courteous, considerate and responsible of all drivers on Australian Outback roads.

These massive vehicles are an integral part of the Australian Outback, just as much as kangaroos, red dust, spinifex and endless shimmering horizons. They can be found in all parts of Australia, but the really big ones are restricted to the Outback. Not surprisingly, they are banned on most roads in the more populated southern and eastern states – they don't mix very well with normal traffic. They also kick up a lot of red dust, making forward visibility hazardous to say the least; it's no fun driving along behind a road train on an unsealed road. In fact, it's probably a good idea to pull over and have a nap until the dust settles.

If you try to overtake one safely and without exceeding the speed limit, it will take you at least 1.75 kilometres (i.e. more than a mile) and 60 seconds to do so - that's an awful long time to be hung out on the wrong side of the road. These brutes deliver over 600 horse power, have fourteen-litre engines that gobble fuel at a rate of one litre per kilometre, which is why many of them have four, 450-litre fuel tanks; at a normal filling station fuel pump (in Australia called bowsers) it would take around 45 minutes just to fill the tanks at the normal flow rate of 40 litres per minute. Thankfully, for large vehicles the flow rate tends to be higher, but you would still have time for lunch.

In 2004, one of the really natty road train rigs would have set you back around 300,000 Australian dollars (£125,000), and they take an awful lot of polishing, if only to remove miscellaneous - and usually unidentifiable - body parts from the roo bars.

Three hours from Perth, I leave the main highway and turn towards the Indian Ocean and the low-lying, scattered settlement of Cervantes, a place named after an American whaler wrecked on a nearby reef in 1844, but a town with a more recent pedigree, being established only in 1962. 259 kilometres north of Perth, and facing out into the Indian Ocean, the pace of life is relaxed here.

When I first visited Cervantes in '98, a new backpacker's hostel had opened less than half a kilometre from the beach, but in the intervening years little has changed...except the influx of German and Japanese tourists and the growth of the rock lobster fishing industry.

Jobs must be few and far between here, and getting those that do come up mightily difficult if an advert in the window of the Sea Breeze Café is anything to go by. They were looking for 'Long-term employees for casual work 'on call', must be expienced (sic). Previous applicants or staff need not apply. Preference will be given to married or single person with no dependants or other job and non-smoker'. So, if you applied before and were rejected, you're obviously not up to it; if you applied and have a job, you're clearly not good enough either, but you couldn't apply anyway because you already have another job, which must be a crap job if the one on offer is better. To qualify you must be married or single. Well, that should fit just about everyone, unless it's meant to exclude divorcees, widows, widowers, gays and lesbians, and people in mutual long-term one-to-one, on-going, non-marital relationships without dependants. And who, out of those who could apply, would be looking for a long-term job that appeared to have no set hours, required you to wait at home by the phone in case there was a sudden run on fish and chips, and which precluded other more gainful employment? Moreover, you had to have had previous experience of selling fish and chips – well, actually it doesn't say that, it just says 'experienced', or is meant to: you could be experienced in selling cars, the Encyclopaedia Australis, double glazing or pornographic videos.

Much as I like Cervantes – and I do – I decide not to apply; I have a dependant dog.

What the tourists come to see is the Pinnacles Desert, a parched landscape of shifting sand and limestone pinnacles projecting from the ground like so many misshapen teeth, hundreds of them, thousands, maybe tens of thousands – to a Selachophobic (someone with a fear of sharks, which is probably most of us, but in terms of having to explain it to your friends nothing like so bad as being Hexakosioihexekontahexaphobic) this must seem like the jaws of Hell.

Along the 17 kilometres (10½-mile) drive from Cervantes to the Pinnacles Desert, kangaroos patrol the roadside like Priapic traffic wardens; the sun is setting, producing long shadows that conceal their huddled forms. The car park is strategically sited so that as you walk from it the actual pinnacles, of which so far I've seen only a few scattered examples, appear with a breathtaking suddenness, clusters of monuments like a prehistoric necropolis stretching to the horizon in every direction, well, stretching as far the coastal dunes, the beaches and the all-embracing bush. Signs ask you not to climb on the pinnacles. Sadly, they're not in German, or Japanese.

My mind doesn't know what to make of this wonderland. So, I wander slowly, aimlessly, among the pinnacles, embracing a few in the way that folk embrace trees and ancient standing stones, as if trying to find a totemic pathway back to the beginning of their beginning.

As I start taking long-shadowed pictures in the setting sun an emu wanders out from behind one of the pinnacles. It has a quizzical, almost pained looked on its tiny face, and wanders off, daintily stepping, ballerina-like into a small pocket of low scrub. I follow, to investigate. I can find its tracks going into the scrub, but circle it as often as I might, I can't find tracks leading out. The scrub can't be more than ten metres across, but somewhere in there, perfectly camouflaged is an adult emu, probably laughing its socks off.

On the way back to Cervantes I pull up at the roadside, kill the engine and get out to listen to the sounds of silence. The air is starting to cool quickly and the sky darkens with a dramatic suddenness. There is no moon, just an endless display of stars, bright enough for me to make out the surrounding bush. Orion is hanging upside down, as, presumably, are Jupiter, Mars and Saturn. But silent is not how I would describe the sounds around me.

There must be over 100,000 species of insect in Australia, and it sounds like most of them are out here tuning up for some antipodean 'Last Night of the Proms'. If sound was colour, this would be a vivid and intense display, a breathtaking Aurore Australis, the sounds focused by the stillness much more so than sounds in a rain forest, or among the billabongs of the northern tropics. I put it down to the dryness. In a way, it's quite melodic:

that's an E flat, another is C, a minor third lower; another comes in at A, and two almost but not quite on G sharp. With a bit of patience and good orchestration, I could probably get this lot to play *Waltzing Matilda*. Forget your Infinite Monkey Theorem, this is much more promising. But, for the moment, I'll let them tune up.

I jest, of course, but the effect is mesmerising. I love this place; the night sounds, the smells, the warm breath of air coming in from the sea, the intensity of the skies above and the blackness all around. It would spook some people, but I feel completely at ease, privileged to be here, in no hurry to be anywhere else. I just stand still; do nothing, except breathe, lightly. It's a wonderful sensation; tranquillity personified. I wouldn't go so far as to say that I was at one with Nature, that's a bit too fanciful, but I certainly feel my body relax, and it's a while before I can spur myself to get back in the car.

This is how I imagined Australia would be.

It hasn't disappointed.

The air temperature is revving up next morning as I set off along the coastal road, northwards, heading for a crayfish baguette at Skeetas in Geraldton and the long drive to Denham and the Shark Bay World Heritage Site. North of Geraldton the road is so straight for so long I'm able to get through four chapters of Andrew Stevenson's *Travels in Outback Australia* as I'm driving before I pull in at the Billabong Roadhouse. On a later visit, I stopped here and realised that I'd been here previously, something I didn't recall until I walked into the bar. The owner is sitting at a table just to the right as I enter, exactly as he had been six years earlier; he's probably still reading the same copy of *The West Australian*, and I swear he's wearing the same shirt. And the coffee is exactly where I'd left it – through into the next room and on the left. But the price has gone up by sixty cents.

Actually, I lie. I think the guy has changed his shirt.

And I only managed three chapters from Andrew Stevenson's book.

Denham is a place everyone should come to. I can't immediately say why; there are so many reasons and all of them corralled in that lovely indulgence that embraces utter relaxation, inertia, contentment and easy-going simplicity. You just should.

It's a modest little place facing out to Dirk Hartog Island, where the first Dutch ship encountered the unknown land of Australia on the 25th October 1616, more than 150 years before the rather better-known but more infamous voyage of Captain Cook. The eponymous Captain Hartog was so pleased with himself for having accidentally discovered a completely barren and infertile spot that he named it after himself. But he wasn't too impressed because he set off north the next day, but, in an early form of public relations management, not before he nailed a pewter plate to a post to mark the occasion informing anyone else who had the misfortune to be lost on these shores that someone had beaten them to it. By whatever manner of ill trade winds was needed, eighty-one years later another Dutchman, Willem de Vlamingh also found the island, and Hartog's plate, which he was cunning enough to remove and replace with his own, but dumb enough to take the original back to Amsterdam, where, as luck would have it, it lay forgotten in the Rijks Museum for over 200 years.

Now, although the Dutch are customarily credited with having been the first Europeans to discover Australia, many authorities think the Portuguese were, almost a hundred years earlier than Hartog, and who am I to argue? As evidence of this, those who support the Portuguese claim suggest that the name of the Abrolhos Islands near present-day Geraldton is a shortened version of Abri vossos olhos, meaning 'Keep your eyes open', a typical mariner's warning.

To be truthful, Denham really has a lot going for it: a sea view that would stretch to Africa, if you could see that far; a heart-warming out-of-the-wayness that makes it feel as if someone has put it in a safe place and forgotten where; the Bay Café still sells the finest snapper and chips I've ever had; one of the hotels has a drive-in bottle shop, a bit like Macdonalds but selling Goundrey Unwooded Chardonnay instead of burgers, and they got rid of the cop who fined me a hundred dollars for speeding six years ago. If I'd known, I'd have been here quicker: in fact, on one visit, I did, racing hell-for-leather to get there in time for snapper and chips, only to find that the Bay Café wasn't open that day.

But Denham, which gets its name from Captain H H Denham who charted the whole of the Shark Bay area in 1858, is only the main settlement at the centre of the Shark Bay World Heritage Site, an area of shallow, heavily saline inlets between the north-west coast of Western Australia, the skinny finger of land leading northwards past Denham into the Peron Peninsula, and the equally skinny Useless Loop and Dirk Hartog Island boundary.

The shoreline runs in a 'W' shape for 1,500 kilometres (almost 1,000 miles), embracing around 22,000 square kilometres, of which about seventy per cent is water. Aboriginal people have lived here for thousands of years, long before Captain Hartog arrived. They, the Nhanda and Malgana tribes, called it Cartharrugudu, meaning two bays. Rampant natural beauty is all around: cliffs, headlands and beaches, below, the ocean and its caves, valleys and hilltops. It is emotionally magnetic, compelling beauty, a vibrant pathway into the spirit...and full of sharks.

In 1688, the first Englishmen reached Australia, or New Holland as the Dutch had christened it, in the form of William Dampier a converted pirate aboard the buccaneer ship the Cygnet under the captainship of John Reed, who sailed into King Sound. Dampier was one of his officers, an educated man despite his piratical tendencies. Soon after leaving King Sound, Dampier gave up piracy and returned to England, a three-year journey, and devoted himself to writing. He was singularly unimpressed, however, both with the land and its inhabitants, '...the miserablest People in the World'. But such was his success as an author that the government decided to send him back to Australia on a legitimate voyage of discovery, as captain of the Roebuck. In 1699, Dampier reached Cartharrugudu, and after spending a week there decided to name it Shark Bay; obviously not a spur-of-the-moment man.

Throughout much of the eighteenth century, Europeans showed little interest in Australia, until the last ten years when both Britain and France showed renewed interest. In 1770, the British claimed Australia at Botany Bay, and two years later the French did the same, reaching the continent at Cape Leeuwin and sailing north to Dirk Hartog Island to formally claim the new land for France having failed to spot Willem de Vlamingh's plaque, which languished until 1818 before another Frenchman, Louis de Freycinet on an early package holiday found de Vlamingh's plaque and took it back to France. Only in 1947 did France decide to return the plaque to Australia; it is now on show in the Fremantle Maritime Museum.

Not long after Denham visited the area, the first of the pastoralists and pearlers came, and by the 1870s several small settlements had appeared along the Shark Bay coastline. Today, the area of Shark Bay thrives on tourism, fishing and a solar salt project at Useless Loop. At least that's what the tourism blurb says.

David Charles works for the Department of Conservation and Land Management, and is manager at the popular Monkey Mia, where bottle-nosed dolphins have been coming in to be fed by humans since the early 1960s. Now around 100,000 visitors a year come here to do the same. I caught up with David after a dolphin-feeding session and asked him what CALM was trying to achieve, given the stance elsewhere in the world that dolphins should be protected and human interaction avoided.

'We have a legacy of forty years' human interaction here,' he said. 'It's not something that can just be stopped overnight, though as a conservationist I'd stop it tomorrow. So, it's a question of educating people, limiting the amount of interaction so that the dolphins don't become dependent on humans for their food. And this is a major scientific research site, one of the best there is. The Dolphin Interaction Area is only a hundred metres wide and has been set up so that the dolphins can continue to visit without being disturbed by swimmers or boats, and the feeding is restricted to the mornings to encourage the dolphins to find food for themselves.'

It isn't only about dolphins though. Green turtles are at their southern limit in Shark Bay, yet they are the most abundant specious in the bay. As I wait to set off on a two-hour catamaran trip around the bay, three appear beside the jetty. Out in the bay, a loggerhead turtle surfaces for air. Loggerheads are thought to be the most endangered turtle species nesting in Australia. During the summer months, numbers around Shark Bay increase when they migrate here to breed.

Jay, who steers the boat with his feet, with his upper body poking through a hatch in the cockpit roof, isn't convinced the dolphin feeding is a good thing. 'The regularly fed dolphins are lazy, compared with wild dolphins,' he told me. 'It can't be right.'

Just then we spot a dugong, one of the 10,000 elusive dugongs that inhabit the shallow seagrass beds of Shark Bay. The dugong residents of Shark Bay account for ten per cent of the world's remaining population. This one obligingly surfaces a couple of times, as if under contract, then disappears. These gentle giants can live for up to seventy years, but have a low reproductive rate, with the females not giving birth until they are between twelve and seventeen years of age, and then only irregularly, at intervals varying from three to seven years.

One of the real oddities of Shark Bay is the sandhill frog, which spends most of its day buried in the sand dunes, and is one of the few frogs that goes through life without ever inhabiting free water. It emerges when it rains or in the night dew, to feed on ants and other insects. Unlike other frogs, the sandhill doesn't produce tadpoles, but young that hatch directly from large eggs buried in the sand.

As I return to the car the temperature has reached forty. There's a heady smell in the air that I normally associate with the hot rocks of a sauna. You wouldn't want to walk barefoot here. I'm getting third degree burns from the steering wheel and gear lever, and anything that hits the windscreen is instantly fried in its own juices.

Shell Beach at first glance looks like a huge sweeping expanse of white sand. But it is composed not of sand but the remains of a tiny cockleshell, Fragum erugatum, which flourish, and quite clearly die, in trillionic numbers. Not far away, at Hamelin Pool, is yet another oddity. First impressions of the rocky lumps strewn around the beach are vague. But the lumps, or stromatolites to give them their proper name, are built by microscopic living organisms – cyanobacteria – similar to the earliest forms of life on earth that appeared 3,500 million years ago. Up to 3,000 million individual organisms per square metre use sediment and organic material – mucous to me and you – to form huge reefs of stromatolites up to 1.5 metres high, something like 10 million times their size. The stromatolite reefs at Hamelin Pool are the finest in the world, and were only discovered by scientists in 1956; in essence they are living fossils growing at a rather relaxed rate of one metre every 2,000 years. For this reason, local conservationists discourage visitors from lopping off huge chunks as souvenirs.

So, all-in-all, Shark Bay has a lot going for it. It's not all wonder and amazement, though. There are some real nasties here. For a start, it's not called Shark Bay just for the hell of it or because Dampier was stuck for word power. But sharks are just part of a venomous hit squad that includes blue-ringed octopus, stingrays, coneshells, stonefish and seasnakes, some or all of which can lay you up in hospital for a while, if you live long enough to get there.

'Yeah,' says David, 'but leave 'em alone, they won't bother you.'

Tell that to the sharks, I'm thinking.

The next morning I'm preparing to leave, but set off first for a morning jog, while the temperature is still only in the high twenties. Within minutes I'm joined by a mother emu and her young that I'd seen taking a constitutional along the foreshore road only half an hour earlier. Trotting alongside one another, I tried to talk about the price of fish and whether it was going to rain. But she wasn't interested, and pushed on ahead with far greater ease than I was managing.

That's true, by the way...except the bit about the fish. What an astoundingly amazing place. Only the night before, accompanied by my family on this occasion, we did manage to get snapper and chips, and all sat fully clothed in the warm waters of the Indian Ocean, eating them, and watching the sun go down...then I remembered box jelly fish...

It wasn't part of my original plan, but the decision to turn off into Murchison Gorge was a good one. This pristine red-hued gorge marks the course of the Murchison River, the second longest river in Western Australia, flowing for about 820 kilometres (510 miles) from the southern edge of the Robinson Ranges to the Indian Ocean at Kalbarri. As a result, today it finds itself as part of the Kalbarri National Park.

Aboriginal people inhabited the area for thousands of years and have a dreaming story about the Rainbow Serpent forming the Murchison River as she came from inland to the coast. Kalbarri is believed to be named after a prominent member of the Aboriginal people known as the Nanda who lived in the area, but it is similar in name to an edible seed – Kalbar – commonly known as the woody pear tree. The Aboriginal name for the area is Wurdimarlu.

The first European people to visit the area were the crew of a trading ship, the Batavia, who, evidently being short of planks to walk, cast two mutinous crew members ashore near Bluff Point, south of the present town, on what was then a most inhospitable place.

The river was named by the explorer George Grey, whose boats were wrecked at its estuary on 1st April 1839. It was no joke; this was his second disastrous exploratory expedition, and he was fast running out of ships. The name commemorates the Scottish geologist Sir Roderick Murchison.

Within a hundred years, the area flanking the estuary and river mouth, so under-appreciated by Grey, was used as a holiday destination by families from the Galena mines, and then as a military holiday camp during the Second World War. Only as recently as 1951 did the town of Kalbarri appear, and by the end of the 1990s, when I first visited, the population was still only around 2,000.

In 1963, the Kalbarri National Park came into being, formally protecting the lower reaches of the river, including the gorge.

The gorge is truly spectacular and of outstanding geological interest, as it exposes a section through the Tumblagooda Sandstone, a geological sequence rich in Ordovician trace fossils. From the rim of the gorge at Hawk's Nest I gazed down on black swans swimming far below in what remained of the river. It was scorchingly hot; very - summer temperatures frequently exceed 40 degrees Celsius - and that prompted a beer and rock lobster session in Kalbarri to cool down, purely in the interests of survival, of course.

By way of entertainment, each day the locals come out to feed the pelicans that inhabit the coastline; it's quite an amusing experience, especially if you get between a pelican and its fish.

It's a tourist thing, of course, and brings in almost a quarter of a million visitors each year, but I've always managed to find secluded spots along to the coast to the south in which to unwind before another culinary session with those delicious rock lobsters.

In a very agreeable way, Kalbarri is uncomplicated, doesn't have pretensions, just gets on with life...the sort of place you could so easily miss...and regret missing.

South of Perth to Margaret River – the caves – Cape Leeuwin- Cape Naturaliste – Fremantle – Rottnest Island and quokkas

South of Perth, once across the Swan River, the countryside is very urban. The Kiriwina Freeway speeds you southwards through a sprawling mass of low-rise houses and commercial buildings that persist until you are well on your way to Bunbury.

I'm heading into the south-west corner of the country, into the wine region of Margaret River. It's so vastly different from the never-ending emptiness of the north-west, but gradually the traffic eases and the houses become fewer and fewer, and I start to warm to the place both emotively and physically; it's thirty-nine centigrade out there, that's over a hundred fahrenheit. The car's air conditioning is permanently in overdrive trying to compete. Road signs flash by advertising mango wine, cooked crabs, roast lunch, Devonshire teas, emu sausages, kangaroo pies and moo poo. Just north of Bunbury there's a wrecked car hanging fifteen feet up in a tree with 'Drive Carefully' painted on its side, and all the way down from Shark Bay I've been passing signs that announce that the local police are targeting, whatever...speeding, seatbelts, drink driving. The best is yet to come: in Bunbury local police are targeting fatigue; presumably by staying in bed. Good news for the drink drivers.

And how does it work anyway?

'Good eye, sir. You'll have seen we're targeting fatigue this week, and we've pulled you over because you're driving seems a trifle erratic. Are you tired?'

'No mate. I'm just pissed.'

'Ah, shame. We did drink driving last week. Take care now.'

I pull off towards the harbour at Bunbury and find a sea view café for a relaxed lunch. As I hover between tables, a vision of youthful loveliness approaches. She must be all of eighteen, blonde, bronzed and shapely in all the right places.

She smiles a greeting. 'Good eye. You wanting lunch?'

'That would be good.'

'Sure thing. I'll just get you a menu.'

When she returns I order garlic prawns and a glass of the local Prevelly Chardonnay.

'You touring around?'

'Yeah. One week down. Six weeks to go. I'm heading for Margaret River.'

'Oh, that's beautiful. You'll enjoy it. Try the caves. And get down to Cape Leeuwin. Some really stunning coastal scenery there.'

There's some stunning scenery here, too, but she's far too young and I'm old enough to be her father, sadly...and married, happily. Everyone is so friendly, so welcoming. They say that if Australia generally comes high on the list of the friendliest places in the world to be, Western Australia is even higher. I can well believe it. I do believe it. Complete strangers smile as you pass them and ask 'How're ya going?'

'Good,' is the answer.

Another waitress goes by. 'Can I get you some water with that?' She returns a moment later with a jug of ice water and lemon. It's nothing in the overall scale of things, but they make you feel as though they care about you. They may be bored witless, but that's not the impression you get.

Another impression is that the town of Margaret River is a one-street town. It isn't, but with all the main shops ranged along the Bussell Highway, it looks that way. I head down to Prevelly Beach to find the outlet of the river, except there is none. The sea is there alright, and so is the river, but the two don't connect. At times of the year there just isn't enough force in the river to keep the river mouth open. So, it sands up and creates a kind of mobile beach until the next great flush of the wet season.

I wander up-river, encountering pied cormorants and black ducks, twelve two-man canoes and twenty-four pairs of shoes. I puzzle over the shoes. Twenty-four is the correct number for twelve canoes, but where are the feet? The answer lies further on. As I move forward through golden sand dunes pinned in place by scrub I can hear the laughter and squeals of Australian yoof at play. Soon they come into view, paddling lazily and inexpertly, their efforts punctuated by lively banter.

'Get out the bloody way, ya stupid drongo.'

'Ah, shut ya gob before ya swaller the river.'

I'm sure they don't mean it.

To the east lies the sea, and between the two is another road, a so-called Tourist Route, the Caves Road. With all the panache of a nation that has the wit to call a cricket with white knees a white-kneed cricket, or an ugly woman a swamp donkey, Caves Road is so-called because along its length, south of Margaret River, lie several limestone caves to which my Bunbury Wish had alluded.

The whole area between Cape Leeuwin in the south, and Cape Naturaliste in the north is, with yet more lexical dexterity, named the Leeuwin-Naturaliste National Park. Within this area there are over 300 caves of varying sizes from small sink holes to huge underground complexes linked by a terrifying maze of interlinking passages – terrifying that is if you're in the least claustrophobic. Four are open to the public, and three of them I was heading off to explore, though 'explore' doesn't hold any of the connotations it did in the nineteenth century when the first real explorers ventured into the dark, labyrinthine world with little more than kerosene-soaked rags for lamps and a vague hope they would find their way out again.

The first recorded discovery of caves here was in 1848, when two caves with underground chambers were found only a short distance north of Augusta, then a struggling township. Fifty years later, a Government-funded investigation into the potential of the south-east area concluded that there were forty-five or so caves in the area, some suitable for development for tourists. The Government was not slow to see the caves, coupled with the agreeable climate here, as a means of encouraging visitors from the east.

Today, if you want to visit the caves you simply drive down Caves Road for half an hour or so, pick up a 'Grand Tour' ticket at the first one you come to - Mammoth Cave - and then use the generously discounted ticket to get you into the other two that are nearby, Lake Cave and Jewel Cave. In the early 1900s, it was quite a different proposition. A package tour of sorts did exist on which visitors travelled to Busselton by steam train, then on horseback to the caves and slept out in the bush for several nights; a lucky few might find a bed in pioneers' homes or the Caves House Hostel. When you did get into the caves, you stumbled along rough pathways in semi-darkness illuminated only by candles. When the tour guide wanted to show you some particular feature he lit a magnesium flare which had two effects; it illuminated the cavern for several seconds in a brilliant light, but effectively blinded everyone for the duration.

Mammoth Cave is self-guided. So, I wander in and pick up my headphones. A silken female voice, of the type that sets a man's pulse racing, tells me how to operate the system, what to do if I want to replay a section, and when to tell that I've come to the end of each section; what it doesn't do is give me her telephone number. I pad off towards the cave entrance, and dutifully press 101. A man's voice, of a type that may set a woman's pulse racing but which does nothing for me, takes up the story. But, in a light interplay of well-rehearsed info-giving, the two speakers alternate and give me time to bring my pulse back to normal before continuing. The explanations are good, informative without being too detailed, helpful without being patronising.

Gasping a little for breath, I climb the hundred-and-odd steps that finally lead out of the cave. I learn later that it's because the caves create a slightly higher than normal build-up of carbon dioxide, and this linked with the effort of climbing steps induces breathlessness – and I thought it was the voice on the tape.

At Jewel Cave the assembled company are greeted by Malcolm, a man dressed in the stereotypical guides' outfit of shirt, shorts, knee-length white socks and Blundstones. He has a beaut of a well-developed lower chest, so well developed in fact that I wonder how he manages to get down the steps into the cave; it would have been a long time since he last saw his feet, and probably even longer since the family jewels had been inspected without the aid of a mirror or some innocent bystander. He gives a brief lecture on what to do and not to do, which amounts to don't touch anything and stay close to the man with the torch. For a group of thirty, that's going to be difficult. But we wander myriad passageways, pottering this way and that, oo-ing and ah-ing in all the right places, dutifully laughing at his jokes – after all, he's the one with the torch and the only one who knows the way out. The last flight of steps back into daylight are steep, and I'm pressed very closely to a tightly packaged pair of nubile buttocks ahead that a red miniskirt does little to conceal. When we reach a short section where the roof lowers and we must bend almost double, the buttocks come even closer. I pray she's not eaten beans or curry in the recent past.

The final cave, Lake Cave, is an altogether more relaxed affair. Debbie is our guide, and she reckons she's got the best of all the caves, but it's a hell of a way down just to make the start. We're a mixed bunch: a couple of Germans, an elderly couple from Singapore, a few West Aussies and a couple from Windsor, doing Australia in two weeks before heading for Fiji. Lake Cave is the only one with water permanently in it. The display is delightful.

Debbie leads us as far as she can; it's only a short cave, less than a hundred metres, but the subtle lighting and the reflections create a memorable impression. Like all cave guides, Debbie can't resist switching the lights off to let us 'see' what total darkness is like – not unlike the after effects of four bottles of McLaren Vale Merlot, I'm thinking.

Later, I head down to Augusta, a neat township scattered along the coast that leads to Cape Leeuwin, the south-westernmost lighthouse in Australia, building in the late nineteenth century overlooking the point where the Indian Ocean meets the Southern Ocean. In one direction lies Africa, in the other nothing much until you hit Antarctica. I can't believe this place hasn't been swamped beneath luxury hotels, restaurants and holiday resort paraphernalia. But, apart from a modest souvenir shop, there's nothing but unadulterated coastal landscape. It's quite fabulous. I perch on a rock above the two oceans and take it in. A splendid fairy wren – that's 'Splendid fairy wren' not splendid 'Fairy wren' – appears from a shrub and regards me, its head cocked to one side. Satisfied that I'm no threat it gives me a companionable nod and hops about its business.

On the way back northwards I turn off and head for Fremantle. This quiet urbane town has been my target for my first full day in Australia each time I've come. It's a relaxing place, and a good spot to unwind from the journey and let your body catch up with Australian time; just a short train ride from Perth.

Wikipedia tells me that 'Fremantle is renowned for a well-preserved architectural heritage, including convict-built colonial-era buildings, an old jetty and port, and prisons; presenting a variety and unity of historic buildings and streetscapes. These were often built in limestone with ornate façades in a succession of architectural styles. Rapid development following the harbour works gave rise to an Edwardian precinct as merchant and shipping companies built in the west end and on reclaimed land.'

But as a rule, since I'm only ever there following the outward flight to Oz, for me it has other qualities: plenty of bars, good eateries, second-hand bookshops, and an amazing emporium-cum-market of all things exotic, bizarre and downright silly. I had my Tarot cards read here: apparently, I'm going to live until I die... which I find comforting; worth the silver-crossed palm in itself, although there was no mention of the heart attack and coronary heart bypass grafts that came along a few years later.

Maybe I didn't play my cards right.

The Fremantle Market opened in 1897, and forms a precinct providing handicrafts, speciality foods, dining halls and fish and vegetable markets, and is the focal point for hosts of buskers and street performers...seriously entertaining and relaxing after a long flight.

On my last visit to Fremantle, at the tail end of another seven-week grand tour, ready for the flights home, I sat on the steps of a jewellery shop, wherein my wife was browsing. I must have looked jiggered, because an Aboriginal man stopped and asked me if I was okay. He wasn't looking too brilliant himself - torn jeans, stubbly beard, missing teeth, line-etched complexion - but he had the good grace to reach out to a fellow being.

Boy, I must have looked rough!

Rottnest Island

Rottnest Island separated from mainland Australia between 10,000 and 6,500 years ago, but not before Aboriginal man wandered across the land bridge.

The island is believed to be a place of spirits, and is known to local Noongar Aboriginal people as Wadjemup, meaning the 'place across the water'. This I find fascinating, not least because it emphasises that the Noongar people were on mainland Australia looking across to Rottnest at some time after the island separated, and that they had no means of getting there, since they lacked the necessary sailing skills. Yet it was only by sailing from Maritime South-east Asia that the original Aboriginal people could have reached Australia in the first place. Admittedly something like 35,000-60,000 years had intervened, which was plenty of time in which to lose one set of skills and acquire others.

Today, the island is the largest in a chain of islands (which includes Garden and Carnac Islands) on the continental shelf opposite Perth, all formed of limestone rocks with a thin covering of sand. The island, with a total land area of only 19 square kilometres (7.3 square miles), is 18 kilometres (11 miles) off the Australian coast, very slightly north of west from Fremantle. It was used as a prison for Aboriginal people until as recently as 1931.

Rottnest Island is a haven for Western Australian flora and fauna. It is a protected A-Class Reserve and home to unusual animals and plants, particularly a small marsupial called the quokka (*Setonix brachyurus*), a pint-sized kangaroo, very popular with resident islanders as a tourist revenue attraction. Now I'm not going to make a habit of listing species of flora and fauna, but I'm making an exception for Rottnest Island. It is, quite simply, a place that naturalists will love to the exclusion of all else, with the possible exception of northern Queensland. Whatever time you may have allocated for Rottnest Island, at least double it; stay on the island, enjoy the moment, you may never want to leave...and I wouldn't blame you if you did...or didn't.

For a start, as the island's excellent website (www.rottnestisland. com) relates, the island is home to many coastal birds including the pied cormorant, osprey, pied oystercatcher, silver gulls, crested tern, fairy tern, bridled tern, rock parrot and reef heron. Elsewhere, feeding on the brine shrimp that inhabit the salt lakes at the eastern end of the island, are large numbers of red-necked avocet, banded stilts, ruddy turnstone, curlew sandpiper, red-capped dotterel, Australian mountain duck, red-necked stint, grey plover, white-fronted chat, Caspian terns and crested terns. I know all of this to be true, without the aid of the website, because I've just consulted my handbook of Australian birds in which I made notes at the time. Trans-equatorial migrants – which breed north of the Arctic Circle and fly to the southern hemisphere during the non-breeding season – have a place here, too: red-necked stint, grey plover, ruddy turnstone, grey-tailed tattler and curlew sandpiper.

Around the coastline are many sea birds, including the yellow-nosed albatross, Cape petrel, Wilson's storm petrel, Australian gannet, great skua and wedge-tailed shearwater. In the melaleuca (myrtle) and acacia woodlands you find tree martin, welcome swallow, silvereye, spotted turtledove, laughing turtledove, fan-tailed cuckoo, red-capped robin, golden whistler, western warbler, singing honey eater and Australian raven.

Three species of frogs are found on Rottnest Island: the delightfully named moaning frog, the western green tree frog and the sandplain froglet. Seventeen species of lizards have been recorded, too, and of these, four are very rare. There are two types of gecko, two types of legless lizard and thirteen types of skink. Commonly seen lizards include the Bobtail, King's Skink, Marbled Gecko, West Coast Ctenotus (another skink) and Burton's Legless Lizard.

There are also two species of snakes present on the island, the Southern Blind Snake and the Dugite. The Southern Blind Snake is a non-venomous burrowing snake, and the Dugite is a slender, dark brown, venomous snake. Dugites are frequently seen during the summer months, often lying on the road harnessing warmth from the sun; I know that because travelling the road just in front of me is a young girl on a bike, oblivious to the fact that she just straddled a Dugite. Thankfully, although venomous, Dugites are timid and non-aggressive – unless you run over them with a bike, I suppose.

This magnificent range of species is typical of so many parts of Australia, but Rottnest is so compact and yet so blessed with natural history that I defy any true-blooded naturalist not to be drawn there. My wife and I were, but for an hour or so it was anything but an agreeable experience, primarily because I had booked a tour on a semi-submersible boat but hadn't allowed for the slightly choppy conditions. It wasn't the most agreeable part of the day, but the island certainly made up for it. Only vehicles that are propelled by human power are today allowed around the island, except for wheelchair transport. So, it's very much a case of 'On yer bike', or walk.

But it is the delightful quokka that visitors mainly come to see. This cat-sized animal was one of the first Australian mammals seen by Europeans. The Dutch mariner Samuel Volckertzoon wrote of sighting '...a wild cat' on Rottnest Island in 1658. In 1696, Willem de Vlamingh mistook them for giant rats and named the island 'Rotte nest', from the Dutch word rattennest meaning 'rat's nest'. Should you find a quokka, however, don't be tempted to pick it up; it isn't going to eat you, but to do so carries a hefty fine, of up to AU$2,000.

Cute, but not cuddly.

CHAPTER FIVE

SYDNEY

Sydney Harbour Bridge Climb – Sydney Rocks – Sydney Opera House – Australian Rules Football – Australian cuisine

I'd be lying if I said I wasn't just a tad apprehensive. But Sarah, who has a smile and a figure that makes me wish I'm forty years younger, tells me not to worry, I'll feel much better afterwards. Where have I heard that before?

I take my place in the queue and study the handout; this is going to be quite something. I've never done anything like this before. Presently Zac Gillett appears, an instantly likeable, cheery, confident, re-assuring, and, as I discover later, much-travelled, entrepreneurial young man. He, too, tells me not to worry. Spotting a way of opting out without losing too much face, I ask him how many people chicken out once they start.

'Hardly any; maybe one or two a day, out of an average of eight hundred.'

No use thinking of getting out that way then. I resign myself to the inevitable, realising I have to be fully committed and trust in Sarah's judgement, after all handling an average of eight hundred clients a day, and up to fourteen hundred at their peak season, I figure they ought to know what they're doing...and that includes making sure everyone is sober – so, we all get breathalysed.

With what for a moment I mistook as clairvoyance, Zac says he'll meet me on the other side as he hands me over to Jo, who takes me through to the changing rooms and suggests, as it is quite warm already, that I should strip down to basics, and slip into something more comfortable.

The two-tone pale grey Babygro jump-suit has a dehumanising look about it, like I've suddenly become one of the uniformed minions of some wicked despot in a James Bond movie, and it's relief to see that everyone has to wear them. At least we all look equally daft. When it gets cold, they supply fleeces; when it rains, out come the waterproofs. Against the sun, they supply a baseball cap, which clips to the top of the jump-suit collar along with the ties for my specs. Nothing is left to chance. I'm even breathalysed and have to pass through a metal detector.

Suddenly, Zac re-appears and fits me into a safety harness, then shows me how to use the security device, which simply clips on at the start, and stays fixed the whole time. Then a little practice getting up and down, turning around and walking with the safety harness, and we're ready.

Zac, donning headphones so that he can talk us through the whole experience, leads the way. And suddenly, suitably encondomed and trussed, I'm face to face with it.

It's huge, much bigger close up than I was expecting, and I'm beginning to wonder if I've done the right thing. But, it seems, there's no turning back.

Sydney Harbour Bridge is the world's largest (but not longest) steel arch bridge and, given its magnificent setting, has become a world-renowned symbol of Australia, affectionately known as the 'Coathanger'. Construction fell to the firm of Dorman Long and Co. Ltd., of Middlesbrough in England, and began on the 28th July 1923, ultimately employing approximately 1,400 people.

The bridge finally opened in March 1932. When the arch was joined on 10pm on the 19th August 1930, north and south Sydney were at last permanently linked; it must have held the same sense of occasion as the Frenchman and the Englishman who shook hands beneath the English Channel in December 1988. The length of the arch span is 503 metres, and the height above sea level at the top of the arch, where I'm going, is 134 metres. The construction used around six million rivets, some weighing as much as 3.5 kilograms and over 395 millimetres in length; most of them look like balls sprayed into the steelwork by an army of wayward golfers. The total weight of the steelwork is 52,800 tonnes, with the arch itself accounting for 39,000 tonnes. By any standards this is a monumental construction.

The official opening day, Saturday, 19th March 1932, was a momentous occasion, drawing huge crowds to the city. The New South Wales premier, John T Lang had the honour of declaring the bridge open, but his moment was upstaged by Captain Francis de Groot of the para-military group, the New Guard, who was faster on the draw and slashed the ribbon prematurely with his sword before the premier could whip his scissors out. The official opening celebrations included a vast cavalcade of decorated floats with marching bands, heading through the streets of Sydney and across the roadway. Ironically, the opening of this expensive monument – it cost $AUS4,217,721 (£137,281,358 in today's money) – coincided with a time of economic depression in New South Wales.

The next day, a young man, who had queued for two days to buy the first rail ticket sold to the public for crossing the bridge became the unwitting catalyst that led to today's BridgeClimb Experience. The young man became the father-in-law of Paul Cave who developed the dream of enabling ordinary people to cross the bridge. In 1998, the BridgeClimb was officially launched, and since then has seen over 3 million folk brave the journey, one of the most recent, a lady from Sydney, to celebrate her 100th birthday. In a few years, the BridgeClimb has already garnered numerous tourism and heritage awards.

Not exactly going where no man had gone before – there have been thousands of marriage proposals at the summit of the bridge –

I launch myself into Zac's wake, as he heads out across an approach span leading to the first of the four abutment towers. The safety gadget clatters across the security cable giving a re-assuring tug at my waist from time to time. It's not yet all that far down to the ground, but a fall would result in the sort of headache paracetamol won't fix. There's a handrail each side of the walkway, and the tendency is to hang on to both, although it's easier just to walk normally. Zac keeps up a constant and informative patter.

When I repeated the climb with my family some years later, the guide told my wife, who was afraid of heights, just to look straight into his eyes, not to look down. He was tall, dark, handsome, suntanned, hypnotic, charismatic – she's still not recovered! – and it wasn't only down to the views we were treated to.

'The four towers are purely decorative', Zac tells me. 'Basically, they don't serve any purpose in terms of support for the bridge; they're just ornamental, to make the bridge look better.'

As we reach the first one, I'm suddenly confronted with the rising steps that climb onto the arch. Zac was right; there's little to worry about. The walkway is wide, with generous shoulders, and if I look up and around instead of down there's no real sense of exposure. In fact, it's profoundly exhilarating. The steps, the first of 1,332 encountered on the climb, have a low rise, so there's no tiring sensation of climbing a tedious flight of stairs, just an easy, relaxed gait. Part way up Zac takes me out onto one of the centre spans, and I shoot off a few pictures of the road deck before resuming the climb.

It is a truly magnificent experience. The wind is a gentle breeze of 18 knots from the south-west, and the air temperature hovering around twenty-four. Inside the jump-suit I'm getting hot and sticky, but the wind is refreshing, and the top of the arch just a few paces ahead. Other groups are queuing for the all-inclusive summit picture, so we wait a while and chat about surfing and travel, and Zac points out a few key landmarks like the Olympic stadium, Government House, the Royal Botanic Garden and the Department of Lands building which as recently as the time the bridge was opened was the tallest building in Sydney. Today, it is lost in a wall of glass-fronted office and hotel towers that huddle protectively around it and the tiny Victorian churches that dot the landscape of the city centre. One thing I notice Zac avoids is talk about the Rugby World Cup, and I'm too discreet, especially at this altitude, to bring up the subject of England's win against Australia. Nor does he mention that the heat can cause the entire bridge to move up or down by as much as 18 centimetres.

On the way down, everyone is facing towards the centre of Sydney, walking into the picture: the Opera House, Circular Quay, Walsh Bay and Darling Harbour. Sleek Captain Cook's Tour boats ply back and forth out of Circular Quay, jostling for space with the more urbane green and yellow ferries and darting water taxis. And in The Rocks below, the Saturday market is a-bustle, and the sound of a live band playing Cajun rock drifts upwards.

From start to finish, the climb takes three-and-a-half hours, but the end comes all too soon. Zac presents me with my certificate to prove I did it, and a complimentary summit photograph; it's not Everest, but for many it is. A personal achievement, a sense of adventure, and a thrill of a lifetime.

You should try it sometime. It's not as though you can visit Sydney and not notice the bridge; it's there, slotting diverse bits of its structure into virtually every angle you can view it from, like an impatient child, beckoning to be noticed. James Michener, an American author, in his 1950 book *Return to Paradise*, however is not so easily impressed, opining that the bridge is very ugly, but that no Australian would admit to that. Well, I do have to admit, it is rather clunky...but majestic, solid, bold and big. A magnificent bridge from the top of which I've witnessed one of the finest sunsets.

TERRY MARSH

The Rocks at the harbour end of George Street is a corner of Sydney with a unique appeal, a charisma all its own, a place that, so the blurb goes, offers 'something for everyone. From home-made jams and designer homewares to a ride on a Harley Davidson, or a Ned Kelly outfit' for those feeling disposed to rob a bank. When I came here twenty years ago there was a guy producing instant and highly imaginative 'space' paintings using the sort of cans of spray used for car body repair work. I expected that he'd long have passed away from CFC poisoning, but no, he was still there five years later. His designs had taken on what was for me an over-elaborate style with pyramids, leaping dolphins and bounding kangaroos; I preferred his earlier 'naïve' style, but then I suppose all forms of art must develop, and he was just doing the same.

The truly amazing thing about The Rocks, apart from the fact that they have their own website (www.therocks.com), is the vast range to choose from. When I first visited, there were crammed into what is really a very small area no fewer 25 cafés, 49 restaurants, 14 bars, 15 hotels, 5 indigenous stores, 24 art galleries, 27 fashion stores, 4 antique stores, 25 jewellery stores, 6 museums, 18 art and craft stores, 51 speciality shops and a visitor centre. I've no reason to doubt these figures, but I find them quite incredible. You can spend a whole day or more here, along with a small fortune... and then come back the next day for something you forgot. It is spectacularly atmospheric, exciting, bustling, frenetic, chaotic, and, should it all get too much, simply step aside, order a glass of Sauvignon Blanc, and watch the world go by; it's remarkably therapeutic.

And some of the buildings are quite stunning. Sergeant Major's Row, built between 1881 and 1883 is an agreeable two-storey run of colonial houses with much intricate wrought-iron work on the balconies. One of the houses became the Swagman's Post Café, another specialises in Irish design. Not far away a closed building, the police station from 1882 until 1974, is built on the site of the First General Hospital in Australia. The original building was demolished in 1796 and rebuilt in 1788. It is classified by the National Trust as part of Australia's Colonial Heritage, one of very few neo-Classical nineteenth-century police stations in the inner city. It was built, the hospital that is, by twelve convict carpenters who worked alongside sixteen men on loan from ships in the harbour.

I have a little time to kill while awaiting a respectable hour to launch myself on Sydney's eateries, so I flip idly through the TV channels and find myself watching a game of Australian Rules Football. After ten minutes I decide that the nearest description I can devise is that it's badly choreographed chaos. I'm not sure about the 'rules', which the name of the game implies must exist somewhere, probably in a darkened vault guarded by fierce three-headed Potteresque hounds that have never seen the light of day nor been fed for over a month. This must be the only football game in the world where you score a point for missing the goal, and I wonder at first if that's intended to be a sop to the unlucky soul who misses so that he doesn't get too upset. I've not yet figured out how many players there are on each team – it isn't unequivocally clear how many teams there are, probably two – because they never stay still for long enough to count them. And the situation is complicated by a number of other individuals on the field of play who run around blowing whistles, bouncing the ball on the ground from time to time but generally running away from what's going on, getting out of harm's way, I suppose.

But I have reached a conclusion about the qualities needed to be a star player. To begin with you have to epitomise the youthful vigour of Australian manhood, you need to be suitably bronzed – though if you don't match up, I guess they probably give you vouchers for free tanning sessions down at the local massage parlour – ruggedly handsome, slim and athletic, rather like the sort of people you meet at a typical Saturday market in England, I suppose. You also have to look good in a sleeveless vest, and exceptionally good in tight-fitting short shorts – so, no room for flabby buttocks or over-sized tadgers...although...no, we won't go there. Oh, and you have to be able to spit nonchalantly whenever the television cameras are on you.

The game starts by one of the supernumerary guys bouncing the ball hard on the ground, like he's using the head of someone he doesn't like too well. The rest of the players meanwhile are gathered round chatting in small groups about what was on the television last night or whose wife they're messing about with, and generally just hanging around until the ball comes back from orbit. Then they all lunge at it. If they can't reach the ball, then it seems to be okay to lunge at the head of one of the opposing team, and, if you can't reach that, then just give him a good kicking. Then they start kicking and throwing the ball all over the place, hoping one of their own team will find it. If they're lucky, the ball arcs beautifully towards one of their team-mates, but, just as he's about to catch it, an opposing player is obliged to thump him in the back of the neck and knock him off balance. And so it goes on, until someone standing in front of four goal posts – the middle two are taller than the others – catches the ball. Then everything goes quiet for a while as he composes himself and then runs towards the goal and tries to kick the ball between the tall posts. Which seems to make everyone happy, as the score goes up by six points. If he misses the tall posts, but gets the ball within the outer small posts, then only one point is scored, and no-one seems very happy with that, except the opposing team. The pitch is oval, presumably because it looks prettier that way, and the chaos is meant to be contained within it. If the ball goes outside the oval, then another of the supernumeraries stands on the line with his back to the players and throws the ball high over his head for the on-field players to start charging about with. Play continues until they all get fed up or someone blows a whistle. And then they go home to watch the edited highlights for the next six days.

If it was left to me, I'd have goal posts that were constantly moving on tracks around the edge of the field...and a square ball.

I've long held the view that one of the best ways of understanding the culture of another country is through its food, or, more precisely, through my stomach. One of the criteria I use for determining the quality of the food I've been given, and by the same token its value for money, is whether I could cook the same thing myself, as well or better. And I don't find it at all curious that among my colleague travel writers there are those with a similar approach, all have better-than-modest talent in the kitchen, but none would aspire to being a chef. We're not being 'superior', but we know the difference between quality cuisine and culinary bullshit.

So, later in the day, looking for somewhere suitable to eat, I wandered down to Circular Quay and along Cahill Walk, taking time out at the Eastbank café bar to have a delightfully chilled glass of Omrah Unoaked Chardonnay 2003, while I indulged in my favourite pastime of watching the world go by and eavesdropping on conversations. The tongues were many and varied: Japanese, Irish, American, English, Indian, Malaysian, and Scouse (that's the language of Liverpool, England, for those that don't know, and it comes with a strong accent which makes it intelligible to very few who live in Liverpool and hardly anyone who doesn't. Fortunately, my great, great grandfather was from Liverpool).

With fruit bats circling overhead in huge numbers, I wandered down to the Opera House, probably the most instantly identifiable building in the world. Clive James, the iconoclastic Australian expat satirist described it as a typewriter full of cockle shells. John Betjeman said, with wonderful imagery, that it reminded him of a rugby scrum of nuns. I'm not sure how many games of rugby played between teams of nuns Mr Betjeman has been to, and I certainly haven't seen any, but I'm prepared to believe him, and the description works so well it does so the other way round. Ask anyone which building in the world might be described as a rugby scrum of nuns, and, after a moment's pause, my betting is that nine out of ten with say Sydney Opera House.

Located right at the end of Bennelong Point, juxtaposed to the harbour and completely to scale in relation to the Harbour Bridge, the sandstone cliff face, Macquarie Street and Circular Quay, the vision of the Opera House is dramatic and unforgettable. My own first visit was greeted by the sight of thousands of fruit bats flying over the huge sails.

The Opera House took 16 years to build, between 1957 and 1973, and by any standards is a masterpiece of modern architectural design, engineering and construction technology. It exhibits the creative genius of its designer, the Pritzker Prize winner, Danish architect Jørn Utzon, alongside the successful engineering of the Danish firm Ove Arup and Partners and the Australian building contractors M R Hornibrook.

Amazingly, the architect, Jørn Utzon was initially rejected by three judges in a 1956 competition to design the Opera House, but his entry was picked out by the fourth judge, renowned American architect Eero Saarinen, who declared it outstanding. Utzon ultimately beat 232 other entrants, and won £5,000 for his design, even though he had never visited the site before entering the design competition, and used his naval experience to study charts of the harbour

The story of its construction was one of great controversy. Complex engineering problems and escalating costs made it a source of great public debate that only subsided when the beauty and achievement of the completed building placed it on the world stage. The technical challenge of how to construct the roof sails alone took four years to solve, based on the geometry of the sphere and Utzon used this to demonstrate the creative potential and the assembly of prefabricated, repeated components.

Today, Sydney Opera House is a national cultural centre that has gained widespread recognition and respect as a performing arts venue, and includes a concert hall, opera and drama theatres, a playhouse and a studio. It is a fitting showcase for many of the world's leading performers. As Utzon envisioned, the Opera House reflects its pivotal place in Australia's creative history '...an individual face for Australia in the world of art'.

Anyway, I digress.

On the way back from the Opera House I'm drawn by the wondrous-sounding dishes of a quayside restaurant, and spend twenty minutes digesting the menu before attempting to digest anything else. How did I feel about caramelised black figs, Persian feta and roquette? Or maybe my palate could be agreeably surprised by the deboned grilled cinnamon quail with roast carrot, ginger and pomegranate salad and grape sauce. But I was very tempted by the dry aged grain-fed rib-eye steak on the bone from the Darling Downs, spinach, ricotta gnocchi and horseradish jus, but no more so than by the ravioli of gorgonzola, ricotta, truffled honey, burnt butter and sage. I'd almost made my mind up when I spotted the sugar-cured ocean trout with tzatziki, salmon roe and mustard cress. I detail all these to illustrate my point. Without exception they had my neglected tummy on the brink of gastronomic joy. I was heading for culinary delight, and would savour every moment.

However...I began with a tomato, pine nut and tuna tart with roquette, but, apart from the roquette, which was fresh and lightly seasoned, the tart was a huge disappointment, being little more than an up-market pizza. So, I was just a little concerned as I waited for the quail, my main course choice. When it arrived there was plenty of it – Australians don't understand the meaning of small when it comes to food, which is no bad thing, and certainly not a fault – but I have this fixation with carrots, which I hope you won't tell anyone about until it becomes legal. I've never quite figured out why restaurant chefs even bother with carrots. They are notoriously difficult to cook and retain flavour, even assuming they had flavour in the first place. Any attempt at boiling simply removes the taste and, as it happens, the goodness, too. And then they are invariably prepared in advance and kept warm, which, alas, is terminal. Mine were supposed to be roasted, which ought to have given them a better chance. But it wasn't to be; they were as bland as the pomegranate salad and grape sauce. Why bother using pomegranate seeds if you can't taste them in the end product?

I wasn't hungry when I finished, but I felt let down. I could have done better myself, and that equated with objecting to paying for it. When I dine out, I want to experience culinary art, to savour the skills and talents of the chef, to appreciate the best produce of the country I'm in prepared by people with ability. I know they can do it, I've eaten well often enough. And I know they can do it in Australia. But my quail, much as I greatly appreciate it giving up its life that I might eat, was done a disservice.

Still there's always tomorrow.

And many more places with much more accomplished chefs.

A trip by boat to Manly – Katoomba and the Blue Mountains – Botany Bay and Captain Cook – Cronulla

One of the delights of Sydney Harbour is the plethora of boats coming and going, and somehow failing to collide; there are some close calls, but generally they contrive not to hit anything. Big boats, little boats, bus boats, taxi boats, private yachts of all shapes, sizes and expense, and tour boats that take you around the harbour and out as far as Manley. You pay at least AU$40 for the privilege, even though you get exactly the same 'cruise' experience on the Manley ferry for around a quarter of that.

Personally, and this may apply only to me, I find Sydney Harbour confusing. If I stand with my back to the Sydney Opera House, facing across the water to Kirribilli, I have the distinct impression that the sea is to my left; it isn't, it's to the right. That's probably because I'm very much a west coast person, with the sea on my left when I face north.

Anyway...Manley.

During the 19th and early 20th century, Manly was renowned as one of Australia's most popular seaside holiday resorts. There is a story, possibly apocryphal, that Manly Beach was the place where a prohibition of daylight sea bathing was first challenged. Clad in a neck to knee costume, in October 1902, William Gocher, swam at midday after announcing his intention to do so in the Manly and North Sydney News. After being ignored by authorities and being publicly critical of them, he swam again and was escorted from the water by the police, although no charges were laid. In November 1903, Manly Council resolved to allow all-day bathing provided a neck to knee swimming costume was worn. During the first official bathing season in 1903, 17 people drowned on Manly Beach. A year later a surf club was formed on the beach to safeguard the public.

For the less adventurous soul, commercial Manly is centred around The Corso, which runs from Manly Wharf to the ocean at Manly Beach. Part of The Corso is a mall which allows outdoor dining for cafés and restaurants. It was here that I met Jo Metcalfe from Leeds, working in a bar where talking to customers for longer than it takes to write down an order was frowned on. But she didn't care; she was coming to the end of her work permit, her boss refused to give her a permanent job, even though she regularly worked 60 hours a week for him, and that lessened her chances of staying in Australia. I never did find out how she got on.

Back in Sydney, where one of the rare privileges of being a travel journalist saw me staying as a guest of a 5-star hotel, I was working my way down a complimentary bottle of champagne – a great investment for the hotel, as I subsequently wrote four long features about the hotel (that's the way it works) – while debating the prospect of a visit to Katoomba and the Blue Mountains, 80 kilometres (50 miles) inland. The trip had not been part of my original plan, but this delectable range of eucalyptus-clad hills was too much to resist.

Katoomba, I find, etymologically challenged. Kedumba or Katta-toon-bah is an Aboriginal term for 'shining falling water', a name that derives from a waterfall plunging into the Jamison valley below the magnificent escarpment for which the area is famed. It aptly describes the location. But before the name Katoomba was adopted in 1877, the site was known as William's Chimney, Collett's Swamp, and in 1874 was named The Crushers, after the name of the railway station that served a nearby quarry. It was around this time that Katoomba started to develop as a tourist destination, in spite of these nomenclatural impediments.

A walk down the main street to Echo Point produces one of the most stunning vistas in Australia: the Three Sisters, a series of rocky pinnacles, backed by the undulating blue haze of forest that makes up the Blue Mountains National Park. These are not mountains in the traditional sense, rather a giant plateau dissected by deep canyons and gorges. Sulphur-crested cockatoos flit across the canopy below, while the sharp calls of unseen birds echo from the walls.

The Blue Mountains National Park is one of the most well-known parks in Australia, part of the Greater Blue Mountains World Heritage Area, being listed for its geographic, botanic and cultural values, including numerous sites of Aboriginal significance.

With care, it is possible to take the Giant's Stairway, a pathway descending 800 steps around the far side of the Three Sisters, precarious in places, to the forest floor, from where a superb trail leads to the nearby settlement of Leura, near enough to make a circular walk well worthwhile. It's a descent I've relished a few times, and always with a hushed sense of privilege. My imagination forever on the cusp of some startling revelation, a previously unknown species of bird, mammal, insect, snake...dragon... The trees are mainly eucalypts, including Sydney peppermint, black ash, red bloodwood, narrow-leafed stringy bark and hard-leaved scribbly gum, turpentines, Sydney red gums and she-oaks. The plants in the understorey have tough, leathery or spiny leaves, hard and unyielding to the touch. It's an eerie place, never quite silent, always with something creaking, whispering or scuttling about.

Sadly, many of today's visitors to the Blue Mountains see the National Park from one of the many lookouts between Wentworth Falls and Blackheath, and rarely actually set foot in the park...well, there's ice cream, burgers and beer up there.

Weighed down by the baggage of reluctance and the products of a trawl through a second-hand bookshop, I head back to the railway station. Tomorrow I must move on...no, tomorrow I must package the books into a parcel and post them home...and then I must move on.

In the event, tomorrow got off to a bad start. A queue for breakfast, a mile walk to get a hire car, a thirty-minute wait at the car hire desk, the drive back to pick up my luggage, and the nightmare of trying to find my way out of Sydney.

I'm heading for Canberra, apparently an insignificant place in the scale of things, but still the nation's capital, and, with evident naivety, I expect some signposting in Sydney to give me a clue. But all I get is the 'Airport' and 'Wallongong'. So, I opt for Wallongong, for no better reason than I like the rhythm of the name, but on the way decide to divert to Botany Bay, expecting some imperious Victorian monument announcing that this was where it all started, even though it wasn't. But Botany Bay, which has the status of a city, is a huge disappointment. Pastel-coloured neo-Colonial shops and houses front one main street. There's a Sir Joseph Banks Hotel and a Captain Cook's Hotel, but little to encourage me to stay and take in the historic significance of the place. And somehow I find that quite sad. This is the heart of Sydney's pan-tiled suburbia, a terracotta panorama fully on view to anyone landing at Sydney airport. On the plus side, there's a high security prison, a container terminal (Port Botany), an oil refinery and a sewerage outlet.

I decide not to stay; it seems after all that I don't have Captain Cook's navigational skills - his landing place is now the south head of Botany Bay National Park, and the spot where the crew of the Endeavour anchored on the 29th April 1770, is marked by a simple red buoy.

But I can't quite bring myself to leave the area, and start following road signs for Cronulla, on the ocean side of the Kurnell Peninsula. Cronulla, is a relaxed and agreeable coastal resort at one end of Sydney's longest beach a ten kilometre stretch that continues as the deserted, dune-backed Wanda Beach. You probably wouldn't come here unless you were a surfer, but this is prime surfing territory, and if you want to watch body-toned, happy young people, male and female, you'd be hard pushed to find a better place.

A wrong turning in Wallangong has me going round in circles so many times children on swings at a roadside park are starting to point me out to their friends. In the end, I resign myself to asking a taxi driver the best way to Canberra. I pronounce it Can-bra; he stresses the second syllable, Can-ber-ra, with a South African accent. Ironically, by all accounts, I was right - Can-bra - and he was wrong. Anyway, his advice is to go back the way I've come and turn off for Picton. This is not news that I receive with good grace, even though it turns out to be good counsel.

CHAPTER SIX

CANBERRA

The birth of Canberra – PM's Question time in Parliament House – Australia's parliamentary system

'Canberra is not, as you might believe, a desolate wasteland of bleak suburbia' (Anthony Sharwood: Columnist, News.com.au)

I really like Canberra, I didn't think I would, but I do. Others are less enamoured, but I can't help it if they are unable to recognise a pearl when they see one.

And while my first impression is that it's wondrously like a real-time MENSA puzzle for motorists, or some enormous theme park with acres and acres of tidy and immaculate open space pinned in place by strategically positioned groups of Norfolk pine – and somewhere, lost in the middle (except there isn't a middle) a city of over 375,000 souls – it does rather grow on you in a very appetising sort of way. Around each bend I'm expecting Mickey Mouse to appear, or a fairy tale castle, or to see a road sweep surreptitiously lifting the edge of the manicured lawns to hide the dust underneath. Except there are no road sweeps – unless they work at night; everywhere is so pristine it can only be self-vacuuming. And, like a theme park, if the place looks hugely contrived, that's because it is. The theme, of course, is politics, and that's not a subject that readily endears itself to the hearts and minds of the good people of Australia. So, politicians are devious, lying, self-interested conniving bastards (their words not mine), and 'politics'

equals 'Canberra', so Canberra is crap, too.
Except that it isn't.

As a child, I collected stamps from Australia, or at least from the different colonies of Australia - New South Wales, Western Australia, Victoria, Tasmania - and I wish I'd kept them because recently I saw individual stamps mounted in tiny frames on sale in Perth for thirty-five dollars. I could have been quite wealthy by now. But what the different stamps illustrated, was that all the component colonies had their own governing bodies, their own fiscal infrastructure, their own constitutions, their own time even. Duty imposed on products traded across a colony boundary, even though they may only be yards apart, was as severe as if they had crossed half a world. The situation was astoundingly ridiculous.

A Federation of the Australian colonies had been discussed as early as 1847, but more than thirty years would elapse before the plans gained any serious support. In 1885, the Federal Council of Australasia was established, minus New South Wales, who refused to join until persuaded of the sense of it by Henry Parkes, the Federation's highest profile advocate, who delivered an inspiring speech declaring that the time was ripe for a centralised system of government. Parkes' sentiments were strongly endorsed at a conference held in Melbourne in 1890, and then, with greater determination, again a year later in Sydney when the conference debated Parkes' first stab at a constitution for the new federation. Presciently, at the conference banquet, Parkes proposed the toast 'One People; One Destiny'. It was to be, but not just yet, and it took some time to sort things out, but the Imperial Parliament in London did little to impede the new development, giving the Bill an almost uninterrupted passage through Parliament, enabling Queen Victoria to give it the Royal Assent on the 9th July 1900. The date set for the inauguration of the Commonwealth of Australia was the 1st January 1901.

On that day, a new nation was born, and three weeks later Queen Victoria died.

Because the competing and substantially equal claims of Melbourne and Sydney to be the new Commonwealth's capital were never going to be amicably resolved, the decision was made to seek an altogether new site for the capital. Advertisements that might just as easily have been selling a second-hand car were placed in metropolitan newspapers inviting people to suggest sites around 64,000 acres in size, that might be suitable as a location for the new capital. The response was overwhelming, though the records don't appear to detail how many sites on offer where from the people who owned the land in question. In the winter of 1902, a group of senators embarked on a tour of twelve sites from Armidale in the north to Eden in the south. It requires little imagination to visualise the expedition as one huge bout of sycophantic junketing with the visitors being entertained magnanimously by local communities, causing one local journalist, who presumably had mislaid his invitation, to peevishly describe the exercise as a 'silly picnic excursion'.

Some picnic.

The selection process was project-managed by Alexander Oliver, President of the Land Court, who ultimately reported that three sites – Orange, Yass or Bombala-Eden – would equally be suitable for the Seat of Government. Years were to disappear into the maw of colonial bias, bickering, controversy and politics before, in late 1908, the House of Representatives voted for Yass-Canberra.

Of course, that was only the start of the process. Having agreed on a general location, it was now necessary to fix a specific location within the Yass-Canberra area. The Constitution itself imposed a certain limitation, requiring that the new capital '...shall be in the State of New South Wales, and be distant not less than one hundred miles from Sydney'. The location was miles from anywhere, stinking hot in summer and decidedly nippy in winter, an outback sheep station divided by the Molonglo River below the Tidbinbilla Hills in the southern part of New South Wales. On New Year's Day, 1911, New South Wales passed 2,360 square kilometres of land, along with a section of Jervis Bay for use as a federal port, to the Commonwealth Government, which then assumed control of the Federal Capital Territory.

All it needed now was a name.

With the sort of foreseeable blend of backroom politicking, scholarly and practical thought, and plain but good-natured silliness I witnessed employed at the time of local government re-organisation in England and Wales in 1974, the good people of Australia, when invited to submit names for the new capital, did their utmost to give the politicians something to chew over. Seven hundred names were put forward including Cookaburra, Wheatwoolgold, Kangaremu, Federatia, Olympus, Paradise, Captain Cook, Shakespeare, Eucalyptia, Sydmelperadbrisho (work that one out for yourself), Meladneyperbane (that one, too) and the politically inane and instantly doomed Swindleville, Gonebroke and Caucus City.

You could almost feel the relief when someone, hopefully casually over a gin and tonic after a lousy day at the abacus, pointed out that the place already had a name that had been in use for almost a century – Kan-berra, meaning 'a meeting place'; how convenient. So, in March 1909 the site known to the indigenous Ngunnawal Aboriginal people as Kamberra was finally accepted. Another waggish interpretation suggested that the name comes from the local Aboriginal word for 'woman's cleavage', because it's nestled between two hills.

Relief there was for sure when at noon on the 12th March 1913, Lady Denman, the wife of the Governor-General, mounted a crimson-draped platform and elegantly declared 'I name the capital of Australia, Canberra. May God bless her, and all who sail in her'.

To be truthful, she didn't say the last bit.

But she did, inadvertently, stress the central syllable – Can-ber-ra – which got the place a bad name from the outset. And they've been queuing up to bash Canberra ever since. The city certainly does seem to have trouble convincing professionals to move there, despite high pay and world-class services. I read that up to 75% of the doctors employed at the emergency department at one of the city's public hospitals, don't live in the city or its surrounds; it's even said that the department head regularly commuted four hours by plane from his home in Perth. Not the most glowing of recommendations, not to mention a tad disloyal if the city's paying his salary. And since The Lodge became the prime minister's official residence in 1927, every PM has lived there except John Howard, who preferred to commute from Sydney and stayed in Kirribilli House, the Prime Minister's residence there.

A lack of nightlife is one of the most common complaints about Canberra, not that I've noticed an issue, but then I'm usually tucked snugly in bed by 10pm. A 'beacon of mediocrity', and a 'pantheon of being ordinary' are other negative soubriquets for Canberra, but, on the plus side (I think), the Australian Capital Territory is Australia's only jurisdiction where making hardcore porn movies is legal, and it has some of the most lax cannabis laws in Australia. But check whether this is still the case before you decide to rush out there.

Detractors aside, what appeals to me about Canberra is its layout. Canberra is a planned city, the inner-city core of which was designed by Walter Burley Griffin, a 20th-century American architect, born in the late 19th century, who must have thought all his birthdays had come at once when someone asked him to design the new capital city of Australia; not a job that drops on your desk too often.

'Okay; I'll just finish inventing the carport and the L-shaped floor plan, and then I'll be right with you.' In the event, it didn't all go according to plan; anyone's plans.

Near Lake Burley Griffin, major roads follow a wheel-and-spoke pattern rather than a grid, and that can be mightily confusing when you first arrive. Griffin's proposal was consumed with geometric patterns, including concentric hexagonal and octagonal streets emanating from several radii. Sounds wonderful; and it is, but not if you have to drive around it, although, to be fair, it's fine once you get the hang of it. And the Canberra drivers do seem to be tolerant of in-bound traffic.

Lake Burley Griffin was intentionally designed so that the orientation of the components was related to various topographical landmarks in Canberra, as Lionel Wigmore's Canberra: History of Australia's National Capital, explains. The lakes stretch from east to west and divide the city in two; a land axis perpendicular to the central basin stretches from Capital Hill - the eventual location of the new Parliament House on a mound on the southern side - across the central basin to the northern banks along Anzac Parade to the Australian War Memorial. This was designed so that looking from Capital Hill, the War Memorial stood directly at the foot of Mount Ainslie. At the south-western end of the land axis was Bimberi Peak, the highest mountain in the ACT (Australian Capital Territory).

The straight edge of the circular segment that formed the central basin of Lake Burley Griffin was perpendicular to the land axis and designated the water axis, and it extended north-west towards Black Mountain...

...are you still with me?

A line parallel to the water axis, on the northern side of the city, was designated the municipal axis. This became the location of Constitution Avenue, which links City Hill in Civic Centre and both Market Centre and the Defence precinct on Russell

Hill. Commonwealth Avenue and Kings Avenue were to run from the southern side from Capital Hill to City Hill and Market Centre on the north respectively, and they formed the western and eastern edges of the central basin. The area enclosed by the three avenues was known as the Parliamentary Triangle, and formed the centrepiece of Griffin's work. The effect of the Griffins' quirky designs is to separate each district by leafy scrub, allowing residents to have a perpetual feeling of being surrounded by the bush.

Griffin, ably assisted by his wife, Marion, assigned spiritual values to Mount Ainslie, Black Mountain, and Red Hill and originally planned to cover each in flowers. That way each hill might be covered with a single, primary colour representing its spiritual value. This part of the plan never came to fruition. World War I slowed construction and planning disputes led to Walter's dismissal by Prime Minister Billy Hughes after the war ended.

Many of Canberra's suburbs are named after former Prime Ministers, famous Australians, early settlers, or use Aboriginal words for their title.

Now just over 100 years old, since 1913, Canberra has only slowly developed its role as the national capital. Another fourteen years were to elapse before Parliament finally moved from the interim seat of government in Melbourne to the building known today as the Old Parliament House. Even so, Canberra was still little more than a bush town with attitude, its growth hindered first by the Great Depression of the 1930s, and then by the Second World War. Development was also limited by Canberra's very position. It lies around 60 kilometres (37 miles) south of the main Sydney to Melbourne road - the Hume Highway - doesn't have a main line railway service, the main route south doesn't really go anywhere, though it is one of only two options if you want to go to Melbourne - the other, involving the said Hume Highway, which traffic-wise has more black spots than a Dalmatian, involves turning round and heading back northwards before you can turn south-west – and its port at Jervis Bay is incredibly difficult to get to, involving unsealed roads through the Morton National Park or a great loop north and east through Goulburn and Nowra.

In the 1950s, Robert Menzies government accelerated the transfer of public service departments to Canberra. A few years later, the Government established the National Capital Development Commission as a statutory authority to '...plan, develop and construct Canberra as the National Capital'. The first Commissioner was John, later Sir John, Overall, who first saw Canberra from the harness of a parachute as the 1st Australian Paratroop Battalion drifted into the city in 1943, and was no doubt appointed because better than anyone else he could take an 'overall' view of his responsibilities. [Sorry.] By the time of his appointment as Commissioner, Canberra '...lacked virtually everything a National Capital, or indeed any major city, should possess. Its...elements consisted of a provisional Parliament House and a War Memorial.'

Nothing quite like starting with a blank canvas, but I have to say that the finished painting is wonderful...I don't care how many hate it, or find reason to knock it...Can-bra is great.

As if to endorse my view, in 2014 the world finally got round to recognising that Canberra is the finest place in the world to live, according a report by the Organisation for Economic Cooperation and Development (OECD). See www.bbc.co.uk/news/business-29531850, if you don't believe me. Canberra led the regional ranking while Australia topped the overall country rankings, followed by Norway.

The OECD ranked 362 regions of its 34 member nations in its survey. It used nine measures of well-being, including income, education, jobs, safety, health and environment. Five Australian cities including Sydney, Melbourne and Perth were also in the top ten.

Parliament House, where 'Governments are formed, great

issues debated and laws for the Nation enacted' (according to the marketing blurb) is one of Canberra's newest buildings, in 1988 replacing the imaginatively named Old Parliament House, which has metamorphosed into the National Art Gallery.

The new building is a monumentally bold and imaginative structure – though I can't imagine what architectural historian Nikolas Pevsner would make of it – and eminently attractive in a contemporary way, fronted by a 14-metre square mosaic based on a dot-style painting called Possum Wallaby Dreaming, by Michael Nelson Tjakamarra, a leading Aboriginal artist from the Papunya community of the Northern Territory. More than 90,000 pieces of hand-guillotined granite in seven colours make up the mosaic. If you arrive by car, you tend not to notice this, which is why I mention it now so that you'll go out and have a look. Cars are shepherded directly from the main drag into a spacious underground car park where there is free parking.

I submit myself to a security inspection, but everyone is easy-going and relaxed, but in a 'Don't try anything funny, mate' kind of way. I figure it's probably not a good idea to joke about explosive devices in my car.

The foyer is stunning, embracing forty-eight marble-clad pillars designed to be evocative of eucalyptus forest. On either side, exquisite marble staircases that it's a privilege to ascend rise easily to the first floor. The marble originates in Europe; the grey-green is Cippolino, the rose-coloured is Atlantide Rosa, and the black is Granitello Nero. I stop at the top of the stairs to figure out the floor plan.

'Is there anything I can do to help you?' asks a man who appears from the shadows and whose lapel badge tells me his name is John Beckett, Parliamentary Guide.

I tell him what I'm doing, and he smartly deduces that I'm not an Australian resident. He's from Suffolk, England, himself, and been in Australia for over thirty years. I comment on the spacious design of the city, and he likens it to 'Milton Keynes on steroids.'

He asks if I'm staying long, and whether I'd like a ticket for Question Time at two that afternoon; he promised a lively debate. I'm quite taken by the fact that you can more or less wander into a Nation's Parliament building and quietly mosey on into the House of Representatives and sit in on PM's Questions, it's only one step short of strolling into the chamber itself pulling up a chair with the PM and having a coffee, 'Good eye, PM, how's it going, mate? Need any advice on the old economy, just give me a bell. Like the tie, PM.' – try doing that in the Palace of Westminster, although, at the time of writing this bit, Theresa May is Prime Minister, and she doesn't wear a tie.

John fixes a ticket for me and sends me off to meet Ginny Paterson, who's doing the mid-day tour. Sadly, today it's cut short because the House is in session, but that gives me time to track down Susan Heyward, the Marketing Co-ordinator for Visitor Services, who provides me with a pack of information about the building and the thousands of people that work here. There are a staggering 4,500 rooms in Parliament House (almost one per person) with a gross floor area of more than 250,000 square metres (about 50 square metres per person – that's about half a tennis court each). It's made of 300,000 cubic metres of concrete, more than enough to build twenty-five Sydney Opera Houses, if you were that way inclined and had nothing to do on a Sunday afternoon. Not surprisingly, it's one of the largest buildings in the southern hemisphere, and cost approximately 1.1 billion Australian dollars, at 1980's prices. The flagpole alone is eighty-one metres high and weighs 20 tonnes.

Everyone is so relaxed it's a wonder they don't simply collapse into limp heaps of inert material, so much so that it's hard to believe you're in a building of such great significance to the Nation; it's more like a huge five-star hotel but without the bustle. In fact, it's a self-contained village, with banking facilities, a travel agent, cash machines, and a post office. The only thing that isn't here are beds – 'for obvious reasons' John comments – whatever does he mean? But what you won't find in Milton Keynes or any other self-contained village is the Magna Carta – yes, the Magna Carta of Runnymede fame – issued by Edward I on the 12th October 1297. This is one of only four known surviving originals of the king's confirmation of the Charter.

At one o'clock I meet up again with John who has wangled me a security pass and leads me down corridors into the non-public, restricted areas of the building, pausing at the reflective pool in the Members' Hall as the leader of the House of Senate strolls by deep in thought. Had he been in conversation with a colleague, it wouldn't have mattered: the centrepiece of the pool is a solid slab of South Australian black granite over which water flows in a way that helps prevent the conversations of senators and members from being overheard. Alas, it doesn't prevent inattentive visitors from trying to make a closer acquaintance: on the occasion of one prestigious gathering one lady of a certain age wasn't paying attention to where she was strolling and measured her length in the pool. Doing her best to regain her composure – and let's face it there's not a lot you can do in that kind of situation – and standing beside the pool, her party frock dripping profusely, she remarked 'Well, this is one day I shall remember for the rest of my life.'

Further on we pause outside the Prime Minister's office, then the Deputy Prime Minister's, having entered the blue-carpeted ministerial section of the building. Uniformed men regard us from security bays, but no-one seems alarmed by our presence. There's a brief commotion as serious-faced gofers scuttle across the corridor, and John suggests we pause for a moment. 'Whenever there's a flurry of activity, you never know quite what to expect. You could suddenly come face to face with the Prime Minister.'

A while later, safely escorted back into the public domain, I surrender my pack and, with my pre-booked ticket, joyously leapfrog the queue waiting to get into the chamber. A member is on his feet, largely repeating himself, playing out time until two o'clock. When the Speaker informs him he still has twenty seconds to go, he starts over again, but his words are drowned in the jeers of gathering members. As the hour is reached, John Howard, the Prime Minister ambles in and takes his seat. There's a brief Parliamentary nicety while the house votes on whether to discuss what they want to discuss, or not. A division – when no-one moves, but it all goes quiet and tellers make a note of voting intentions – consumes five minutes or so, ending in a decision to allow the discussion, by a vote in favour of 78 for and 62 against. But then there's another motion while the House, having decided that it will discuss the topic for discussion, has to decide whether it will do so now, or at some other time, or not at all – or something like that. Again, the voting is 78 for and 62 against, a fairly predictable outcome as the look of the face of the Speaker relates.

Finally, the Prime Minister gets to his feet and spends the next twenty minutes telling the House how the Leader of the Opposition, Mark Latham, had been misleading the House by saying he (Mark Latham, that is) had had discussions with officials over the War in Iraq – apparently, the Leader of the Opposition is new to the job, and the Government are determined to rough him up a bit before he gets too settled. He didn't seem all that ruffled to me; indeed, at one point he got up and wandered off, returning a few minutes later with a cup of coffee, much to the PM's evident irritation.

When the Prime Minister finally sits down, having told the House the same thing three times (at least, to my counting, but I confess I was starting to glaze over), the Leader of the Opposition gets to his feet, jibes at how sad it is to see a politician (like the Prime Minister) at the end of his career, thrashing around for an issue (and I must agree, it was a fairly pathetic premise – and that's a non-partisan observation, by the way); how he (the Prime

Minister) was so carried away with his own sense of power that he thinks he can mislead the House by suggesting that he was privy to information from within the Labour Shadow Cabinet – that's the party of Opposition – rather as though he had been the 'minute taker' at their meetings; and how he was evidently 'asleep at the wheel' because he (the Leader of the Opposition, that is) had indeed had meetings with officials about the War in Iraq and Weapons of Mass Destruction.

After forty minutes of this exchange, from which I could only deduce that politicians get paid by the word, I regret to say I had become terminally indifferent. My head was already resting on the shoulder of the person next to me as I slipped towards the catatonic, and I was on the verge of drooling unrestrainedly, a downhill slide from which I was roused only by a sudden outburst of yobbish Government jeers of 'Yah-di-wuf-ti-muggerhuff, ha ha ha', reminiscent of the British House of Commons at PM questions.

But it had all been hugely entertaining, in a toe-nail clipping kind of way.

In the following weekend's *Weekend Australian* ('Howard plays the man', 3-4 April 2004), Editor-at-large, Paul Kelly said of Mark Latham's typecasting of the Prime Minister as having '...an echo of Gough Whitlam's 1972 dismissal of Billy McMahon.' Whether the current exchange would lead to a similar change in fortunes remained to be seen.

It didn't; Latham resigned from politics in January 2005 on grounds of ill health. Eight months later, he published The Latham Diaries, in which he attacked many of his former colleagues and members of the media, as well as condemning the general state of political life in Australia. He went on to write A Conga Line of Suckholes, a book of quotations collected and used by Mark Latham during his public life.

From this you might deduce that the ethos of the Parliamentary system in Australia is just the same as the one in London, but with attitude. I find this quite exquisitely appealing, in a rainy day kind of way, although it's a while before I rid myself of Joe Simpson's pertinent observation (Touching the Void) that a politician is '... someone who looks deeply at the surface of things'.

The Australian Constitution provides for two houses in the Federal Parliament - the Senate, in which there are 76 senators, and the House of Representatives, which has approximately twice as many members as the Senate, usually around 150, though the number varies for complex demographic reasons - or, as some would have it, political chicanery. Both chambers are open to visitors though the Senate, rather like the British House of Lords, doesn't seem to do very much, except quibble and generally delay things until the lower house gets seriously pissed off with them for prattling about and takes matters into their own hands. The Senate is tastefully furnished in somniferous shades of red, and the House of Representatives in eucalyptic shades of vomit.

In one of the long rooms is the obligatory gallery of prime ministerial paintings. Actually, the paintings, as works of art, are astonishingly good, though the term in office of some of the prime ministers was so woefully short I wouldn't have been surprised to learn that some of the paintings were really enlarged Polaroids, or at the very least still wet when hung. In the early years, few managed more than a matter of months: Alfred Deakin's Protectionist Party completed seven months, Chris Watson, who followed him fared even less well, his Labor Party surviving for just four months. George Reid's Free Trade Party managed eleven months, and Andrew Fisher's Labor Party clocked up seven months before surrendering to Alfred Deakin's revival of the Protectionist Party, which managed three months longer than his earlier term in office. Taking minimalism to political extremes, Arthur Fadden, the Country Party, ran the Nation for thirty-nine days, and Earle Page, who was brought to power on the 7th April 1939, didn't even see out the month, lasting just nineteen days. But the prize for the shortest term in office goes to Frank Forde, who in July 1945, representing the Australian Labor Party, hung on in there for a whole seven days: not even time enough to draw his pay cheque, and certainly less time in office than he had to spend posing for his portrait. Fortunately, for the development of Australia at least, subsequent Prime Ministers have succeeded in hanging onto power for significantly longer periods.

The Telstra Tower – the Australian National Botanic Gardens

Well, first off, it's no longer the Telstra Tower. These days it's known as Black Mountain Tower, a telecommunication tower situated above the summit of Black Mountain. Rising 195.2 metres above the mountain summit, it is not only a landmark in Canberra, but one that offers panoramic views of the city and its surrounding countryside from an indoor observation deck, two outdoor viewing platforms and the tower's 80-minute revolving restaurant. It's well worth a visit for the view alone.

Black Mountain Tower has become one of the most symbolic landmarks in Canberra, and a major tourist attraction with a total of over six million visitors, twice as many as the Sydney Harbour BridgeClimb, so finding a day to visit that is going to be quiet isn't promising. In 1989, the World Federation of Great Towers invited the tower to join such distinguished monuments as the CN Tower in Toronto, Blackpool Tower in England and the Empire State Building in New York...can't help wondering where they hold their annual general meeting.

In my view, botanical gardens are to the Bush, what zoos are to the Serengeti. So, the prospect of wandering around Australia's pride and joy in the flower department didn't have my pulse racing. But this largest living collection of native Australian flora is on a par with Canberra itself for delaying you when you really ought to be driving on. The synergy of both places is quite surprising. You arrive in Canberra expecting to do the whirlwind tour, and three days later wonder why you're still there - although that may have something to do with road design. The botanical gardens are the same. If flowers are your thing, expect to be delayed.

For me, they are not; so I wasn't.

The king who never was

Since Canberra is the centre of all things political, administrative and constitutional, it seems appropriate to record here the seemingly bizarre fact that a small town of barely 1,000 inhabitants, Jerilderie in the southern Riverina region of New South Wales, is the current place of residence of the true monarch of Britain.

Forget your Elizabeth, the Georges, Victoria, even Henry VIII and his train of wives; they, it seems, are all founded on an illegitimacy, namely that of Edward IV (1461-1483).

Academic research has revealed, with a high degree of probability, that the father of Edward IV was not Richard, Duke of York, but rather some humble archer of the Royal court with whom Richard's wife, Cecily Neville, despite pious countenance and demeanour, had a dalliance while the said Richard was known to be absent from the marital bed.

Edward was born on 28 April 1442. No contemporary evidence refers to him as being born prematurely, as it would have been (although this is contested). Accordingly, counting back nine months from birth would date his conception to late July 1441, when Rouen Cathedral Chapter records the duke's absence. Moreover, the baptism of Edward is said to have taken place secretly in a side chapel at Rouen cathedral, rather than with full pomp and ceremony in the main body of the cathedral as was bestowed on his brother George.

A 2004 Channel 4 television documentary (*Britain's Real*

Monarch) examined records in the archives of Rouen cathedral, which indicated that from 14 July to 21 August 1441 Richard, Duke of York, was away on campaign at Pontoise, several days' march from Rouen (where Cecily of York was based), and that prayers were being offered at the cathedral for his safety.

So how did Cecily become pregnant? How it has been deduced that it was down to being 'serviced' by an archer is unclear, but if the duke was away, then clearly someone else had caught Cecily Neville's eye, and found their way to other parts of her anatomy, too.

Richard, Duke of York, would have had a duty, to challenge the child's paternity if it was in doubt; refusing to do so, and allowing a child he knew was not his to remain an heir to the English throne, was tantamount to treason. Moreover, the Duke of York was not a man of great physical stature, but Edward was, formidable, in fact. Also, it seems that when Edward, supposedly an heir to the throne, was baptised, it was done secretly in a side chapel, not with all the pomp and ceremony you might expect.

But if Edward IV was indeed illegitimate, then that affected the long line of those who came after him: Edward V, Richard III, Henry VII and VIII, Edward VI, Mary I, Elizabeth I and so on.

So, who is the rightful monarch?

By tracing the correct monarchical path through George, the Duke of Clarence, Edward's younger but legitimate brother, it was revealed that British-born Michael Abney-Hastings, 14th Earl of Loudoun, who migrated to Jerilderie in the 1960s, was the true King of England and the Commonwealth, a senior descendant of George Plantagenet, and, ironically, a republican, having voted for an Australian republic in the 1999 referendum. Until his death in 2012, he worked for a Rice Research Institute, and has a family that include Prince Simon (the alternative Prince of Wales), and the princes Marcus, Zak, Caleb, Jet and Riley, along with princesses Lisa and Isabella.

Prince Simon, the 15th Earl of Loudon, following his father's death, would have become the rightful monarch of England under this alternative path of succession, rather than Elizabeth II.

Long live the king.

Leaving Canberra along the Hume Highway – through the Snowy Mountains – the town with its own submarine (Holbrook) – Glenrowan and Ned Kelly

I was most reluctant to leave Canberra. I was really becoming fond of the place and just about getting the hang of the road network. Whatever the Aussies may say against it, and most of what they do say is directed to the politicians, not to Canberra itself, it's a unique and fascinating place, and I wish I had more time to spend here. I've been here three times now, and each time been sidetracked and hopelessly delayed.

But, having already stayed in Canberra longer than I had planned, the Hume Highway calls, as I head northwards to Yass to join it. The countryside is very easy on the eye and agreeably attractive. The scenery undulates by, which helps to make the driving easier, but to deflect any tedium I was armed with CDs of Meat Loaf, Simply Red and various extracts from the classical works to sing along to, though Ravel's Daphnis and Chloe was more of a hummer in places.

Holbrook, 356 kilometres (222½ miles) north-east of Melbourne and 491 kilometres (307 miles) south-west of Sydney between Tarcutta and Albury, is Australia's underwater centre, it says. Given that it's a fair old yomp from the sea – somewhat akin to the Swiss Coastal Path Walk – you may be forgiven for querying that observation; in fact, I'd be worried if you didn't. But it's founded on the presence in the High Street of a World War II submarine, not a replica, but the real thing – the sort of thing you'd expect to find on any conventional High Street in Warwickshire, for example. It's conceivable, of course, that Holbrook has declared UDI and is in the process of forming its own navy, but, if so, they have a few teething problems to sort out first, not least being finding somewhere convenient to float the damned thing.

The explorers Hume and Hovell were the first known Europeans in this area, travelling through in 1824 looking for new grazing country in the south of the colony of New South Wales. The area was then inhabited by the Wiradjuri people, and originally called Ten Mile Creek. The first buildings were erected in 1836, and a German immigrant, John Christopher Pabst, became the publican of the Woolpack Hotel on 29 July 1840, and the area became known as 'The Germans'. By 1858, the name had evolved into 'Germanton', although the postal area retained the name Ten Mile Creek. In 1876, the name Germanton was gazetted and the old name Ten Mile Creek consigned to history. During World War I, the town name was deemed unpatriotic, so on 24 August 1915 the town was renamed Holbrook in honour of Lt. Norman Douglas Holbrook, a decorated wartime submarine captain and winner of the Victoria Cross. Lt. Holbrook commanded the submarine HMS B11, which is the scale model you find in the town today. To further honour Lieutenant Holbrook, the local town council acquired a portion of the hull of HMAS Otway, a Oberon class submarine when it was decommissioned by the Royal Australian Navy in 1995. The Navy gifted the fin from the submarine, and this led to a drive to bid for the whole submarine. This was successful in raising $100,000, almost all a gift from Holbrook's widow. However, this amount was insufficient to purchase all of the Otway. So, they settled for the outside skin of the Otway above the waterline. This part of the Otway is now displayed in Germanton Park in the heart of Holbrook, having been dedicated in June 1997.

A few miles beyond Wangaratta, I reach Glenrowan, a one-street town doing its utmost to cash in on the fact that Ned Kelly made his last stand here. When you see Glenrowan, you'll understand why he made it his last stand, though I would hardly describe it as a place to die for. 'Ned's this' and 'Kelly's that' flank the main street at the southern end of which a huge effigy of the villain himself tries to give the impression that here was a larger than life character. With a little more effort, it could all be mind-blowingly naff; as it is there's a huge amount to be desired, and I suppose I have to be grateful for the fact that ninety per cent of what is tasteless and tacky about the Australian souvenir market has been corralled into Glenrowan's shops and museums. But I have been there, I've seen what it's like, and I think that if I was the mayor of Glenrowan, I'd make what I could of this bushranger-cum-villain-cum-folk hero.

Ned Kelly himself, as John Beckett had pointed out back in Canberra, was a thieving, murderous Irish-Australian who killed policemen, but who remains, paradoxically, a national icon. An antipodean Robin Hood, though in the case of Ned Kelly there is rather more substance, not to mention historical accuracy, to the legend. Inevitably, the tales of Kelly's deeds are many and varied, but then as now you can't go around killing policemen and expect to get a pat on the back from the authorities.

Boasting that he had never robbed a poor person or harmed a woman, it was ironic that Kelly was ultimately brought down by a schoolteacher. In June 1880, Ned and his gang were occupying the hotel in Glenrowan. Here, believing in his own propaganda and indestructibility he dreamt up the mad idea of derailing a train bringing police to hunt for him. The gang compelled track repairers to pull up sections of the rail track at the first turning after reaching Glenrowan, at a culvert and on an incline. While Kelly and his gang awaited the arrival of the train, a schoolteacher managed to escape the hotel and stopped the train before it reached the damaged section. The police surrounded the hotel, and burned it down, killing three of Kelly's cohorts. But the man himself, mad as ever, donned his home-made armour and shot it out with the police until a bullet to his unprotected legs brought him down. He was taken to Melbourne, tried and hanged in November of that year.

The memory of Kelly lived on, then as now. To the dispossessed, Ned Kelly's death symbolised an unwillingness that many felt to submit to the morality of the English. For this he was apotheosised into a folk hero, a man who brought down the vane and proud, stole from the rich and sought to highlight what he saw as the corrupt inadequacies of the law.

CHAPTER SEVEN

Adelaide and the Great Ocean Road

Adelaide – the Barossa valley wines – Yorke Peninsula

I have arrived in Adelaide by a number of means: by air from Perth; twice on The Ghan from Alice Springs, firstly before the line northwards was opened, and then all the way from Darwin itself, and by car following the long drive from Darwin. If I had to choose one city in Australia to live, this would be it. Much as I love Perth (a close second, and Hobart, and Cairns, and Alice Springs), there's something about Adelaide that I find agreeably appealing. It may have something to do with the proximity of some of Australia's finest vineyards, the wealth of its surrounding countryside and the closeness (in Australian terms) of such mesmeric places as Kangaroo Island.

The square mile city centre, founded in 1836, is a captivating blend of historic Colonial buildings, wide streets, cafés and restaurants surrounded by State Heritage Listed parklands. But its most important characteristic is its grid-iron street layout, which makes life for the disoriented over-imbiber a doddle...just cling to the walls and keep going until you find where you want to be; you won't get lost until you need to cross the road. So, before setting out, decide on a pub that can be reached by either going left or right from your home, but not both.

Adelaide is a city for the curious and the fun-loving, whatever your age, a quintessential modern city, filled with amazing things that wait on street corners, along little lanes, behind the big hotels and offices, or just below the city's sparkling veneer. In 2013, it ranked equal fifth, below Melbourne (which was number one), but above Sydney, in a 'Liveability report' by The Economist Intelligence Unit.

The Adelaide Plains around today's city were mainly bushland, and originally inhabited by the Kaurna tribe, the territory extending from what is now Cape Jervis to Port Broughton. The Kaurna lived in family groups called yerta, a word that also referred to a large area of land from and on which the family group lived. Each yerta was the responsibility of the adults, who inherited the land and had knowledge of its resources and features. The Kaurna led a nomadic existence within the Yerta in family groups of around thirty. They knew the area where Adelaide city centre now stands as 'Tarndanya', meaning 'Male red kangaroo rock'. Kaurna numbers were greatly reduced by epidemics of smallpox, which preceded European settlement. When the European settlers did arrive in 1836, estimates of the Kaurna population barely exceeded 1,000 people.

What I especially like about the early history of Australia is that its discovery went on for such a long time; visitors just kept finding new bits and wondering if they were attached to anything that had already been discovered; were they just part of a huge geographical jigsaw? The area that was to become Adelaide was no exception.

British Captain Matthew Flinders and French Captain Nicolas Baudin independently charted the southern coast of Australia. In 1802, Flinders named Mount Lofty, 15 kilometres (9 miles) east of Adelaide, and reaching to 710 metres (2,330 feet), but recorded little of the area that is now Adelaide.

In 1830, Charles Sturt explored the Murray River, and was impressed with what he saw, writing:

'Hurried...as my view of it was, my eye never fell on a country of more promising aspect, or more favourable position, than that which occupies the space between the lake (Lake Alexandrina) and the ranges of the St. Vincent Gulf, and, continuing northerly from Mount Barker stretches away, without any visible boundary.'

Captain Collet Barker, sent by New South Wales Governor Ralph Darling, conducted a more thorough survey of the area in 1831. After swimming the mouth of the Murray River, Barker was killed by natives. Despite this, his more detailed survey led Sturt to conclude in his 1833 report:

'It would appear that a spot has at last been found upon the south coast of New Holland to which the colonists might venture with every prospect of success ... All who have ever landed upon the eastern shore of the St. Vincent's Gulf agree as to the richness of its soil and the abundance of its pastures.'

Inevitably, someone was going to hit on the idea of colonising this new and vast country by means more conventional than dumping the scum of Britain there. All they had to do was persuade folk that it was a prime example of location, location, location...'Careful not to step on that snake, Mary'.

A group, led by an enterprising Edward Gibbon Wakefield, a British politician, were proposing to start a colony based on free settlement rather than convict labour. After problems in other Australian colonies, the time seemed right to form a more utilitarian approach to establishing a colony. In 1829, an imprisoned Wakefield - always a good position to start from, with plenty of thinking time - wrote about systematic colonisation in a daily newspaper.

Wakefield, by all accounts, was quite a lad. Not only was he the driving force behind much of the early colonisation of South Australia, and later New Zealand, a practice that was to bring him criticism in Karl Marx's Das Kapital, but he was imprisoned for 3 years in 1827 for his role as a primary protagonist in the so-called Shrigley abduction. The abduction was to do with a forced marriage by Wakefield to the 15-year-old heiress Ellen Turner of Pott Shrigley in Cheshire. Wakefield conspired with his brother

William to marry Ellen for her inheritance The couple were married in Gretna Green, Scotland and travelled to Calais before Turner's father, a High Sheriff of Cheshire, was able to notify the authorities and intervene. The marriage was annulled by Parliament, and Turner was legally married two years later, at the age of 17, to a wealthy neighbour of her class.

However, this wasn't the first time Wakefield had tried it on. At the age of 20, he had eloped to Scotland with a 17-year-old heiress, Eliza Pattle. Her mother reluctantly accepted the marriage and settled £70,000 on the young couple, with the promise of more to come. Unfortunately, Eliza died four years later in 1820 after giving birth to her third child. But Wakefield had political ambitions and needed more money. He tried to break his father-in-law's will and was suspected of perjury and forgery. Then he came up with the plan to marry Ellen Turner in the expectation that her parents would respond as Mrs Pattle had. Alas, he picked on the wrong family.

But what a splendid, inventive and altruistic fellow to cultivate and inspire notions of ordered antipodean settlement...some might say.

He suggested that instead of granting free land to settlers as had happened in other colonies, the land should be sold. The money from land purchases would be used solely to transport labourers to the colony free of charge, who were to be responsible and skilled workers rather than paupers and convicts. Try to move to Australia these days, and you'll find this policy still applies.

What is so astoundingly arrogant about the proposal is the assumption that the land was owned by someone in a position to sell it. Now, I wonder if that someone was Aboriginal...oh, no, I forgot, the Europeans offered the Aborigines the 'precious gift of their civilization' in return for the right to use the wealth of their land.

Well, that's alright then.

Named in honour of Adelaide of Saxe-Meiningen, queen consort to King William IV, the city was founded in 1836 as the planned capital for Australia's first freely settled colony in Australia. Although he subsequently became side-lined by the Australian authorities, Wakefield's plans did eventually come to some sort of fruition, when a certain Colonel Light completed the survey of Adelaide and designed its grid layout, thereby helping many an inebriate to see the light.

The Barossa valley is a great escape. Its leafy hills and valleys have inspired many artists; it's a place rich in history, culture, food and wine.

Now, I ask you to consider this offering: 'The week-long Barossa Vintage Festival is held biennially, in odd-numbered years. The festival runs for around a week, and celebrates the completion of the year's vintage season. A variety of wine-themed events are held during the festival, including competitions, musical events, food events with local produce, balls and parades.'

This is a party to be invited to. Look at the evidence. In one week you consume so much wine, get involved with wine-themed events – such as wine drinking, wine tasting, wine sipping, probably wine bathing, I shouldn't wonder – enjoy so much music, dancing and generally parading about, that it takes you two whole years to recover. Is no-one sober enough to organise it every year? This is Australia's oldest and longest-running wine festival, run continuously since 1947, when it was started to celebrate the end of the Second World War.

Bear in mind the 'odd-numbered years' should you be heading that way, and the fact that no-one actually knows whether it's a week or something vaguely 'around' a week. My guess is, who cares?

There are 13,256 hectares of vineyard in the Barossa, the majority planted with Shiraz, with other varieties such as Grenache, Cabernet Sauvignon, Mataro, Riesling and Semillon, also part of the Barossa wine canvas. More than 750 grape growers each tend an average vineyard size of 17.7 hectares. In 2009, the state shipped out 118 million gallons (448 million litres) of wine, with 2003-04 topping that and producing about 194 million gallons (733 million litres) of wine.

And that's only what they ship out. What do they keep for themselves?

With a couple of days in hand, I decided to move out from Adelaide, to see what the Yorke Peninsula held in store. Located west-ish of Adelaide, between Spencer Gulf on the west and Gulf St Vincent on the east, and about a 90-minute drive away, the peninsula is a major grain producing area, and, bolstered by some excellent beaches and coastal resorts along its 700 kilometres (440 miles) of coastline, turned out to be a perfect place to unwind for a few bottles.

Before white settlement, around 1840, the peninsula was home to the Narungga people, whose descendants still live there, in the community at Point Pearce, near the northern end of Gulf St Vincent.

Maintaining the same biennial approach to festivals as Adelaide, the Yorke Peninsula hosts the world's largest Cornish Festival. Rich in Cornish heritage, the towns of Moonta, Wallaroo and Kadina, known as 'Australia's Little Cornwall', host the week-long Kernewek Lowender – which translates from the Cornish language as 'Cornish Happiness'. Well, at least they know this one lasts a week; a home-from-home for Cornish pasty lovers.

My only disappointment with the peninsula was that time started to become an issue, and I had a mini-schedule to adhere to. I could seriously chill here, on a regular basis; it's a place with in-built inertia, and a pace of life set at andante moderato.

TERRY MARSH

Fleurie and Kangaroo Island – the world's largest war memorial (the Great Ocean Road) – Australia's Big Things

Projecting like a stubby thumb into the Southern Ocean, the Fleurieu Peninsula might be largely unknown but for the happy coincidence of climate and landscape that makes this one of Australia's finest wine growing areas. Pull off the southbound highway from Adelaide and turn into McLaren Vale and you will be left in no doubt: pennants line the road into town proclaiming the many vineyards compressed into this wide and fertile valley. Virtually the first building you encounter is an information centre devoted to the wines of the region.

Less than an hour's drive from the capital city, the Fleurieu Peninsula was named after the French Navy Minister, Charles Pierre Claret, Comte de Fleurieu, by the French explorer Nicholas Baudin who in the early 19th century, was busy 'discovering' the coast of Australia in the way explorers say they're doing when they're lost.

I arrive late into McLaren Vale, and, after a quick meal collapse into bed. In the morning I find a naked woman in my room, and it takes a few minutes for me to register that she's on a painting, on the wall. I was staying in what I was to discover was a delightful guest house on the edge of town, run by a charming lady, Jo, short for Josephine, whose taste in furnishings and all things domestic were, well, tending towards the risqué, but without offending.

In the evening, Jo joined me on the veranda topping up the wine I'd consumed during the day with yet more, while we watched the moon rise and fill the sky and the surrounding countryside with subtle blue light. It was all rather surreal, and the moonlight just hallmarked an impression that was already growing hazy.

'How long have you been here?' I asked at some point in the evening.

'Jim and I came out from Kent around fifteen years ago. He

worked in banking in London, so we weren't short of a bob or two. Flew straight into Sydney, and on to Adelaide the next day. We had no plan; no intentions, other than to spend some time here, relax and work out the rest of our lives together.'

I could tell from the tone of her voice that something hadn't worked out quite as they might have hoped. Jo was quiet for a while, then said: 'And then the bastard went and had a stroke and died within a day. And I've been here ever since.'

I made sympathetic noises, but she waved them away.

'You just have to get on. And there's nowhere better than this.'

She was right. Just then, at that moment, with the moon rolling across the sky, the distant lights of Adelaide scorching the northern sky, crickets chirruping away in the spinifex and a warming red washing around my insides, there was nowhere else I wanted to be. From the merlot-fuddled recesses of my mind I distinctly remember thinking, if it's like this with one moon, what must it be like on Mars?

Finally, Jo got up and stretched, pointing towards the bush beyond the house.

'He's over there, somewhere. Scattered his ashes in the bush, where I can keep an eye on him.'

I confess, as Jo stretched, I admired every sculpted contour of her still youthful body, and couldn't help thinking that she must be one hell of a creative lover.

But not tonight, Josephine...

Until you make that turning into McLaren Vale, the impression is that you are driving through an unduly extended suburb of Adelaide, a place of bolt-on domesticity and commerce. But the transformation is instant and enchanting, and the unassuming town of McLaren Vale a neo-colonial outpost with a new twist, a tight-knit community that welcomes visitors. To be fair, there is a suggestion that things are on the brink of change well before you get to McLaren Vale. Instead of urban scatter, the countryside is intermittently lush and green with neatly partitioned zones of vines: shiraz, grenache, cabernet sauvignon and chardonnay, although to an uninitiated eye like mine, all grapes look the same until they've found their way into a bottle...and after a while, all the bottles look the same.

That wine is king is beyond question, as over sixty 'cellar doors' - Aussie-speak for what the French call dégustation and the English a free snifter - testify. But, as if the opportunity to drop in to a few days' worth of tippling isn't enough, the commercially minded locals have invented a splendid wheeze in the form of a 'Cheese and Wine Trail', here raised to the level of operatic art. Central to the plot is Blessed Cheese, a café-cum-cheesery-with-attitude. It's a modest place in itself, but the focal point for three trails that take you round the vineyards, four per trail. For a fee you are provided with eskis (chilled picnic hampers) filled with biscuits, cheese, dried fruits, nuts, humus, fish and meat snacks, knives and forks, and sent out to find the vineyards linked to the trail of your choice. When you get there, simply introduce yourself, and you'll be offered a tasting of wine that best compliments the snacks in your hamper - which, incidentally, are numbered so you don't scoff them all at the first sitting, or get your Gippsland Blue tangled with your Kervella Affine.

It's an extraordinary way of spending three or more hours, depending, of course, on who's doing the driving, as drink-drive laws in Australia are fairly inflexible, and that does rather tend to colour your view. Stretch the whole thing out to a day - two vineyards in a morning, then two in the afternoon, with a relaxed lunch (if you can manage more food), and you should be within the limits. But don't complain to me if you aren't; I'm only the messenger.

From a wider perspective, the Fleurieu Peninsula rattles the cages of those who believe that if it isn't Sydney or salt bush then it isn't Australia. And if you can escape the velvet embrace of

Adelaide, surely Australia's most under-appreciated city (which in some ways is a blessing), then exploring Fleurieu opens your eyes to whole new domains of Australian culture like Deep Creek Conservation Park, which you'll be obliged to share with the tiny western pygmy possum, the short-nosed bandicoot and hordes of kangaroo grazing as the sun goes down. Along the coast towns like Goolwa, Port Elliot, Normanville and Aldinga are not far from small but ideal beaches and fishing jetties where the metronome of life ticks slowly.

Victor Harbor by contrast is one of Australia's fastest developing resorts, reached by an agreeable journey through undulating farmlands. VH caters for the tourist and doesn't mind who knows it. In a most agreeable sense, there is still something of a colonial feeling about the architecture of this modest coastal town, a pedigree endorsed by the use of steam trains as a tourist attraction. But it is the stunning coastal setting and the attraction of the fairy penguins on nearby Granite Island, plus the chance of spotting southern right whales offshore, that is the great draw.

From Victor Harbor it's about an hour's easy drive to the ferry terminal at Cape Jervis where Kangaroo Island beckons across the quixotically named Backstairs Passage.

Once occupied by the Aboriginal people, the native population disappeared as the land became an island following rising sea levels several thousand years ago. It was resettled in the early 19th century onwards, at first by sealers and whalers, and then as part of the colony of South Australia from 1836. The island, named by Matthew Flinders, a contemporary of Baudin, is a gem, best suited to those with time to take in nature and the wildlife for which the island is renowned. Indecent haste is not an ingredient that will enhance the flavour of Australia's third largest island. A leisurely approach, spread over three days or so, is perfect, for then it is that you get to see into all the nooks and crannies this natural wonderland of pristine wilderness has in store, including some awesome coastal scenery and secluded sandy beaches like Stokes Bay, that I'm not even going to mention, much less draw attention to.

The beauty of Kangaroo Island is its unspoiled condition, a place untouched for thousands of years, where the wildlife exists much as it once did on the Australian mainland. Words don't really do it justice, in some ways they can spoil the moment; nor do pictures, for that matter.

Kangaroo Island is a stunning wildlife sanctuary, suffering less from the impact of European settlement, because of its isolation from the mainland. As a result, it retains more than half of its native 'old-growth' vegetation – a vast area of over 2,250 square kilometres (869 square miles). The chance to see such primeval conditions so close to urban Australia is an opportunity to be savoured. But it requires a particular attitude of mind: I couldn't help smiling when I overheard a non-Australian tourist bemoaning the lack of wildlife, in much the same loud voice I'd earlier heard him yacketing on to anyone within hearing distance about the cost of his son's education, the trouble with his laptop, the price of fish... Small wonder he saw nothing; it was long gone.

You can, of course, do your own thing, hire a vehicle on the island (mainland hire cars cannot be taken to Kangaroo Island), and wander the dirt roads. But I got much more for my time by taking a two-day trip with Jon Marsden from Kangaroo Island Odysseys. Door-to-door service with a barbie thrown in (not literally) around lunchtime, and the knowledge and experience of trained rangers, is a recipe certain to expose the best this island has to offer.

The ferry docks at Penneshaw on the Dudley Peninsula in the east of the island, and from there it is an easy drive to Seal Bay, an aquatic reserve where as part of a guided tour you can stroll among Australian sea lions basking on the beach. On the way there's a better than average chance of spotting wedge-tailed eagle, swamp harrier, black-winged kite, pelican and white-bellied sea eagle as well as the timid echidna, a bizarre link with prehistoric times.

Aboriginal prehistory is much less evident; although the island was uninhabited at the time of European settlement in the 1800s, Aboriginal people lived here as early as 16,000 years ago, occupying simple camps around the coast and inland lagoons, hunting and gathering what they needed to survive.

Not to put too fine a point on it, the Remarkable Rocks are, well, remarkable. Part of the Flinders Chase National Park, this impressive gathering forms what appear to be a cluster of precariously balanced granite boulders. This amazing work of nature has been shaped by the erosive forces of wind, sea spray and rain over some 500 million years. The golden orange lichen covering some of the rocks offers visitors wonderful photo opportunities at different times of the day; all of the visitors on the day I was there went around in spellbound silence. It's that kind of place; hushed, secularly reverential.

Perfect.

Melbourne was calling and it was a toss-up between a quick flight or a more leisurely drive. I opted for the drive, little realising that I would be driving what is the world's longest war memorial.

The Great Ocean Road is an Australian National Heritage-listed 243 kilometres (152 miles) stretch of road along the south-eastern coast of Australia between the Victorian cities of Torquay and Allansford, near Warrnamboul in the west. Built by over 3,000 servicemen between 1919 and 1932 and dedicated to their colleagues killed during World War I, the road is, in effect, the world's largest war memorial. At the time of its construction, this part of southern Australia was accessible only by sea or a very rough bush track. The soldiers were paid 10 shillings and 6 pence for an eight-hour day.

The road flirts with rain forests, as well as beaches and cliffs of limestone and sandstone, and travels via Anglesea, Lorne, Apollo

Bay, and Port Campbell, the latter notable for its natural limestone and sandstone rock formations including Loch Ard Gorge, The Grotto, London Arch and the Twelve Apostles.

The London Arch, a neat offshore island, used to be known as London Bridge, having two major arches that connected a small promontory with the mainland. But in 1990, a huge chunk of it collapsed leaving two tourists stranded, and London Bridge became London Arch. I can't help wondering if there was a 'Wow, did the earth move for you, darling' moment before they realised their plight.

The Twelve Apostles experienced the same formative and destructive processes, but should you start to think you've had one too many stubbies, there are only nine stacks...well, not even that, because in 2005, one of them collapsed, leaving eight remaining. But with a rate of erosion of two centimetres per year, it may not be long before their number increases...or decreases further. It's a salutary reminder of how forceful the seas around Australia can be, bludgeoning the land in often katabatic fury, writhing across the emptiness all the way from Antarctica.

The delight of the Great Ocean Road, and the whole of Australia for that matter, is the way it ambushes your expectations, and throws surprises at you with wilful regularity. This is how I came to meet the Big Lobster, at Kingston, a modest town about 297 kilometres (186 miles) south-east of Adelaide. Known locally as 'Larry', the Big Lobster - 17 metres high, 15.2 metres long and is 13.7 metres wide, with an approximate weight of 4 tonnes - was designed and built by Paul Kelly as a means of attracting attention to a nearby visitor centre and restaurant. It was built in six months from a steel frame with a fibreglass shell. The size is said to have been an error: the original plans were drawn in feet, but the designer misinterpreted them to be metres...and, er, no-one noticed? Larry is just one of around 150 'Big Things' dotted around Australia, a loosely related set of novelty architecture and sculptures. The first was the Big Scotsman in Medindie, Adelaide, built in 1963. Every state in Australia has at least one of these big things, and they just underpin the odd-ball but splendid sense of humour that threads the tapestry of Australia. Today, they are something of a cult phenomenon, but they were originally intended as tourist traps...be warned.

As for the road, it was, I have to say, one of the finest drives in Australia, and one I didn't want to end. Whatever they may say, you can't get too much of a good thing, and on the Great Ocean Road I surfeited on one wondrous littoral experience after another.

TERRY MARSH

CHAPTER EIGHT

Melbourne

Liveability – Small world – Floored by a right hook – Batman cometh – the Hoddle Grid and the laneways – Botanic Gardens – Matthew Flinders – Australia's lost Prime Minister

According to a 2013 'Liveability report' by *The Economist* Intelligence Unit, the best quality of life of any of the world's urbanites is enjoyed by Melburnians. For the third year in a row Australia's second city stayed a whisker ahead of Vienna in Austria and Vancouver in Canada. On a complex system of scoring Melbourne hit 97.5% for stability, healthcare, culture, environment, education and infrastructure. Writing in February 2014, for BBC Magazine, Lynne O'Donnell, Australian reporter and author of *High Tea in Mosul*, points out that the judges came to that conclusion while overlooking some other, equally important, qualities: '...like food and wine, beaches and forests, and vineyards an hour's drive from the city centre'.

For the visitor, from the moment you arrive, there is a pulsating sense of all things good, a city vibrant with confidence, bright, bustling and good-naturedly brash. This is a place that breeds celebrities: the city is the birthplace of no less than Cate Blanchett, Pat Cash, Barry Humphries (aka Dame Edna Everage), Dame Nellie Melba, Danii and Kylie Minogue, Rupert Murdoch, Olivia Newton-John and three Prime Ministers, plus a couple who lived here but weren't born here.

On my first visit to Melbourne, I stayed at a backpackers' hostel, and in the morning asked for a lift to the ferry port for onward journeying to Tasmania. A young girl with a Union Jack on her T-shirt was doing the driving.

'Where are you from?' I asked.

'England.' Yeah, got that much unaided.

'Where in England?'

'Up North. Lancashire.'

'Really? Where in Lancashire?'

'Near Blackburn. A place called Chorley. You may not know it.'

Okay...

'Where in Chorley do you come from?'

'Clayton Green' she said, now sounding a bit puzzled, and peering at me in the rear view mirror.

'Ah,' said I. 'So you shop at the same ASDA supermarket as me, then?'

'Really?'

Really.

Small world.

I got the drive for free.

The following year I was back in Melbourne, exposing my wife to the delights of 'Death by Chocolate' at a Lanes restaurant, and, following the long and gorgeous drive from Adelaide, confident that I could handle anything Melbourne city's traffic could throw a me, not least because I used to be a driving instructor, and therefore a smartarse know-it-all when it comes to driving techniques. Actually, being a driving instructor didn't make me a better driver than anyone else, it just meant that when I screwed up, I made a professional job of it.

Well, Melbourne floored me with its right hook. I've heard of reptiles, birds and animals being endemic, but a driving technique? That was a new one on me, and if you are a driver from a country where everyone drives on the right (unlike Australia, which follows

UK rules) then you may need to lie down for half an hour in a darkened room after experiencing the hook turn.

It's all to do with trams.

A hook turn is a right turn from the left lane.

Think about that for a moment, if you're from the UK. Turn right, from the left-hand lane; I know folk do it at a roundabout close by where I live. But that's because they're either stupid, visiting strangers or not thinking too much about the imminent prospect of a nasty collision. But this manoeuvre-to-beat-all-manoeuvres has the endorsement of the Victorian government no less. But, should anyone be unduly alarmed by this quirk of traffic management, then relax; it applies only in the Central Business District, and that isn't too large an area.

So, here's how it goes:

> If turning right at an intersection with traffic lights and a 'Right Turn from Left Only' hook turn sign, you must make a hook turn so as not to delay trams.
>
> To do a hook turn you must:
> – approach the intersection in the left lane and indicate that you intend to turn right
> – on a green light move forward to the far left side of the intersection, keeping clear of pedestrian crossings
> – remain stopped until the traffic lights on the road you are turning into have changed to green, then complete the right turn.

It sounds simple, and, although I chickened out a few times and turned left, then did a U-turn and went back across the intersection, I did eventually get the hang of it, without any casualties. But it is all somewhat alarming to be parked in a vulnerable position at an intersection, with throbbing Toyota Land Cruisers on your left waiting to mow you down. But, apparently, if they do so, while you might not live to recount the experience, they will get in very serious trouble for not giving you the priority you have. In any case, there is a delay on their green light to give you time to make your turn.

It's all to do with avoiding having your car trashed by a marauding tram – which is a good thing, methinks. If you Google 'Melbourne Hook Turn' you'll get to a number of YouTube videos demonstrating the technique.

Brilliant; just like the rest of the city.

The history of how Melbourne came to be is fascinating, hallmarked at times by the arrogance of the British government's representatives, and imbued with scepticism. It largely concerned a man by the name of John Batman, a young settler and grazier from Tasmania, or Van Diemen's Land as it was then known.

In April 1835, Batman, sailed from Launceston on Tasmania, aboard the schooner Rebecca, in search of fresh grazing land on mainland Australia. He crossed Bass Strait, into the bay of Port Phillip, and arrived at the mouth of the Yarra River in May. After exploring the surrounding area, he met with the elders of the indigenous Aboriginal group, the Wurundjeri of the Kulin nation alliance, and negotiated a transaction for 500,000 acres of land, which later became known as Batman's Treaty, an event thought to have taken place on the bank of Merri Creek (near the modern day suburb of Northcote). The consideration consisted of an offering of 20 pairs of blankets, 30 tomahawks, 100 knives and scissors, 30 Looking Glasses, 200 handkerchiefs, 100 pounds of flour, and 6 shirts, in addition to a yearly Rent or Tribute of 100 pairs of blankets, 100 knives, 100 tomahawks, 50 suits of clothing, 50 Looking glasses, 50 pairs of scissors, and 5 tons of flour.

The deed, sometimes called the Batman Treaty, the Dutigullar

Deed, the Dutigullar Treaty (variously spelt) or the Melbourne Deed, is available to view online in the State Library of Victoria, along with a transcript that is fascinating in itself:

> *Know all Persons that We Three Brothers Jagajaga, Jagajaga, Jagajaga, being the Principal Chiefs, and also Cooloolock Bungarie, Yanyan, Moowhip and Mommarmalar being the Chiefs of a certain Native Tribe called Dutigallar situate at and near Port Phillip, Called by us. The above mentioned Chiefs Iramoo being possessed of the tract of Land hereinafter mentioned for and in consideration of Twenty Pair of Blankets, Thirty Tomahawks, One Hundred Knives Scissors, Thirty Looking Glasses, Two Hundred Handkerchiefs, and one Hundred Pounds of Flour, and Six Shirts delivered to Us by John Batman residing in Van Diemens Land Esquire but at present sojourning with us and our Tribe Do for ourselves our Heirs and Successors Give Grant Enfeoff and confirm unto the said John Batman his heirs and assigns All that tract of Country situate and being at Port Phillip, Runing (sic) from the branch of the River at the top of the Port about 7 Miles from the mouth of the River, Forty Miles North East and from thence - West. Forty Miles across Iramoo Downs or Plains and from thence South South West across Mount Vilanmarnartar to Geelong Harbour at the head of the same and containing about Five Hundred Thousand more or less Acres as the same hath been before the execution of these presents delineated and marked out by Us according to the custom of our Tribe by certain marks made upon the Trees growing along the boundaries of the said Tract of Land To hold the said Tract of Land, with all advantages belonging thereto unto and To the Use of the said John Batman his heirs and assigns for ever To the Intent that the said John Batman his heirs and assigns may occupy and possess the said tract of Land and place thereon Sheep and Cattle Yielding and delivering to us and our heirs or successors the yearly Rent or Tribute of One Hundred Pair of Blankets, One Hundred*

Knives, One Hundred Tomahawks, Fifty Suits of Clothing Fifty Looking glasses, Fifty Pair Scissors and Five Tons Flour.

In Witness whereof We Jagajaga, Jagajaga, Jagajaga, the above mentioned Principal Chiefs, and Cooloolock, Bungarie, Yanyan, Moowhip & Mommarmalar the Chiefs of the said Tribe have hereunto affixed our seals to these presents and have signed the same Dated according to the Christian Aera this Sixth day of June One thousand eight hundred and thirty five.

The last sentence of Batman's journal entry for Monday, 8th June 1835 (also in the State Library of Victoria) is said to pinpoint the founding moment of the settlement: "I am glad to state about six miles up found the River all good water, and very deep - this will be the place for a village."

The National Museum of Australia, however, are not convinced about any of this, adding the words 'Or so he said' to the explanation that Batman had purchased land in exchange for goods. It goes on to say of the occasion, '...the eight 'chiefs' each made their mark. They understood. Or so he said'; adding 'The next day he made copies of the documents and began the journey home, impatient to tell the story. I am the greatest landowner in the world.' So he said.'

I may be mistaken in thinking this, but I detect a lack of conviction in that, even though you can read a copy of the actual deed in the State Library.

Upon returning to Tasmania, however, Batman's treaty was deemed invalid by the Governor of New South Wales, Richard Bourke, in the belief that the Aboriginal people did not have any recognised claims to the lands of Australia. The proclamation formally declared, under the doctrine of *Terra nullius* - an expression used in international law to describe territory that has never been subject to the sovereignty of any state - that the Crown owned the whole of the Australian continent and that it alone could sell and distribute land. It was, if analysed, a very simple 19th-century expression of 'Finders Keepers'; I found it, ergo, it's mine (shades of Descartes 'Cogito ergo sum', perhaps).

Well, we can lay the blame for that legal nicety at the door of the Romans. And, if it's not sticking my head too far above the parapet, if the doctrine of Terra nullius had applied when the Aboriginal people first arrived in Australia, wouldn't they have enjoyed the same rights of ownership? Or is it a case of 'Well, you may have lived here for 50,000 years, mate, but you don't own the land until we say you do.' Which sort of misses the point that the Aboriginal people see things the other way round; they belong to the land, not the land to them. Mind you, it didn't stop the brothers Jagajaga trying to sell off something they could not, by their culture, have owned. But in their defence, they did only admit to 'possessing' the land they were disposing of, not actually 'owning' it. Probably not the first time Batman got it wrong.

However, at the time of Bourke's proclamation a prominent businessman, also from Van Diemen's Land, John Pascoe Fawkner, had funded an expedition to the area, which sailed from George Town aboard the schooner Enterprize.

On the 29th August 1835, the settlement party aboard the Enterprize entered the Yarra River, and anchored close to the site chosen by Batman. The party went ashore the following day (near what is today William Street; on what is now Melbourne Day) and landed stores and livestock, and began to construct the settlement. When he found out about the new visitors, Batman was dismayed and informed the settlers that they were trespassing. However, under the Proclamation of Governor Bourke, both parties were trespassing on land that allegedly belonged to the Crown. When Fawkner arrived in October, negotiations were made for land to be shared equally, regardless of the proclamation, which in the meantime had gained approval from the Colonial Office. Fawkner knew that cooperation would be vital if the settlement was to continue to exist fait accompli. So, land was divided, and the settlement existed peacefully. It was referred to by a number of names, including: 'Batmania' and 'Bearbrass', of which the latter was agreed upon by Batman and Fawkner. In 1836, the Secretary of State for the Colonies, Charles Grant, recognised the settlement's fait accompli, and authorised Governor Bourke to transfer Bearbrass to a Crown settlement. Batman and the Port Phillip Association he was conjoined with were compensated £7,000 for the land. In March 1837, it was officially renamed Melbourne in honour of the Prime Minister of the United Kingdom, William Lamb (the Lord Melbourne).

I may be a sceptic, but it strikes me that £7,000, at 1836 prices, showed a considerable profit for a few handkerchiefs, blankets, tomahawks and looking glasses. Today, that's worth in excess of £677,100, and surely they could have got them on eBay for much less.

The Hoddle Grid is home to the city's famed alleyways and arcades, and renowned for a distinct mélange of contemporary and Victorian architecture, as well as expansive parks and gardens around its edges. This remarkable layout of the streets in the centre was pioneered in 1837 by Robert Hoddle. All major streets are one-and-a-half chains (Remember those? 66 feet = 20.1168m = 22 yards = 100 links = 4 rods. Of course you do.) in width, while all blocks are exactly 10 chains square (that's a square furlong – if you're still paying attention – there being 10 chains in a furlong). It is one mile (1.6 km) long by half a mile wide (0.80 km). What this created was an area of laneways, invariably missed by tourists, and a colourful reminder of the city's past.

With ten latitudinal and nine longitudinal streets, this hidden inner city area was a flamboyant centre of business, banking and chic shopping, that evolved to provide access for horse-drawn carriages. During the gold rush years of the 1850s and 60s, however, the lanes did nothing to enhance Melbourne's reputation, quite the opposite, with many lanes becoming the haunts of criminals, and buildings reinventing themselves as brothels, opium dens and speakeasy gaming parlours. Even until as recently as the 1980s, while suburbia flourished, the lanes were dark, dismal and dirty. But with the urban renewal of the 1990s, Melbourne's lanes felt the breath of new life – they must have known I was on my way and wanted to spruce the place up a bit in welcome.

Today, Melbourne's laneways are a wonderland of narrow enclaves wherein mainstream culture takes a back seat to allow for unique, quirky boutiques, galleries, tiny cafés, dim sum eateries, Japanese tea houses and hidden jazz bars. This is a whole new experience in itself. Melbourne's 200 laneways, are a journey of discovery, stuffed with artistic graffiti to artisan boutique retailers and of course all those magical coffee bars. Take a wander, but make sure you make the time to look around very carefully. If it's hidden, it's going to be a treasure worth uncovering. Every time I've visited I've been unable to retrace my steps from earlier years; it's like a ceaselessly shape-shifting warren that seems different from one day to the next...and probably is.

Just keep it to yourself.

ACDC Lane (formerly the somewhat unimaginative Corporation Lane) was renamed in memory of one of Australia's most successful musical exports, to AC/DC what Matthew Street in Liverpool, England is to The Beatles.

Formerly Brown's Alley, Dame Edna Place, terminally linked with another bizarre Aussie export, is located off Little Collins Street, between Swanston and Elizabeth streets. I wasn't there, but by all accounts it was crowded with Dame Edna impersonators and interested lunchtime 'possums' for the launch on the 8th March 2007.

Breakfast in the heart of the Flinders Quarter, in and around the lanes and alleys branching off Flinders Lane between Swanston and Elizabeth Streets is a real treat. The atmosphere is modern, with high fashion and crowded cafés, and yet paradoxically charming and old-fashioned. In this enclave, Degraves Street and Centre Place are two of the most popular, a place where Melbourne's love affair with coffee explores its roots in the many European-inspired cafés crammed almost uncomfortably into the slender alleyways.

George Parade, off the top end of Collins Street, boasts several excellent basement restaurants and below-ground eateries. Block Place is another alternative, where jazz rhythms soar above the clamour of patrons shoe-horned into snug wood-panelled cafés. But the beating heart of Melbourne's renaissance is Hardware Lane, a thoroughfare that epitomises the enchanting atmosphere of the laneways culture. The architecture of Hardware Lane is a picturesque historical portrait, with early 1900s' warehouses, originally home to blacksmiths and their ilk, still intact. Today, however, they host restaurants: the original façades remain, enhancing the pukka nature of this precinct while complementing its regeneration as an area of fun and leisure.

So, it was something of a shock to find in 2014 that the city fathers have been selling some of the lanes to property developers. In the preceding two years, the council earned more than two million Australian dollars (£1.1million) from laneway sales, although they are very reluctant to spell out the details. In December, 2013, Jason Dowling, City Editor of The Age, reported that a spokesman for the council said it '...periodically considers the discontinuance and sale of roads and laneways', adding that the portions of laneways sold usually relate to small pieces of land surplus to council requirements, and that 'All proposals to discontinue and sell public roads and laneways are advertised and are sold at market valuations'.

Now, is that a new brand of Eau de Cologne? Or do I smell a rat?

Wherever you travel in Australia you encounter flora in some form or another: a staggering 24,000 species of native plants have been identified compared to England's 1,700 native plants, and there are probably still more they have yet to find. So, while it's a delight to find some of them growing wild, it's equally welcome to encounter them in a zoo, or, in this case Melbourne's Botanical Garden. There are other botanical gardens, of course, all over Australia, but that in Melbourne has a quality that is paradoxically relaxing and buzzing with interest.

The Australian government's own website explains that it was William Dampier who first introduced Europeans to Australian plants in 1703 in his book A voyage to New Holland. On Captain Cook's voyage in 1770, Joseph Banks and Daniel Solander collected over 30,000 botanical specimens and Sydney Parkinson made 674 drawings on the voyage - an obsession that goes some way to explaining how Botany Bay got its name. French naturalists and scientists, such as Labillardiere, extensively promoted Australian plants with the publication of seven volumes. Napoleon's wife, Josephine, patronised botanists and the growing of Australian plants - growing over 100 Australian plants including grevilleas, banksias, eucalypts and casuarinas at Malmaison, outside Paris. Today, many of the central parts of Madeira are cloaked in eucalyptus trees, acacias and cycads that originated in Australia. Remarkably, Australian architect Robin Boyd in his book, The Australian Ugliness (1960) wrote that many people regarded even eucalypts and acacias as '...primitive landscape and elements - unfamiliar, strangely primeval - which must be eradicated from the home environment'. Boyd's was a caustic polemic on the stylistic cowardice of the suburbs, and the unsightliness of post-war Australian suburban design, and it would have taken courage to call Australia ugly. The country has never bragged about its beauty, that's left to the likes of me, but we must question the necessity to challenge the presence of native species of plants.

Plants are important to Australia in many ways, not least because in 1912, the wattle was incorporated into the design of the Australian Coat of Arms, and each Australian state and territory has chosen a flower native to its region as an official floral emblem. These are: Australian Capital Territory - Royal Bluebell (Wahlenbergia gloriosa); New South Wales - Waratah (Telopea speciosissima); Northern Territory - Sturt's Desert Rose (Gossypium sturtianum); Queensland - Cooktown Orchid (Dendrobium phalaenopsis); South Australia - Sturt's Desert Pea (Swainsona formosa); Tasmania - Tasmanian Blue Gum (Eucalyptus globulus); Victoria - Common Heath (Epacris impressa), and Western Australia - Red and Green Kangaroo Paw (Anigozanthos manglesii).

I knew you wanted to know.

As botanical gardens go, that in Melbourne is most agreeable; it's not far from the city centre for a start, and is a great lung of greenness in which to relax. The ornamental lake is sure to have black swans busy a-swanning, while the greater area encourages familiarity with some of the country's amazing species. One inmate, for a time, however, was the cause for concern, adding the dubious delights of being aerially brained to a visit to the garden. Falling cones from the Bunya Bunya Pines (Araucaria bidwillii) are not something you want to encounter. The pine is a large evergreen coniferous tree, native to Queensland, that can grow to 45m. There are nineteen in Melbourne Gardens. The cones are 20-35cm in diameter and house as many as 50 large (3-4cm) seeds or nuts. The spiky green cones weigh anything up to 5kg and have been described as 'spiky green footballs'. For safety reasons, the garden teams are trying to remove the cones. Curator of Arboriculture Will Jones said: 'We removed 150 cones from 5 trees in a week. They often hit a branch on the way down, bouncing through the canopy, sometimes hitting the ground well beyond the drip-line of the tree. So perhaps take a few steps back and admire the trees from afar'.

Sound advice, methinks.

TERRY MARSH

The lost prime minister

From time to time we all lose things. I can lose for days and weeks something I put down on my desk only a few moments ago. It's a particular kind of skill, something that requires practice, and one I hope will give me endless hours of occupation in my dotage, or next week, whichever comes first. But to lose something, in this case a 'someone' as prominent and evident as a human being, a prime minister to boot, may, in some circles, be considered a mite careless, and smacks of not taking life too seriously.

But our antipodean brethren did just that.

The year 2017 sees the 50th anniversary of the unsolved and rather sensational disappearance of Australia's 17th prime minister, Harold Holt, off a remote Victorian beach on 17th December 1967. But the lack of a body launched an avalanche of wild and importunate theories about Mr Holt's exit, many ascribed to Cold War scenarios, others to more mundane suggestions that he simply faked his death. On that unhappy day, Prime Minister Holt went missing in rough seas whilst swimming at a favoured spot, Victoria's Cheviot Beach, near Point Nepean. As an aside, Cheviot Beach may well be a place to avoid: it is named after the SS Cheviot which broke up and sank nearby with the loss of 35 lives on 20 October 1887.

As for Holt, Police concluded it was an accidental drowning of an experienced swimmer in dreadful conditions, a theory confirmed, somewhat belatedly in a Victorian coronial inquest in 2005. Clearly, they needed time to think about it, and to be sure that he simply wasn't in prescient collusion with Lord Lucan, who disappeared just seven years after Holt.

Conspiracy theories abounded, including the predictable: that he had committed suicide or been picked up by a UFO. Yet something did not quite add up.

A letter from an American lawyer, Jay E Darlington, dated

133

the day after Holt's disappearance, reads: 'My "hunch", from fragmentary press reports, is: There is better than a 50% chance that Mr Holt's death was not "accidental", but resulted from expert sabotage, probably foreign.' Darlington suggests that several subtle methods might have been used on Mr Holt, including: 'Some delayed-effect drug which he might have got in refreshments on his way to the beach. This would be revealed by expert autopsy, unless it is one of the new "disappearing" ones'. More likely, he goes on, is expert sabotage of his diving equipment. This and other Cold War theories can be found on the Australian National Archives website (www.naa.gov.au).

Other letter writers believed Mr Holt was still alive, and that he had either faked his death and run off with an alleged mistress, or was taken by the communists. A letter dated 8th January 1968 from Miss W Shonhan, a retired school teacher from Sydney, posited what became a popular theory that Holt was kidnapped for political interrogation due to his close relationship with United States President Lyndon B Johnson.

There are numerous letters in the National Archive, of which about one-third came from overseas, like the one from D Dharman of the Society of Astrologe of Sri Mahakalidevi, who claimed to be '...in a position to announce the present position and the whereabouts of the body of the Late Primer [sic] of Australia.'.

But the Holt mystery still intrigues, not least because it occurred during the Cold War. The most obvious reason for this is the lack of a body: no body, no evidence of actual death. Enquiries were made of local fishermen, who suggested two possibilities for the failure to find a body. One, that the body was carried out to sea by tides, or lodged in rock crevices. Two, attack by marine life '...in the form of sea lice, crayfish, etc..', which are adept at stripping flesh from a body within 8 to 14 hours, according to the official Police Report.

The most outrageous theory was that he was abducted by

a Chinese submarine. But officials testify that it had been demonstrated that there was no way a submarine could have operated in the waters off Cheviot Beach. 'Anyway as [his wife] Zara Holt said, Harold Holt didn't even like Chinese cooking.'

Yes; really.

In The Living Australia magazine (Issue 87), all of the above is totally ignored, and the disappearance summed up in the sentence: 'He was a keen skin diver, and in December 1967, he drowned in heavy surf near Portsea, Victoria' – much as the coroner decided in 2005.

In the end, the view was taken that the Prime Minister's demise was nothing more than a tragic accident.

Goodbye Harold Holt, Hello John McEwen, although he didn't hang around for too long.

CHAPTER NINE

TASMANIA

Introducing Tassie – Police escort – North-West: A walk around The Nut – Did the earth move for you Stanley? – The cleanest air in Australia

Tasmania has everything.

That's not tourism-speak: that's my assessment. It is quite simply a wonderful, scenically voluptuous, historically well-endowed and all-round mega-outstanding place to be. Space; wilderness; lakes; mountains; wildlife; good, clean air; the freshest sea food you'll find anywhere; the first parking meter in Australia; some very dark secrets, and the sort of sensayuma and laid back approach to life that regards mainland Australia as the off-shore island.

If I had just one week to spend in Australia, I would choose to spend it on Tasmania. Alas, I've a feeling I may have said that about somewhere else, too.

Among those who travel widely, Tasmania is regarded as one of the loveliest places on earth: its west coast beaches are awe-inspiring, the Bay of Fires Conservation Area on the north-eastern coast is a stunning region of white beaches, blue water and orange-hued granite; its mountain ranges, too, rugged, lush, cloud-rending peaks, and dripping, dense forests, home to the beautiful Huon pine, many of which have lived for over 2,000 years, and, some will have you believe, still home to the famed 'Tassie' tiger. It doesn't surprise me in the least that in 2014 Tasmania came fourth in Lonely Planet's 'Top 10 Regions to visit in 2015' despite being left off some Australian maps and the Commonwealth Games kit for 2014. It is the only Australian destination to make it into the ranking. So, outshining the rest of the country.

On top of that – and I'm guessing that many Scottish distillers will baulk at the claim – in 2014 Sullivans Cove whiskey was voted the best single malt in the world, and because supplies are dwindling it is reported that for one of the 516 bottles that came from Barrel 525 some are offering as much as AU$20,000.

Here are some more interesting facts about Tasmania:
- The first telephone call in Australia was made in Tasmania, between Launceston and Campbell Town in 1874
- The first parking meters in Australia were installed in Collins Street, Hobart, in 1955
- Tasmania has more visitors per year than its entire population
- Australia's first legal casino was opened in Hobart in 1973
- Australia's oldest live theatre venue, the Theatre Royal, is in Hobart
- The Gaiety Theatre in Zeehan was Australia's first theatre-hotel
- Tasmania has the cleanest air in the world, measured at Cape Grim on the north-west coast
- Tasmania was the first Australian state to introduce a compulsory state education system in 1868
- In April 2003, the Tasmanian town of Coles Bay, on the Freycinet Peninsula, was the first town in Australia to ban plastic bags
- Australia's oldest brewery, Cascade Brewery is in Hobart
- Australia's oldest golf course is at Bothwell, in the Tasmanian midlands
- Tasmania has the lowest crime rate of any Australian state
- Australia's oldest bridge still in use is the 1823, convict-built Richmond Bridge

- The longest single-span chairlift in the world is across Launceston's Cataract Gorge
- Hobart is the second driest capital city in Australia, after Adelaide
- The world's smallest marsupial, the pygmy possum, is native to Tasmania
- Ricky Ponting, one of the best cricketing batsmen of the modern era, was born in Launceston
- In 2014, Tasmania-born Richard Flanagan, a descendant of Irish convicts transported to Australia in 1840, won the Man Booker Prize for his novel The Narrow Road to the Deep North

Tasmania was not confirmed to be an island until 1798

The 14-hour *Spirit of Tasmania* ferry crossing of the 140-mile wide Bass Strait can be a hugely bumpy affair; good reason for booking a comfy berth and stocking up on travel sickness tablets. But it really is the only way to bridge the gap to this wonderful, far-flung byword for remoteness: come back by air, by all means, but do the sea crossing at least once. You have to earn the right to visit Tasmania, and this rite of passage is the test; you just have to put up with the comfy berths, the excellent food and wine, and the starry, starry skies.

Within minutes of arriving in Tasmania, I was in a police car, handcuffed and bound in chains, heading for the nearby town of Devonport.

Actually, not all of that is true.

On this occasion, all I had done was to fail to find the person with the key to my hire car. It was a small-ish company and so didn't have its own kiosk at the ferry terminal, but I didn't know that. So, having not found them, I set off to walk the three miles into town to their offices, leaving my wife at the terminal, perched on our suitcases. Thankfully, no sooner was I under foot, than a police car pulled up beside me. Within was an ex-pat Brit, Thomas

Wilson from Doncaster, 25 years in Oz, and happy to give me a lift into Devonport. He was less happy to give me a lift back when it was discovered that the hire company really were at the ferry terminal, wondering where I was. But, for me, the outcome was welcome. I'd hired a Toyota Corolla; they only had a new 3-litre Holden, big enough to live in...not that we did.

Tasmania has always been a secret place, both in myth and history. Some saw it as Elysium, others, less fortunate, as beyond the gates to Hell.

Under the name of Van Diemen's Land, for the first 50 years of its history, Tasmania was Britain's most distant penal colony, as Nicholas Shakespeare describes (In Tasmania), '...[an] open panopticon to 76,000 convicts gathered from many pockets of the Empire, the majority of them thieves.' The majority of these villains were despatched 'beyond the seas' by English judges, a journey that could take as much as eight months in itself, and following which they served an average sentence of seven years, alas without a return ticket. Not surprising then that many viewed it as the end of the world. It was a place where wickedness flourished alongside depravity and cannibalism; a place synonymous with terror and dread. Yet, by the middle of the 19th century, now under the name Tasmania, the island's exceptional natural history, fertile earth and temperate climate made it popular as a health resort for those tired of the English weather. For that to become possible, however, something had to be done about the native Aboriginal people; a recurring problem, as many saw it.

Initial encounters with Aboriginal communities were hostile, but to the surprise of many it became increasingly evident that the natives were actually friendly and hospitable. French explorers wrote of their purity and perfection. The stage was set for a measure of peaceful co-existence. But who wants utopia when you can so easily have dystopia?

So, by the early years of the 19th century, the British arrogance and sense of dominance and superiority of weapons set them off on a path of destruction that before the century was out saw the extinction of the Tasmanian Aboriginal people. What happened became known as the Black War, or Van Dieman's Land war, a period of conflict fought between the 1824 and 1831, largely as a guerrilla war by both sides which claimed the lives of at least 450 European colonists and between 600 and 900 Aboriginal people. In accordance with a solar rhythm, the conflict mainly consisted of hundreds of ambushes on Aborigines' camps by night, and on colonists' huts by day. Eastern Van Diemen's Land was the site of the most intense frontier conflict in the whole of Australia, and appears to have been the breeding ground for an especially sordid strain of white violence; a place where men 'consider[ed] the massacre of these people [blacks] an honour.'

The near-destruction of the Tasmanian Aborigines, however, and the frequent incidence of mass killings, has sparked debate among historians over whether the Black War should be defined as an act of genocide. Nicholas Clements in his profound and scholarly PhD thesis – *Frontier Conflict in Van Diemen's Land* – says that

'A key source of white violence was sex deprivation. European women being extremely scarce, so frontiersmen sought black females any way they could. Later, revenge and self-defence also motivated them to kill. Aborigines attacked whites to resist invasion, avenge mounting insults, and to plunder food and blankets. Both lived in suffocating fear, terrified of their enigmatic foes. Likewise, both saw themselves victims, and both felt justified in victimising the other. It was not a battle between good and evil, but a struggle between desperate human beings.'

Clements goes on to reveal:

'...the essentially human character of the conflict, dispelling the myth that modern Tasmania was forged in a battle between good and evil.

Moreover, [he shows] that the traditional literary dichotomies of strong and weak, cowardly and courageous, victim and victimiser do not stand up to criticism. Practically everyone saw themselves as the victims. White and black alike, most were just trying to survive the nightmare in which they found themselves. There were of course many cruel individuals, but they too were victims of their circumstances, assumptions, hatreds, frustrations, fears and sadnesses.'

What the Black War does achieve is a somewhat different perspective on what many view as 'an indelible stain on a callous empire'. For those involved it was a 'cycle of violence, misery and fear, compounded on both sides by the incomprehensibility of the enemy'. Never was a war fought between such fundamentally different people.

My one regret about Stanley is that I don't have enough time to allow me to stay overnight, perhaps in one of the many restored colonial cottages; the whole town is utterly charming, a place preserved in 19th-century aspic. The town, though it is barely more than a generously spread-out village, nestles at the base of a volcanic plug described by Matthew Flinders as a '...cliffy round lump resembling a Christmas cake' - evidently, mum's cooking not up to much then.

This north-western part of Tasmania was discovered by Flinders and George Bass in 1798 during the voyage that proved the existence of a strait between Van Diemen's Land and New Holland. First impressions were not encouraging: the coastline was '...dismal and barren' and they viewed the inland peaks with '...astonishment and horror'. Twenty-five years later, however, Captain Charles Browne Hardwicke noted the abundance of 'fish, quail and natives' and deemed the land 'suitable for all purposes, to any extent of building'. A year later, James Hobbs appears on the scene opining that '...this would make an excellent estate for one or two persons with capital'. Such persons existed, and in May

1824 the Van Diemen's Land Company (VDL) was formed with a view to buying the land to raise sheep for wool.

With the arrival of the first colonists aboard the brig Tranmere, Stanley was born as a company town, and cottages hastily constructed for the senior personnel. The merino sheep that everyone hoped would produce a handsome profit, alas, were not a success, succumbing to harassment by dingoes and hyenas that ravaged the flocks. Out went the sheep, and in came cattle and horses. Generous inducements were offered to prospective settlers to come to the north-west, and many did, aided, once they got there, by the ingenuity of Edward Curr, the company's agent, who contrived to overcome seemingly endless adversity ranging from loss of sheep and crops, to discord between free settlers and the servants assigned to them, the difficulties of the dense forest that surrounded them, which proved as impenetrable for Curr as it did for those who had been before him. Above all else, there was a soul-destroying isolation, and many years were to pass before roads were to reach Stanley, the first a track through the bush linking the town with the next nearest settlement, Port Sorell, more than 150 kilometres to the east.

As I wandered the streets, I couldn't help thinking that for once 'charm' and 'quaint' weren't so much clichéd descriptions as a way of life. There is a keen other-worldliness that sits like a gentle mantle on the town and its people. At the bottom end of town, after passing rows of porticoed shops, the Bay View Hotel and numerous pretty cottages with railed gardens and weatherboarded façades stands the cottage, now a small museum, that was the birthplace of Joseph Lyons, the only Tasmanian-born Prime Minister of Australia, the tenth. Lyons was the grandson of Irish immigrants, one of the most genuinely popular men to hold the office of Prime Minister; his death caused widespread grief. He is the only person in Australian history to have been Prime Minister, Premier of a State, and Leader of the Opposition in both the

Federal Parliament and a State Parliament.

I took the chairlift up onto The Nut, though there is a perfectly serviceable path, and wandered around its expansive summit, peering down at vertical sea cliffs, off-shore islands and the wharf. During the construction of the wharf in 1892, the builders set off 5,000 pounds of dynamite to blast away a large section of the cliff for stone. Bang!...but nothing happened, which must have left the shotfirers rather nonplussed and everyone else edging towards the back of the queue in case it came to volunteering to find out what had gone wrong. Twelve years later fractures caused by the blast finally gave way, dropping over 200,000 tons of rock on the wharf side. Somehow, I can't resist the fanciful speculation that at the very moment the earth moved, somewhere among the long grasses of The Nut a young couple were reaching the climax of their amorous activities: it would be the sort of thing that could do a chap's ego no end of good.

As for Stanley and the Nut, I did the best I could in the time available, and even stayed for lunch until long after I should have been a hundred miles away. But it was worth it. Stanley is in a time warp, and long may it remain so.

In the extreme north-western tip of Tasmania is a pocket-handkerchief sized piece of land known as Cape Grim, discovered and named by Matthew Flinders on 7 December 1798, as he sailed from the east in the Norfolk and found a long swell issuing from the south-west, confirming for the first time that Van Diemen's Land was separated from the Australian mainland by a strait, which he named Bass Strait. What makes Cape Grim unique is its geographic location: the next land mass directly west of Cape Grim is not Africa, as might be supposed, but the southern tip of Argentina.

I can tell you; it's windy.

If it's fresh air you want, this is the place to come, and the reason why you find here the Cape Grim Baseline Air Pollution

Station, operated by the Australian Bureau of Meteorology in a joint programme with the Commonwealth Scientific and Industrial Research Organisation. The Station was established in 1976 and has been operating ever since.

Sadly, Cape Grim is renowned for another of the numerous massacres that characterise the early European history of Tasmania. The Cape Grim Massacre – today a by-word for the cruelty of colonialism – occurred on 10 February 1828, when four shepherds with muskets are alleged to have ambushed over thirty Aborigines from the Pennemukeer tribe, killing them and throwing their bodies over a 60 metres (200 feet) cliff into the sea. The hill where the massacre occurred was then called Victory Hill by the shepherds.

In a way that typifies the obscure truth of this difficult period in Australian history, there is some almost inevitable scepticism about this account, largely founded on the implausibility that four shepherds with slow-loading muskets with limited effective range, could have killed thirty natives. And among so many accounts of such barbarity that still exist it is easy to see how the truth could never be winnowed from the chaff.

Strahan and Macquarie Harbour – Sarah Island penal colony – the man-eating prisoner – The Ship that never was

I came to Strahan (pronounced 'Strawn') from the west, and later took a boat through Hell's Gates, a notoriously shallow and dangerous channel entrance into the large inlet of Macquarie Harbour, and named by convicts who came this way to their own personal Hell. The passage was a bit bumpy; a racing tide was running in from the sea.

Historically, Strahan has been a port to a small fishing fleet, and as well as the gateway to Hell, it was, and is, the gateway to the great south-west wilderness, a place more dense and impenetrable than the Amazon. Originally developed as a port of access for the mining settlements in the area, Strahan was of key importance to the timber industry that existed around Macquarie Harbour.

But Macquarie Harbour was famed for a rather more sinister reason. A penal station was established here, on Sarah Island, as a place of banishment within the Australian colonies, to take the worst convicts and those who had escaped from other settlements. The isolated island was ideally suited for its purpose, separated as it was from the mainland by treacherous seas, surrounded by a mountainous wilderness and hundreds of miles away from the colony's other settled areas. The only seaward access was through Hell's Gates. Sarah Island was a penal settlement for just eleven years, from 1822 to 1833, established, before the more well-known Port Arthur, in an attempt to control the uncontrollable.

Over the years, about 1,200 men and women were sent to Sarah Island. Most had committed further offences while serving their original sentences; others came as 'remittance men', skilled tradesmen who worked at the settlement in exchange for remission of their sentence. They were supervised by military detachments of several regiments, and by a company of civilian officers, supervisors and constables, many of whom were themselves ex-convicts. The population in 1828 was a total of 531, including about 380 convicts, 95 military, 14 women and 27 children.

It must have been a grim place to bring up children. The surveyor who mapped Sarah Island concluded that the chances of escape were '...next to impossible'. Yet, despite its isolation, a number of convicts did attempt to escape. Matthew Brady, a bushranger, was among a party that escaped to Hobart in 1824 after tying up their overseer and seizing a boat, a feat all the more remarkable when you consider that to get to Hobart by sea took over ten weeks. Another convict, James Goodwin was pardoned after his 1828 escape, and in a paradoxical use of evident talent, was subsequently employed to make official surveys of the wilderness he had passed through.

Over time, the island has gained a reputation as a place of unspeakable horrors, largely due to the exploits of one of the island's inmates, Alexander Pearce, its most infamous escapee, who managed to get away twice. On both occasions, he cannibalised his fellow escapees, eating in total the flesh of six. The island also found notoriety in a novel, For the Term of His Natural Life, by Marcus Clark. Although based on actual events, the novel is a work of fiction, and set out to portray Sarah Island as a living hell for its hero, Rufus Dawes.

If I was once again the office boss I used to be, I'd want Kiah Davey working for me. When I visited Strahan she was chatting away cheerfully to tourists from behind the counter of the Visitor Centre. Later in the evening she appeared alongside Heather as the principal actors, actually the only actors, of the Round Earth Theatre Company in an uproariously hilarious interpretation of the last great escape from Sarah Island – The Ship that never was. The year was 1834. The Frederick, the last ship built at Sarah Island, is about to sail for the new prison at Port Arthur. Ten convict shipwrights have other ideas, and figure that they could use the ship in which to escape. So begins this story of an amazing escape, an extraordinary voyage and with a surprising twist in the tail. I'm half tempted to tell the story here, but it would be so much more enjoyable if you went to see the play for yourself.

For me, it was worth coming 18,000 miles for this experience alone. It was fast, furious, and highly accomplished, and has been running since 1993. Time for the London stage methinks – but on the other hand, there's a lot to be said for an open stage protected only by large sheets of canvas (appropriately enough) and wooden benches, though you can help yourself to cushions to sit on and blankets to wrap around your legs.

The next day, Kiah was the tour guide for the trip to Sarah Island, and by the time the boat arrived back from its extended trip up the Gordon River, she was waiting on the pier ready with microphone to tell everyone about the Huon Pine Saw Mill.

Quite a lass. I wouldn't be surprised if she also filled in as the village taxi driver, fire brigade and parish priest...I'm not going to be unkind enough to suggest anything else.

Queenstown – the Gold Rush Motel; Franklin-Gordon National Park (untamed wilderness)

Queenstown, certainly for the rest of my life, will be Tasmania's finest example of how Man's insensitivity to his environment can render virtually irreparable damage. It's so unremittingly grim, but bizarrely you can't help liking the place. The landscape around this time-lagged town is as badly scarred by mining as the backs of the prisoners on Sarah Island in nearby Macquarie Harbour were from flogging. Amazingly, there was a time, in the 1970s, when the local tourist board used to actively promote the battle-scarred lunar landscape that surrounds the town, until someone wised-up to the notion that this wasn't one of the better marketing ploys in a world that was becoming increasingly green. So, they switched instead to promoting the history of the penal colony in Macquarie Harbour, a place reserved for the recidivists of the criminal world and which is associated, as John West in his History of Tasmania writes, '... with the remembrance of inexpressible depravity, degradation and woe.'

Nice move.

To be fair, the unsightliness of Queenstown becomes apparent only a few minutes before arrival; it's not as though you are driving towards it for hours on end. This has been a mining town since 1883 when Mick and Bill McDonough and Steve Karlsson for the want of something better to do struggled through heavy undergrowth up the valley of Conglomerate Creek to the saddle between mounts Lyell and Owen and descended into the Linda valley, then known as 'The Vale of Chimouni'. The next day, Steve and Mick discovered a huge ironstone outcrop. This was what became the famous Iron Blow, where mining began. Two weeks later, the three diggers had pegged out a 50-acre lease, strongly suspecting that the blow was the source of the gold they found washed in the creek below the outcrop. They were right, and the Iron Blow was worked as a gold mine for many years. But the three finders soon lost control as they admitted more men into their syndicate. Early in 1888, the Mount Lyell Gold Mining Company was formed in Launceston, and the gold-bearing gossan averaged about two ounces of gold per day. Ironically, so obsessed was the company with digging out the gold that they ignored millions of pounds' worth of copper. The whole process produced the uninspiring landscape that surround the town today. But sulphur fumes from the smelters are not entirely responsible for the bare hills around Queenstown. Between 1896 and 1922, eleven furnaces were in operation around Mount Lyell. To fire the furnaces, hundreds of timber cutters were employed. Between them they accounted for three million tons of timber. As this was all of the rain forest varieties, they had no chance of natural regeneration because the sulphur fumes killed the re-growth. Wild fires, to which the area was prone, wind and heavy rainfall did the rest, scouring and devastating the landscape, and leaving it void of vegetation.

Today, Queenstown has all the feel of a Wild West mining town, with wide streets and corrugated iron-roofed weatherboarded houses. A promotional hand-out says, on a tantalisingly optimistic note, that 'Approaching the town of Queenstown you can't help but be taken aback by the sight of the barren hillsides, hauntingly bare yet strangely beautiful. This lunar landscape has a majestic, captivating quality.' I confess I have to admire the sheer audacity of the statement, while at the same time acknowledging that it touches a note of empathy within me. And in an especially perverse way, the industrial legacy is something they could make a lot more of; a great deal more. I just wish someone would. Maybe it's time to combine the harsh brutality of Sarah Island with the different kind of brutality that existed around Queenstown...and do it soon, Nature is already reclaiming the tattered hills.

I'm booked into the Gold Rush Motel, which has a restaurant that isn't open on Sundays. I arrive on a Sunday. In fact, the restaurant, which boasts '...excellent cuisine supported by friendly staff, pine-lined surroundings, small but well-stocked bar and a cosy fire' isn't, in spite of its evident appeal to a weary traveller and the notable lack of real culinary competition in town, open all the time at all, although tomorrow I can have room service dinner, but presumably not the cosy fire, or the friendly staff. And breakfast is not in the dining room that isn't a restaurant (except presumably on those days when it is, but that's not today or tomorrow). Tomorrow's breakfast, which I have to pre-order by 8pm today, is delivered to my room tonight. Just as well I haven't asked for scrambled eggs, unless, of course, it all comes as a DIY package. Anyway, according to the hotel room information, they want me to feel at home while I enjoy my meal, which will, it assures me, be 'mouth-watering good'. Now, will that be the 'at home' that is my bedroom, or the 'at home' that isn't a restaurant? Because I'm perverse by nature, well, actually, it's because I want to pick up on an invitation to visit Sarah Island, I book in at the hotel for an extra night. Three nights in Queenstown ought to get me a medal of some kind.

Meanwhile, I head into town in case there's a gun fight about to take place or someone is about to be flung from the Empire Saloon for bad mouthing a lady, falling over drunk, kicking the cat, or whatever you get flung from saloons for. Eagerly, I make for the Mount Lyell Motor Inn Restaurant and wander warily into a room, which as I approach I can see is filled with ranks of hunched and silent munchers. I can feel the turgid atmosphere weighing heavily on my shoulders and penetrating eyes stabbing into my back as I walk to the only empty table, set for ten, and I'm beginning to think I've gate-crashed a convention of the Tasmanian Mourners and Psychologically Oppressed Neurotics Society (or TAMPONS, for short: motto; Up Yours).

In a corner of the room, hung just below the ceiling, is a small television screen displaying the numbers of some cyclical game of Lotto. They are up to game 923, and I have an eerie feeling some in the room have been here since the start. I watch for a few moments, then take a card from a receptacle on the table – where most conventional dining establishments would place the condiments – and start marking off numbers. As each new number appears on the screen, I let out an audible but restrained, 'Yes', repeating this for around ten consecutive numbers. I feel the air around me starting to buzz as other Lotto addicts become distracted, shovelling up peas with a pencil and trying to write with a fork, as they pick up on my apparent success. Of course it's all a hoax; I don't have any of the numbers, and if I have I wouldn't dare claim that I've won – I'll never get out of the place. So, I slump back into my chair and think suitably gloomy thoughts to make me feel more at ease until my Chicken Kiev arrives.

Back in my motel room, I turn on the television and switch to the movie channel. They're showing Night of the Living Dead. What else?

The next evening – and I'm telling you this because maybe you can figure it out better than me – I'm driving out of the hotel when I notice that the restaurant lights are on. So, I stop and head for reception and ask if the restaurant is open. No, I'm told, but we're doing room service for dinner. Now I'm having a modicum of difficulty grasping why, if the restaurant is open enough to have its lights on, and within there is a chef and a kitchen bustling away with dinner orders, and someone then delivering the orders over a one-acre site, it isn't possible to say 'Hang on a mo, we'll set you a table', rather than watch me drive into town and spend my money elsewhere. I mean, how does this work? Say I decide to stay in my room and have a three-course meal. Do all the courses come at the same time? Or do they keep bobbing back to see if I've finished my soup, or the fish course or the sticky fig pudding. And if all twenty apartments are doing the same, how can I be sure I get the soup I ordered and not the soup that is intended for someone else – except by not ordering soup in the first place?

Earlier in the day I had ventured into the Empire Hotel. I had a recollection that there was something vaguely interesting about the staircase. Well, there is. It's made from Tasmanian blackwood, but all the virgin timber was shipped over to England in 1904 to be fashioned into a staircase, and then shipped back and assembled on site. I stood at reception for a while waiting to converse with someone in order to check out the accuracy of my recollection. There were three people behind the desk. After five minutes of being ignored I said in an overloud voice: 'Is there any chance of getting some fucking attention here. I'm after five nights in your best room, with five nights of dinner, with an expensive wine, and maybe a few lunches. And if you could rustle up a couple of women, that would be good, too.'

Nobody flinched, probably that was because my comments were no more than thoughts. But, after five minutes of standing at the reception waiting to be noticed by any of the three people, all of whom were less than five feet from me, I gave up and walked out. So, if you're heading this way, just wander in, find an empty room and settle in. No-one seems to give a toss. Meanwhile, I'll head off to find a psychiatrist to see if I can have my self-esteem revived. I never did get to see the pine-lined surroundings of my hotel's restaurant, with its small but well-stocked bar and a cosy fire. A cosy fire would have been good; especially a cosy fire with a couple of decent cognacs. And as for the friendly staff...

I left Queenstown with quite a few backward glances. In the right hands this ugly duckling could be turned, once again, into a much-prized swan.

Anyway, I'm up early, feeling bright and perky, and ready to tackle a modest amount of bush walking. First stop along the heavily bush-flanked Lyell Highway were the Nelson Falls, along the Nelson River and lying within the Franklin-Gordon Wild Rivers National Park. The thing about Franklin-Gordon is that we're talking heavy-duty wilderness, and I mean potentially lost without a cat in hell's chance of coming back alive. If Tasmanian Tigers are still about, this is where they are, just waiting for unsuspecting bush walkers to drop in for lunch. It's not the sort of place you go for a Sunday stroll.

Later, I stop at the start of the trail to a prominent peak, Frenchman's Cap. It doesn't seem all that far away. Maybe I can just jog along there, and be back in time for dinner. That was the plan, at least until I read the sign at the start of the track which says 'Frenchman's Cap: 3-5 days'. Three to five days, but I can see it; it's just over there, behind that green hill, and over that undulating section of bush, past that large stretch of what looks like bog. Undaunted, well, just a little fazed, I set off along the track, purely to see how things go, though I confess my optimism is rapidly waning. Within ten minutes I arrive at the Franklin River. Crossing it isn't a problem, as there's a neat aluminium bridge, about a foot wide; one of those that bounces in a reassuring way as you walk across; one of those that also sways rather alarming when you're out in the middle; one of those you'd rather wish you'd never started to cross. I decide to retreat and re-gather my thoughts. That's when I notice the small print on the notice board beside the bridge:

'The track is difficult to follow and in poor weather you will need to navigate in untracked country. The Franklin River can be difficult to cross as you need to swim and the river is deep and cold.'

Enough said. Back to the car. I've been in this bush country before, and I know there are things out there that can do you a serious mischief...and the wildlife is just as bad.

The Franklin-Gordon Wild Rivers National Park has a rich and remarkable heritage. It contains the last remaining truly wild rivers of Australia, and contains many Aboriginal sites that bear testimony to an Aboriginal heritage on Tasmania extending back over 36,000 years. More recently, it has been the scene of a strong European heritage of convicts and piners, and the stage for the largest conservation battle in Australian history – a battle which ultimately led to the Tasmanian Wilderness World Heritage listing.

One of the most recent episodes in the complex history of the region, however, unfolded during the summer of 1982-3, when the village of Strahan became the focus of the largest conservation battle ever fought in Australia: the battle to save the Franklin River. This mighty wild watercourse was under threat. A few years earlier, in 1979, the Hydro-Electric Commission (HEC) formulated a plan to construct a 180 megawatt power scheme that would result in the inundation of 37 kilometres of the middle reaches of the Gordon River and 33 kilometres of the Franklin River valley. The issue dominated Tasmanian politics throughout the late 1970s and early 1980s and caused great rifts between those who supported the construction of the dam and those who sought the preservation of the wilderness.

In 1981, a referendum was held in the hope of resolving the issue, giving the Tasmanian people the opportunity to express their support for the construction of either of two alternative schemes. The option of 'No dams', which had previously been on the table, however, was withdrawn. This resulted in 44% of the electorate casting an informal vote by writing, 'No Dams' across their ballot.

During the height of the campaign, the Tasmanian Government rejected AUS$500 million offered by Prime Minister Malcolm Fraser to construct an alternative power scheme outside the boundaries of the World Heritage Area. Further offers by the newly-elected Labor Government under Bob Hawke were similarly turned down. Then, at the end of March 1983, the Hawke Government, elected on an anti-dam platform, passed regulations forbidding HEC works within the World Heritage Area. Despite this, the HEC continued with the construction of works while the Tasmanian Government's challenge to the validity of the legislation was heard in the High Court. It was the decision of the High Court on the 1st July 1983 which, after a four to three majority ruling, prevented the damming of the Franklin River. The Federal Government subsequently provided the Tasmanian Government with AU$276 million in compensation, and the Franklin river was saved.

In a cradle's embrace – Lake St Clair – bush walk – an encounter with a tiger snake

A year before I first visited the Cradle Mountain-Lake St Clair National Park, a colleague writer went there and returned with tales not of a land filled with milk and honey, but of fabulous lakes and landscapes, wildlife and views, and of an ascent of Cradle Mountain in a snowstorm. I didn't like the sound of the last bit, but it still didn't put me off wanting to see for myself. There is one particular picture of the mountain and the adjacent Little Horn from pandani-flanked Dove Lake that stuck with me during the weeks of travel through Australia that finally led to this location. If ever a picture lured me into its embrace, this was it.

I had to go.

[Pandani, by the way, is found only in Tasmania and is the largest heath plant in the world similar but unrelated to the pandanus palm of tropical and south-east Asia. I knew you were wondering.]

Today, much investment has been poured into tourist development to cater for the increasing numbers who want to visit one of Tasmania's most extravagant settings. And while I recall a hotel of sorts from my first visit, things have moved on apace, and now you'll find a rather plush hotel – just to soothe the pain of having to cope with such stunning scenery. Thankfully, when I arrived, there was no room at the hotel: 'thankfully' because that meant I had to rent one of the self-catering lodges, not that I intended to do any self-catering, but the isolation was what I needed in order to shunt my mindset more towards a nature writer's perspective of the place, rather than leaving it to the tourist gaze.

That visitors come here at all is down to one man, Gustav Weindorfer, an Austrian-born Australian amateur botanist, lodge-keeper and promoter of the Cradle Mountains National Park. He and his wife climbed Cradle Mountain with friends in 1910, and waxed lyrical about the need for others to see the landscapes for themselves. So, he set about building a chalet that would allow tourists to stay in the valley. Hundreds of acres were bought, and in March 1912, Weindorfer began work on a building he was to call Waldheim, or 'Home in the Forest', using locally harvested King Billy pine. By Christmas 1912, stage one was ready for the first visitors, with a living and dining room and two bedrooms.

The lodge I stayed in – a lounge, kitchen and bedroom combined – was meant for six, but I like rooms that are spacious. It was warm, snug and had a dramatic view of the ragged summit ridge of Cradle Mountain. It also had a nocturnal visitor in the form of a brush-tailed possum and its young that perched on the roof supports looking very wide-eyed, appealing and food expectant – tough!

At Derwent Bridge I pull onto a side road leading down to Lake St Clair, at 167 metres, the deepest freshwater lake in Australia. Along its western shores rise the wooded and craggy heights of Mount Olympus, and across the base, just above the shoreline, the final stages of the Overland Track, a 65-km, six-day trek through the heart of the Cradle Mountain-Lake St Clair National Park.

I walked the first and last sections of this trail in 1998. The first in order to climb Cradle Mountain; and the latter after having sailed up the lake aboard the Ida Clair, and been dropped off at the northern end to face a five-hour walk back to Derwent Bridge. The walk starts at Ronny Creek in Cradle valley and journeys through a landscape of spectacular glacially carved valleys, rainforests, eucalypt forest, golden buttongrass moorlands and stunning alpine meadows covered in a wide variety of alpine and sub-alpine vegetation, including the colourful deciduous beech, something of an anomaly given that most Australian native flora is evergreen.

Most walkers end their walk at Narcissus Hut at the head of Lake St Clair, where they board a small ferry which takes them to the Lake St Clair Visitor Centre at Cynthia Bay. I was going the other way, taking the ferry up to Narcissus Hut and bush walking back out to Derwent Bridge from there.

As I came ashore near the hut, I noticed a separate building, built high on stilts, with steps leading up to it. I wondered what it was, and why it was built so high: turns out it was the toilet, built so high because the trail I was about to follow is renowned as a favoured habitat of tiger snakes, as I discovered later when one slithered across the track, passing between my legs, and inducing a sudden and impromptu rendition of the St Vitas Dance – really not the thing to do!

I lived to tell the tale, but it was some time before my legs stopped trembling, and coming face-to-face with one while inclined at forty-five degrees, so to speak, is not something I care to think too much about.

The bush walk is just under 18km, it took me five hours and there did come a point when I wondered if the bush would ever end. Snakes or no snakes, the scenery is awe-inspiring, at least for me, with more than a hint of the loveliness of remoter parts of Scotland.

The view of Cradle Mountain across Dove Lake is something no self-respecting hill walker can resist; it is so alluring. Rising to 1,545 metres (5,069 feet), it is the fifth highest mountain in Tasmania, and one of the principal tourist sites, composed of dolerite columns, similar to many of the other mountains in the area.

Raised on the hills of Britain and the mountains of the French Alps and Pyrenees, Cradle Mountain was a most enjoyable experience, and one over which I lingered for most of the day. But I could see how, in spite of a clear path all the way, walkers with less experience might find the top section of large boulders and blocks reason enough to turn back, or satisfy themselves with the walk around Dove Lake.

The sheer majesty of the Tasmanian landscape, typified by Cradle Mountain, cannot be over-stated; it possesses a natural beauty that stops you in your tracks (except when tiger snakes are about), and force feeds you with the diversity, the flora and fauna. So, it's not surprising that in December 1982, the World Heritage Committee included the Western Tasmanian Wilderness National Parks in the World Heritage List. In 1989 this was expanded to encompass around 1.4 million hectares – almost a fifth of the total area of the island. In a region that has been subjected to severe glaciation, these parks and reserves, with their steep gorges constitute one of the last expanses of temperate rainforest in the world. Remains found in limestone caves attest to the human occupation of the area for more than 20,000 years. What is eminently satisfying, if you like wilderness, is that the Western Tasmanian Wilderness National Parks World Heritage Area had satisfied all the Unesco criteria for listing as a natural property in addition to three of the six cultural criteria. In doing so, the listing had satisfied more criteria than any other World Heritage Area on Earth.

Some of my notes taken at the time must have come from some promotional leaflet, the contents of which have since found their way onto the internet, but it tells you all you need to know: 'The Tasmanian Wilderness World Heritage Area offers all people, for all time, the opportunity to seek joy and inspiration amidst the untrammelled grandeur of nature, and refuge from an increasingly artificial world. It is waiting for you to discover it, and, perhaps, discover a part of yourself.'

So, what are you waiting for?

Hobart: the corpse in the fountain – Errol Flynn

I'm staying at a hotel overlooking the Railway Roundabout. It's at the end of the Brooker Highway, but – and I'm not maligning any of them – few of the young population of the city would be able to remember the railway from which it got its name; that's long gone. In its place, you'll find a fountain, a modestly proportioned fountain, but, as I gaze on it now, an attractive one nonetheless, a tall, slender phallus played on erotically by varying jets of water and a range of coloured lights. It was built by the citizens of Hobart as a monument to the Mayors and Lord Mayors of the City who have held office since 1853, all forty-seven of them: a delightful change from the usual 'rogues' gallery of photographs hidden away in some civic corridor of power. The design, which incorporates three subway entrances under the busy roadway leading into a small three-tiered garden with the fountain as the centrepiece, was decided by competition. In late 1999, it gained some unwanted notoriety when the naked and burned body of a man was found in it. He turned out to be William George Fisher, a vagrant, who died of drowning while apparently attempting to ease the pain of third-degree burns he had acquired half a kilometre away where his burnt clothes were found. But how he finally met his end will never be known. I'm just hoping his spirit isn't still lingering about.

Not far away, at 52 Warwick Street, is the boarding house where the Hollywood movie star, Errol Flynn lived as a child – and I'm betting there's not many around who could tell you that Flynn was a Tasmanian, although during his time in Hollywood he liked to refer to himself as Irish. This swashbuckling hero of almost fifty films, notably Captain Blood (1935) and The Adventures of Robin Hood (1938) was born in 1909 and roamed the streets of Hobart as a child, living in a succession of houses of increasing standard as his father's employment improved. But in time he abandoned Tasmania and became a naturalised American citizen in 1942.

By all accounts Flynn lived up to the image he liked to portray on screen. By his own account (*My Wicked, Wicked Ways*, 1959), he concluded his formal education at Sydney Church of England Grammar School (Shore School) with being expelled for theft, and having been caught in a romantic assignation with the school's laundress.

Flynn had a reputation for womanising, hard drinking and narcotic abuse, and this lifestyle caught up with him in 1942 when two underage girls accused him of rape. The scandal received immense press attention with many of Flynn's movie fans refusing to accept that the charges were true (one such group that publicly organised to this end was 'The American Boys' Club for the Defense of Errol Flynn (ABCDEF)', claiming that the image of Flynn's screen persona was a reflection of his actual character in real life. The trial took place early in 1943, and Flynn was acquitted after a successfully aggressive defence by his lawyer. Although Flynn was acquitted of the charges, the trial's sexually lurid nature created a notorious public reputation of Flynn as a ladies' man, and permanently damaged his screen image as an idealised romantic lead player, which Warner Bros had expended much time and resources establishing in the eyes of female movie-going audiences. For Flynn it was the beginning of what was to be a sad end.

For all his fame, however, Flynn was not the first Australian to find movie picture success in America. That distinction goes to Louise Lovely, born Nellie Louise Alberti, in Paddington, Sydney to Ferruccio Carlo Alberti, an Italian musician father, and a Swiss mother. She made her professional debut at age nine as Eva in the classic Uncle Tom's Cabin. Lovely eventually returned to Hobart, where she lived to be 85 years old, dying as recently as 1985.

There is something about the marina-like atmosphere of Hobart that I find instantly appealing, a measure of which has to do with the excellent barramundi and chips to be had on the quayside. There is a dazzling and bustling street market along the waterfront, and from somewhere deep within it come the sounds of a didgeridoo being played exceedingly well. It turns out to be Dave Johnson (http://didgera.net), who also contrives to play electronic percussion drums at the same time. My immediate impression is that he has about six or seven arms, and lungs the size of a walrus, not that you get walrus in Tasmania. After a few dazed minutes during which this young man's accomplishment becomes increasingly clear, I find a chair, order a coffee and hang around while he plays '...a wholesome, penetrating explosion of sound and rhythm that awakens in the audience a soul-filled feeling.'

That last bit comes from his website, but I couldn't have put it better myself; which is why I didn't. I'm mesmerised, and not sure how many coffees I got through, but I didn't sleep for days afterwards.

Twanging with caffeine and feeling peckish I steam into the city in search of an eatery; it isn't a wise move. Such restaurants as there are have large bronzed and very muscular men standing outside them dragging people in off the streets, otherwise they'd be empty. One such is the Dragon Palace. I'd walked past it earlier in search of something a little more salubrious, now I wish I'd placed an order as I did so, because I end up back there waiting an age for each stage of the meal. I'm paying the service a compliment when I tell you it's slow. When I went in, there were only two goldfish in the aquarium; when I came out there were ten. Don't go there if you're in a hurry, but if you do, take something to liven things up a bit while you're waiting, like a freshly painted door to watch as it dries.

I lied about the bronzed and muscular men.

And the goldfish.

And that was all of fifteen years ago. Today, it's like a completely different place: super-cool and 'boutique' as the Lonely Planet guide puts it, buzzing with excitement and self-belief.

Bruny Island – Port Arthur penal settlement and the Port Arthur Massacre

First discovered by Abel Tasman and later visited by Furneaux, Cook, Bruni d'Entrecasteaux (after whom the island is named), Bass, Flinders and Bligh, Bruny Island lies to the south of Hobart, and is separated from the Tasmanian mainland by the d'Entrecasteaux Channel or simply, 'The Channel', which provides a large, sheltered, waterway some 60 kilometres long with numerous bays, islands and inlets to explore and fish.

It was a desire to cross the narrow neck of land joining North and South Bruny that led us that way. It's a short ferry ride from Kettering onto the north island, and then by way of Bruny Island Main Road, sandwiched between Adventure Bay to the east and Great Bay, linking to the south island, much of which is given to the South Bruny National Park.

Bruny Island is identified by BirdLife International, a global partnership of conservation organisations, as an area of global importance for the conservation of birds population because it hosts the world's largest population of the endangered Forty-spotted Pardalote (no, I'm not making this up), a third of the world population of the Swift Parrot, 13 of Tasmania's 14 endemic bird species, and up to 240,000 breeding pairs of the Short-tailed Shearwater (aka the Tasmanian Muttonbird). For ornithologists it is nirvana.

In the past, the timber industry was dominant on Bruny Island, with many eucalypts being milled and exported. Later, a sandstone quarry exported its stone, mainly to Victoria. A number of public buildings in Melbourne were built from Bruny 'freestone'. Agriculture has always been important, too, and the original settlers had to be self-sufficient until more recent times and the advent of the ferry service that replaced the old 'Channel Boats'. Apple trees, the first in Australia, were planted in Adventure Bay by Captain Bligh (of 'Mutiny on the Bounty' fame) and for many years the fruit and orchard industries provided employment for many locals. Fishing, too, has always been a local activity with scallops, oysters, mussels, blacklip abalone and crayfish in abundance together with a large variety of scale-fish. Eco-tourism is now a growing feature of the island's economy with birdwatching tours and sea trips.

Today, little remains of the old industries and although there are still huge tracts of State Forest and National Parks, there are only two small sawmills in operation. Farming too, has diminished, although many of the locals still have a few sheep and cows.

On the way back to the ferry we stopped off to walk out onto the sands of Adventure Bay and collect shells, something we probably should not admit to. Anyway, the place was deserted with just the soughing of the wind across the sands and the distant call of a lorikeet to give voice to the place. Reliably mapped by early explorers and offering abundant fresh water and game, Adventure Bay became a popular anchorage for European explorers. In the nineteenth century, the Bay became the site of a whaling station, and was later used by the timber industry. Today it is a tourist destination, and, when we visited, a very quiet one...and, I have to say, a very special one.

Port Arthur, on an almost-island 60 kilometres south-east of Hobart named after George Arthur, the Lieutenant Governor of Van Diemen's Land, is a peaceful tourist destination today, but its history is mind-blowing. This is one of Australia's most significant heritage areas and an open air museum. The site forms part of the Australian Convict Sites, a World Heritage location, and one of '...the best surviving examples of large-scale convict transportation and the colonial expansion of European powers through the presence and labour of convicts.'

The drive from Hobart, along the Tasman Highway to Sorell and the Arthur Highway to Port Arthur, takes around 90 minutes, and nothing along what is an appealing and scenic route can prepare you for what lies at journey's end.

It would be folly to suggest that wandering around this former penal colony, with or without the services of a guide, gives more than the vaguest of notions of what conditions were like. You're just looking a walls and rooms 1.65 metres long and 1.05 metres wide in which prisoners were kept in solitary confinement, and they are saying nothing. The Port Arthur peninsula is a naturally secure site, surrounded by water rumoured to be shark-infested. The only connection to the mainland, the 30m-wide isthmus of Eaglehawk Neck was fenced and guarded by soldiers, man traps and half-starved dogs. Yet prisoners did escape and attracted a reward of fifty sovereigns '...to any person or persons who shall apprehend or cause to be apprehended and lodged in safe custody...the said Felons'. Should the person doing the apprehending be a convict themselves, then a pardon awaited...a conditional pardon.

From 1833 until 1853, Port Arthur was the destination, and for over 1,500 the final resting place, for the hardest of British criminals, mainly malefactors who had re-offended after their arrival in Australia. Rebellious personalities from other convict stations were also sent here to face the strictest security measures of the British penal system.

The layout of the prison was symmetrical, a cross shape with exercise yards at each corner. The prisoner wings were connected to the surveillance core of the prison as well as the chapel in the Central Hall. From this surveillance hub each wing could be clearly seen, although individual cells could not. This 'Separate Prison System', as it was known, also signalled a shift from physical punishment to psychological punishment. Hard corporal punishment, such as whippings, used in other penal stations served only to harden criminals. So, at Port Arthur, food was used to reward well-behaved prisoners and as punishment for troublemakers: a well-behaved prisoner might receive larger amounts of food or allowances of tea, sugar and tobacco. As punishment, the prisoners would receive the bare minimum of bread and water. Under this system of punishment a 'Silent System' was implemented in which prisoners were hooded and made to stay silent, to 'allow time for the prisoner to reflect upon the actions which had brought him there'. As a result, many prisoners deprived of light and sound developed mental illness, an unintended outcome.

In spite of its reputation as a pioneering institution for the enlightened view of imprisonment, Port Arthur was in reality as harsh and brutal as other penal settlements. Some critics suggesting that its use of psychological punishment, compounded with no hope of escape, made it one of the worst. Some tales suggest that prisoners committed murder (an offence punishable by death) in order to escape the desolation of life at the camp.

Little remains today of Point Puer where boy convicts, between ten and eighteen years of age were jailed, most for theft. Their age brought them no benefits and they were treated as brutally as adult prisoners. Solitary confinement was commonplace and sustenance limited to just 450 grams of bread a day and a small amount of water.

Today, Port Arthur is officially Tasmania's top tourist attraction. It was even viewed as a tourist attraction long before it was abandoned as a prison. But right from the beginning, Port Arthur's potential as a tourist site was remarked upon. David Burn (An Excursion to Port Arthur in 1842, Melbourne 1972), visiting the settlement in 1842, when it was only twelve years old, was much struck by the scenery of the Tasman Peninsula, and declared that: 'Here at some future...day, when penitentiary and penal settlements have ceased to exist...the Tasmanian steams will flock with their joyous freightage of watering-place visitors.' Anthony Trollope (Australia, 1873, Brisbane 1967) took the view that when the buildings had long since fallen down, 'Men might then make "unfrequent excursions to visit the strange ruins"'. In the Tasmanian Guide Book, published in 1871, the description of this peninsula goes only as far as Dunalley, as if the coastline had been snapped off at Eaglehawk Neck. But an earlier publication, no doubt aimed at wealthier tourists had no compunction about including the settlement: 'To get into Port Arthur', it said, 'is about as troublesome as going into Russia, and it has rather more complicated passport regulations'.

Well, it's a lot easier these days, and, if nothing else, serves to highlight developing trends in black tourism, although on a lighter note the location is also used to give chamber music recitals. In November 2014, the Australia Chamber Orchestra returned to Port Arthur to perform a concert of Scandinavian works by Nielson, Sibelius and Sinding '...in the intimate surrounds of the Asylum Hall'. I can't help feeling there's something not quite as wholesome about that choice of words as the programme makers would have you believe, something unfeelingly sadistic about performing glorious music in surroundings where people were deprived of sight and sound to the point of madness, and something just a little ghoulish and unthinking about bringing to the site of the second most horrific massacre by a single person in world history (see below) music from the country where the worst such massacre took place.

Maybe I'm just not connected to the dark side of tourism. You can even have a pre-concert meal in the Felons Bistro featuring such delights as wallaby, funky fresh salads, pickled octopus, venison and rabbit pies.

But, I guess, that's just Australia for you; all part of being weird and yet wonderful at the same time.

Port Arthur, however, has a modern history of crime that ranks as one of the deadliest shootings committed by a single person; it still remains the deadliest in the English-speaking world.

In 1996, just two years before my first visit to the destination, 28-year-old Martin Bryant from Hobart, loaded his car with guns and ammunition and went to Port Arthur. There he killed 35 people and wounded 21 others, and was taken into custody after an overnight standoff and was given 35 life sentences for the murders without the possibility of parole. Bryant instantly became the most vilified individual in Australian history and was rapidly enlisted in the serial killers' hall of infamy. His rampage was the deadliest shooting by a lone gunman in history until 2011 when Anders Behring Breivik shot and killed 69 people at a summer camp on a Norwegian island having already killed 8 people in a car bombing in Oslo.

It is impossible to imagine the scenes at Port Arthur that day, to understand what happened, or why. All I can offer is the sense I felt when I first visited that the massacre was still fresh in people's minds, as if a cloak of terror and dismay still draped itself across the place. Bad enough that Port Arthur was one of the most reviled prison colonies in the world, but for it later to become the scene of, arguably, even greater horror is something that cannot be ignored. It was still being talked about when I returned six years later.

Tassie wildlife – the Tasmanian Tiger; Tasmanian Devil

So, what about that Tassie Tiger? Is it real? Is it a myth fomented in some inebriated imagination? The adventurer in me wants to find out, but the coward just wants another beer.

The thylacine was the largest known carnivorous marsupial

of modern times. Because it had a prominently striped back, it became known as the Tasmanian tiger. Native to continental mainland Australia, Tasmania and New Guinea, the Tassie tiger is thought to have become extinct during the 20th century, the last extant member of its family, Thylacinidae.

The thylacine became rare or extinct on the Australian mainland about 2,000 years ago, but it continued to survive on Tasmania along with other endemic species, including the Tasmanian devil. Hunting encouraged by bounties is generally blamed for its extinction, but other contributing factors were in play, notably disease, dogs, human encroachment into its habitat and the concurrent extinction of its prey species. Yet in spite of its official listing as extinct, sightings are still reported, though none has been conclusively proven.

Notwithstanding its fate elsewhere, the thylacine survived into the 1930s on Tasmania. At the time of the first settlement, the heaviest distributions were in the north-east, north-west and north-midland regions. They were rarely sighted during this time, but slowly began to be credited with attacks on sheep, that hardy standby (which usually also mentions the killing of children) hauled out whenever there is a perceived need to demonise an animal or bird, cf wolf, dingo, eagle. As early as 1830, the Van Diemen's Land Company introduced bounties on the thylacine, and between 1888 and 1909 the Tasmanian government paid £1 per head for dead adult thylacines and ten shillings for pups. In all they paid out over 2,000 bounties, but it is thought that many more thylacine were killed than were claimed for. Whatever the reason, the thylacine had become very rare in the wild by the late 1920s. Yet, despite the fact that the thylacine was widely believed to be responsible for attacks on sheep, in 1928 the Tasmanian Advisory Committee for Native Fauna recommended a reserve to protect any remaining thylacines, with potential sites of suitable habitat including the Arthur-Pieman area of western Tasmania.

The last known thylacine to be killed in the wild was shot in 1930 by Wilf Batty, a farmer from Mawbanna, in the north-east of the state. The animal, believed to have been a male, had been seen around Batty's house for several weeks.

But does the Tassie tiger still exist?

The Australian Rare Fauna Research Association (www.arfra.org) has almost 4,000 sightings on file from mainland Australia since the 1936 extinction date, while the Mysterious Animal Research Centre of Australia (www.mysteriousaustralia.com) recorded 138 up to 1998, and the Department of Conservation and Land Management recorded 65 in Western Australia over the same period. Independent thylacine researchers on Tasmania report 360 Tasmanian and 269 mainland post-extinction 20th-century sightings. What evidently makes it difficult to find is that it is a crepuscular and night-time hunter, and would you go wandering off into the forest just as it's going dark?

I must confess to a longing that this exquisite creature – there are plenty of images by which to judge its beauty – somehow still survives deep in the Tasmanian forests, biding its time before emerging in army sized numbers to gobble up all the sheep – well, give a Tassie tiger a bad name.

But it is acutely worrying that no-one has managed a confirmed sighting, and that's a problem compounded by significant numbers of 'sightings' that are unconfirmed. When will some antipodean David Attenborough go off in search of the truth? They always find what they're looking for, usually on the last day, at the eleventh hour, just before they have to leave.

On another visit to Cradle valley a few years later, my wife and I spent half an hour watching a wombat going about its business, a huge, hairy, amorphous, tailless wonder that no-one seems to take seriously, even depictions of the animal in Dreamtime portray it as of little worth. But, we found it cute…not that we were tempted to give it a pat on the head; while normally docile, they have an irascible and unpredictable temperament, a fine set of teeth and a pair of back legs that can kick like a donkey.

Wombats don't seem to be any more popular in the animal world either, since Tasmanian devils, and dingos, like to prey on them, and Aboriginal people are known to have hunted wombats for food. The UK *Independent* newspaper, reported that in April 2010, a 59-year-old man from rural Victoria state was mauled by a wombat, causing a number of cuts and bite marks that needed hospital treatment. He resorted to killing it with an axe. And while it is always a pleasure to spot a wombat, it has nothing, for reasons that are unclear, like the cultural significance of other native animals such as the koala, kangaroo or the dingo.

So, what about that other Tasmanian delight, the devil (Sarcophilus harrisii)? Well, when you see one you can't help thinking that only a mother could love it...there are no words on the 'cute' theme that apply to the Tasmanian devil. These squat little beasts are stocky and muscular, have black fur, a strongly pungent odour, extremely loud and disturbing screech, keen sense of smell, and ferocity when feeding...and those are its good points. For good measure, they have the strongest bite per unit body mass of any extant mammal land predator; crunching through bones is like eating a snack. So, having one as a pet is not a good idea... and yet it is the iconic symbol of Tasmania, the symbol of the Tasmanian National Parks and Wildlife Service.

Since the late 1990s, however, devil facial tumour disease has majorly reduced the devil population and today threatens the survival of the species, which in 2008 was declared to be endangered. Like the Tassie tiger, the devil was also branded with the sheep killing iron, and it, too, fell under the terminal fist of the bounty hunters.

Because devils tend to be nocturnal, and I'm not daft enough to go wandering dense forest in the dark, I have yet to see one in the wild. Sadly, those I've seen in zoos, which I care not to publicise, are desperately in need of being released – but that's just my take on zoos generally.

With fewer introduced predators and a larger tracts of intact habitat, Tasmania is quite probably the last refuge for many animal species. The diversity of the island's vegetation is also remarkable and includes examples of the most ancient plant species on Earth; the tallest flowering trees; the oldest plant clones and a high proportion of endemic species such as the eastern quoll and twelve species of bird found nowhere else on Earth. Yet you don't need to go off on safari to track down enough Tassie wildlife to make your day a satisfying one: you can find pademelon in the suburbs of Hobart, and elsewhere widely evident – and no, that's not something you buy on a fruit stall in a market, although these small kangaroos were highly regarded as a food item by the early Australian settlers.

TERRY MARSH

CHAPTER TEN

Queensland

Cairns – the Great Barrier Reef – Port Douglas Rainforest Habitat and a champagne breakfast with the birds

Cairns is about 1,700 kilometres (1,100 miles) north from Brisbane, a popular travel destination for tourists because of its tropical climate and its convenience as a starting point for anyone wanting to visit the Great Barrier Reef and Far North Queensland, which was why I came, and returned...and came back again.

The first thing you notice about Cairns, apart from its bright and sparkling outlook on life, is that it's hot and humid, a condition I describe as clammytropic. And when it rains, it comes down like organ pipes and bounces two feet back in the air. Coming from the north of England I was well used to torrential downpours, but in Queensland it's like being inside a waterfall surrounded by a fearful and resounding roar. At times the raindrops conjoin to form a solid cube of water into which only the foolhardy would venture. In terms of rainfall, Queensland is in the Premier League. It's wise to remain indoors when it's like this; that's what the geckos do, anyway. I've spent many a happy hour sharing an audiobook with a few House Dtella (*Gehyra australis*), a cute little creature with something like thirty-plus cousin species in Queensland alone. On the plus side, the rain is quite warm. So, if you need a shower and can't be bothered dealing with the intricacies of Queensland plumbing, just strip off and stand on the balcony for a while; you can be sure the rain will reach places you never knew you had.

DOWN UNDER DREAMING

Prior to British settlement, the Cairns region was predominantly mangrove swamps and sand ridges, populated by the Mandingalbay Yidinji and the Gimuy Walubara Yidinji people, who still claim Native Title rights. In 1770, James Cook mapped the future site of Cairns, naming it Trinity Bay, but it was another 100 years before Cairns was founded in 1876, a development hastened by the need to export gold from the tablelands to the west of the inlet. Even then it was at the distant end of a less-than-perfect jungle highway, shrouded in luxurious foliage and populated by a madness of eccentrics, loners and chancers of dubious intent and purpose.

On my first visit, keen on sampling the tropical joie de vivre for which Cairns was renowned, I trundled out of town from the airport shuttle drop-off, rucksack on my back and a slightly smaller one on my front, to track down one of the numerous backpackers' hostels. Here as elsewhere standards vary, and the hostels often accommodate a species of humanity endowed with a wide range of hygiene and moralistic deficiencies, often setting new standards for both as I discovered when I tried to sleep through the acoustics of the seven or eight occupants of the adjoining room taking a night-long Waltzing Matilda approach to sexual activity. I'd witnessed the ribald prelude in the bar earlier in the evening, a place that made the bar in Star Wars look like a care home for genteel ladies; there were certainly some who were not of this world. In the morning, I found that someone had kindly deposited a yard of vomit outside my room door and not reclaimed it. Thankfully, the hostel staff take this sort of thing in their stride. Well, in the context of vomit, not literally in their stride.

When I returned a few years later, and then later still, I opted for more conventional hotel accommodation, and delighted on a daily basis to a chilled beer on the terrace, gazing out across the turquoise waters of the Pacific, and poring over the day's copy of *The Cairns Post*. I do rather like getting local newspapers, wherever I go, and reading about places I know virtually nothing about

– in France it gives the impression to any casual passer-by that I understand French. There is something soothing to find that other nations have just the same problems as your own: that politician's I've never heard of also fiddle their expenses and put it down as a 'simple mistake' that anyone could make; that celebrity infidelity is commonplace, and that people are murdered or go missing. I will now never go to live in Australia; that was a long-ago prospect. But it's still interesting to see what sort of property I could buy for AUS$500,000, even assuming I had AUS$500,000.

I can't admit to understanding the economics of Queensland; it's not the sort of thing you think too much about on holiday, except when you're reading newspapers. I thought Cairns in particular was a pretty nifty, go-ahead place with little need for improvement, a bit sweaty but you can't do much about that. But in 2015, an apparently long-awaited Northern Australia White Paper, launched in Cairns by Prime Minister Tony Abbott, unveiled a grand vision for the state's Far North, set to be unleashed through a vast range of measures tapping into the region's economic potential. Clearly, the Federal Government saw Queensland as a major growth area. Perhaps they've found a new, rich vein of gold. But I certainly hope that the 'grand' vision doesn't involve cutting down precious rain forest.

The Great Barrier Reef, which I was certainly intent on visiting even though I swim like a rock, is the largest living thing on Earth, visible even from outer space and one of the modern Seven Wonders of the World, and one of Australia's nineteen World Heritage Sites. This 2,300km-long ecosystem comprises over 2,900 individual reefs and 900 islands made of more than 600 types of hard and soft coral, and attracts over 2 million visitors each year. The reef is greater in size than the United Kingdom, Holland and Switzerland combined, and about half the size of Texas. It is also home to countless species of colourful fish, molluscs and starfish, plus turtles, dolphins and sharks...some of which will kill you, although it's rarely personal.

What you don't expect if you go out on one of the many dive boats that operates day-long trips to the reef is to resurface and find your boat has gone and left you floating more than thirty miles off shore. But that's exactly the situation that faced childhood sweethearts Thomas and Eileen Lonergan in 1998, in a bizarre and conspiracy laden disappearance that was not discovered until two days after the event.

The Lonergans, from Baton Rouge in Louisiana, USA, were scuba diving at St Crispin's reef when the boat that had transported the group to the dive site departed before they returned from the water. None of the vessel's crew or passengers noticed that the two had not come back aboard. The Lonergans were never found and are presumed to have died at sea. It was not until two days later, on 27 January, 1998, that the pair was discovered to be missing when a bag containing their belongings was found on board the dive boat. A huge air and sea search involving 12 planes, 3 helicopters and a flotilla of boats took place over the following three days.

Against many odds, they appear to have survived their first perilous night. Months later a fisherman 100 miles north of the site found a dive slate which records their thoughts as dawn broke in the morning. In faded scrawl, Tom Lonergan had written: '[Mo]nday Jan 26; 1998 08am. To anyone [who] can help us: We have been abandoned on A[gin]court Reef by MV *Outer Edge* 25 Jan 98 3pm. Please help us [come] to rescue us before we die. Help!!!'

Inflatable dive jackets marked with Tom and Eileen's names were later washed ashore north of Port Douglas, along with their tanks – still buoyed up by a few remnants of air – and one of Eileen's fins. Port Douglas is miles away from where they were lost, indicating that they drowned, their bodies were never found, and the truth of their disappearance remains a mystery. Their story, transported to the Caribbean, nevertheless found its way into the

2003 American psychological horror drama film, *Open Water*.

Less than an hour's drive north of Cairns, the Port Douglas Rainforest Habitat is a curious place. Billed as Australia's leading environmental wildlife experience, I came to the conclusion that if there have to be zoos, then this is how they should be. Fundamentally, this centre allows you to get up close and possible personal with a wide range of species, although you might want to think twice about chummying up to the crocs.

On my first visit I was lying prone, the better to get a good camera angle on some magpie geese (Anseranas semipalmata), when one clambered onto my back and started nibbling affectionately at the back of my neck. It was only afterwards that I realised that this gesture of friendliness was actually a prelude to the bird relieving itself, which it did generously and with lasting aromatic consequence. Thankfully it wasn't a prelude to anything else of a romantic nature.

Elsewhere, birds featured largely in the business plan of the Centre, not least in the well-publicised invitation to enjoy a champagne breakfast with the birds. What the blurb says is: 'Guests are immersed within the Wetlands environment whilst enjoying the cacophony of sounds and colours of Wildlife as they wander freely amongst the guests'. What it means is: 'Come and pay AUS$54 for a delicious breakfast of custard apple, dragon fruit, mangostein and assorted pastries in the hope of getting some into your mouth before the marauding birds beat you to it'.

Actually, that's a little unfair of me. Not all the birds like custard apple.

A train ride to Kuranda (I'm bitten by a parrot) – giants of the rainforest

I'm booked on the early morning train up to Kuranda, the so-called 'Village in the Rain Forest'. My one regret is that I couldn't have seen it fifty years ago, before the tourism pros discovered what a stunning place it was. Now there is an awful lot of tourist tat, and it was here that I first went into paroxysms of self-inflicted anguish over whether a didgeridoo made here by an Aboriginal person and hand-painted by him was an authentic didgeridoo, or a tourist trinket. I could have resolved this dilemma by wandering off into the Bush, finding an Aboriginal person with a didgeridoo and buying it from him. But thankfully my stomach was calling and it had an appointment with a chunk of damper. More accurately, it was my curiosity that had the appointment; my stomach didn't forgive me for days. In any case, if I had found a didge-playing bush whacker, he may well have bought his didge from the man in Kuranda.

Damper is a traditional Australian soda bread traditionally baked in the coals of a campfire and customarily eaten by swagmen, drovers, stockmen and other travellers. It is an iconic Australian dish, and that was probably why I wanted to try it. This brick of bread was originally developed by stockmen travelling in remote areas for prolonged periods. The basic ingredients were flour, water and sometimes milk, which was then normally cooked in the ashes of the camp fire.

Damper became a popular dish for recreational campers and has become available in bakeries. Many variations and recipes exist, some authentic, others using the name to sell a more palatable bread product to the urban public and tourists. I'm not sure which version I sampled, but - let's put it this way - I've never had it since.

The train ride up to Kuranda - just under two hours - was without incident, rising steadily through a steaming tropical rainforest, past spectacular waterfalls and into the awesome Barron Gorge, and inordinately tranquil in a clackety-clack sort of way. This famous railway was built between 1882 and 1891 and even today is considered an engineering feat of tremendous magnitude involving hundreds of men to construct 15 hand-made tunnels and 37 bridges.

For a more elevated approach to Kuranda there is the Skyrail Rainforest Cableway, spanning 7.5km, and traversing the McAlister Range, through the Barron Gorge National Park; it's certainly much quicker...and quieter.

The land around Kuranda has been home to the Djabugay Aboriginal people for more than 10,000 years and this indigenous culture still thrives today. Back in Cairns I'd pulled a few strings to get me an appointment with one of the Aboriginal spokespeople in Kuranda. I'll call him Tom so that he doesn't invite the wrath of his spirits for speaking to a Gadja (ghost spirit, or white man).

'Djabuguy', he tells me, 'is the name of the Aboriginal people who lived in the Kuranda region, long time past. Kuranda village was Ngunbay, the place of platypus. Good fishing and hunting. But all this changed when gold and tin were discovered. Access was on the trails of the rainforest people, and through their country.'

I knew what was coming.

'This was not popular with the Djabugay, who killed bullocks and the occasional white man. They took workmen's food, because traditional gathering and hunting grounds were destroyed by the settlers, and overhunted by men working on the railway line.'

Because I had already read *Conspiracy of Silence* by Timothy Bottom, I knew that the Queensland frontier was more violent than any other Australian colony. Yet what we know about these killing times is swept aside it seems in favour of the great pioneer myth. As white pastoralists moved into new parts of country, violence inevitably followed. Over 50,000 Aboriginals were killed on the Queensland frontier alone, a quarter of the original population. Europeans were killed too, but not in anything like the same numbers.

Kuranda was originally surveyed by Irish-born Thomas Behan, in 1888, and the building of the railway and road from the port of Cairns paved the way for trade and the movement of people across the inland mountains. At 380 metres above sea level, coffee was the crop of choice in and around Kuranda until frosts in the 1900s wiped out the harvest. Later, Kuranda became a destination for locals on holiday with word soon spreading of the magnificent Barron Falls and the vibrancy of the rainforest. In the late 1960s, Kuranda was the place to be: spectacular scenery, wonderful climate, cheap living, grow your own food, do your own thing. Not surprisingly, then, hippy communes flourished until new settlers arrived in the 1970s – musicians and people with artistic talents and imagination pursuing an alternative lifestyle.

At the top end of town is Birdworld where, for reasons that escape me, I poked my finger into the cage of an Eclectus parrot, with predictable results; I still bear the scar to this day, which serves as a useful reminder not to go poking anything into anything.

Time precluded a more extensive visit to the Atherton Tablelands above Cairns, but I was determined to go off in search of some giants of the rainforest, the acclaimed fig trees of Atherton. In the event, they were remarkably easy to find, being barely 50m from the road, and now popular with tourists.

The Curtain Fig Tree, just out of Yungaburra, is one of the largest trees in tropical North Queensland, and one of the best-known attractions on the Atherton Tableland. The tree is a strangler fig (*Ficus virens*), which germinate on top of a host tree and send roots into the ground. Once rooted, the fig grows quickly, finally killing the host tree and growing on independently. In this case, the aerial roots drops 15 metres (49 feet) to the ground. The Curtain Fig Tree and the nearby Cathedral Fig in Danbulla National Park are more than 500 years old. Although these figs kill their hosts, they are an epiphyte which feeds from the ground, unlike a parasitic plant which feeds from the sap of the host.

When I visited, my only company was a small group of grey-headed robin and a brace of orange-footed scrubfowl that stalked about the forest floor uncaring of yet another visitor.

Oh, I forgot to mention the zillion mossies, but you do get used to them...in a bizarre, self-inflicted masochistic way.

Daintree Rain Forest – Crocodylus Tented Village – a night walk in the forest – encounters with poisonous frogs, giant spiders, lizards and snakes – Cape Tribulation

I awake in the dark and leap out of bed, uncertain where I am, until I bump into a chair I haven't got. Then I remember: Daintree, part way up the pointy bit at the top right of Australia.

I am also much entangled in mosquito netting, without which the night would have been something of an ordeal as the buzzing beasties of northern Australia tend to look on me as a rather tasty al fresco snack. As it was, the undulating curves of my half-sleeping form become a nocturnal playground for the Daintree's own mousey delight, melomys, which scuttles backward and forwards across me for much of the night, resisting my swinging-leg attempts to persuade it to try someone else's bed. In the morning, I find a tidy pile of the remains of a white-kneed cricket on the edge of the bed; a present from my nocturnal visitor. You don't get that in Blackpool – well, not the white-kneed crickets.

Daintree is a tropical rainforest and listed as a World Heritage Site in 1988, with over 700 species of plants and animals that can only be found there. Daintree is home to the bull kauri, the biggest conifer in the world; the tallest cycad in the world, Hope's cycad, as well as the smallest cycad in Australia, the Bowenia. Mammals, like tree kangaroos, bats and tropical bettongs live here. Birds include the cassowary; a potentially nasty piece of work that can make a real mess of you if it puts its mind to it.

The Daintree rainforest is believed to be 180 million years old, some tens of millions of years older than the Amazon rainforest. This is part of the Kuku Yalanji country, its people having lived in this area for thousands of years, and their songs and legends continue to give special meaning to this landscape today.

On my travels, I'd heard much about Crocodylus, a tented village way deep in the rainforest on the road north to Cape Tribulation, and wanted to see for myself. Nothing could have prepared me for the experience. On a scale of one to ten of a blend of bizarre, wonderful and downright deadly, this is heading for fifteen.

The road from Cairns is Queensland at its best, faithfully paralleling the numerous indentations of the coast, with lazy sweeps of sandy bays, endless beaches fanned by gently swaying palms, and the sparkling sea, or to be more precise, the edge of Pacific Ocean, never far distant. It was a tropical wonderland.

Beyond Port Douglas and Mossman the swaying ranks of roadside sugar cane give way to luxuriously green tropical mountains, a convoluted lush chaos of trees and ferns and shrubbery, which seems to grow down to the very edges of the road, leaving me with a lasting impression that the road may be overgrown and impassable by the time I come back, so quickly does Nature regenerate in these fecund conditions.

I head first for the riverside village of Daintree itself, a place with a delightful country-western ramshackle appeal, somewhere you almost expect to see horses hitched to a rail outside the saloon. There was a saloon, but, sadly, no horses, unless you count those under the bonnets of the ranked Holdens and dusty Land Cruisers that seem to be the hallmark hereabouts of those who want to give the impression they are hardened bush pioneers. I shun the croc cruises and croc burgers and retreat a few kilometres to turn down a side road that leads to the occasionally croc-infested Daintree River. The only way across is by an ancient and arthritic car ferry that hauls itself along on rusting cables. It's a truly cathartic experience, a gateway to another world, something deeply mystical and enthusing.

Having paid the ferryman, I ease wide-eyed into this verdant wonderland. Butterflies of iridescent hues sweep down to greet me and dance about the car. These lightweight natives of the forest seem to be saying 'Welcome'; at least, that's the spin I'm putting on it because I've heard there are some rather heavyweight spiders in this neck of the woods and I've no wish to run afoul of them by upsetting the welcoming committee.

Humidity is rising towards 100 per cent. I've made it to the famed wet tropics. I have the air conditioning on maximum and I'm still weeping sweat. But that's a trivial price to pay for the privilege of entry into this magnificent green underworld. As I motor along, vines hang over the road, occasionally swiping at the car as if trying to get a firm grip and whisk us off for lunch.

Named in honour of an Englishman, Richard Daintree, this is the largest surviving tract of tropical lowland rainforest on the Australian continent. Much of what lies ahead of me is inaccessible wilderness where jungle-clad mountains sweep down to meet the coral sea. A fierce campaign during the 1980s saved it from the developers and led to its status as a Wet Tropics World Heritage Area. The Daintree River, 140 kilometres in length, rises on the eastern edges of the Mount Carbine and Mount Windsor tablelands to the south and west, along the Great Dividing Range. It rains here, though rain is not so constant a factor in rainforest as might be suspected; scientists more correctly refer to these forests as 'closed' forests. Even so, it has one of the wettest climates in Australia, where seasons are determined by rainfall, or the lack of it. As a result, 'Wet' and 'Dry' replace the four seasons we know so well in the northern hemisphere.

Daintree is so diverse that it is home to eighty per cent of the endemic species of marsupials, birds, reptiles and frogs in the whole of Australia's rainforests, and that's before you start cataloguing the thousands of butterflies, ants, spiders, moths, wasps, snails, cicadas, bees, millipedes and microscopic organisms.

It's dark in the rainforest as I pull into Crocodylus and wander along a narrow path to reception, flanked by the six-foot webs of the golden orb spider, wait-a-while wands and the eerily amplified sound of something scuttling about the undergrowth. I'm having second thoughts...and third. The receptionist beams a welcoming smile – anything less would have had me turning tail and heading out faster than I came in – and suggests I take some mossie coils to help reduce the problem in the tents. I thought of asking for a tent without the problems, but something stopped me.

All the tents have names, which I thought was heart-warming, and mine lies somewhere deep in the jungle. So off I set looking for Kookaburra Dreaming. It's mid-day, but very little light penetrates the canopy, and what there is casts a gloomy half-light that makes me wary about where I'm putting my feet. Five feet off the path, a metre-long Boyd's forest dragon clings to a tree, watching me go by, and further in I pick up the vivid green of a tree snake; harmless enough, but just a touch scary if you're not expecting this sort of thing.

My tent is huge; in fact, my tent is bigger than the ground floor of my house back home. Four sets of bunk beds line the walls, and in a recess is a double bed with a mosquito net hanging over it. Business is quiet, and I get the tent to myself. I start unpacking, but then wonder if this is a good idea. The receptionist had warned me about melomys, which, friendly as it is, isn't too fussy what it eats or where it carries out its ablutions. So, I opt for hanging my sack from one of the posts of a bunkbed hoping that will suffice, and, tucking the bottoms of my trousers into my socks, decide to explore. As I reach the door some impulse causes me to pause: a buff-breasted paradise kingfisher is perched on a branch just a few feet away. I hold my breath and watch. There are more birds endemic to this region that anywhere else in the country – and this is one of them.

There is also a whole encyclopaedia of things that can do me harm, including a rather nasty species of tree, which Australian understatement modestly names the stinging tree. In fact, there are three species of stinging tree in Australia, two are found in Daintree. The main offender, the Hairy-leaf Stinger, sometimes called the Gympie Stinger or Gympie Gympie, is widespread here, and there's one not far away. To describe the effect as a sting is on a par with likening the after effects of being hit by a 50-metre road train travelling at 100 kilometres an hour as a bit of a headache.

The point is underlined later that evening when I meet up with Anthony Border, a forest guide who aspires to lead a group of worried faces on a night tour of the forest: a couple of young German guys putting a brave face on things; three young ladies from Brisbane who seem less confident; two backpackers of indeterminate origin, and me, just indeterminate. To the sound of something primeval screeching in the dark, steaming, tropical rainforest, Anthony cloaks us all in waterproof ponchos and equips us with powerful torches run from a heavy-duty battery that we tether around our waists.

'Where we're going,' he tells us, smiling broadly, 'there are many things that can cause you grief. So, stick to the path and don't stray.'

Suddenly, I want to be carried.

We all huddle closer together, each intent on following immediately and very, very faithfully in Anthony's footsteps. If it was daylight we'd be so scared by the worried looks we probably wouldn't start. As it is, we put our trust in Anthony; he's a likeable, bright faced young man and clearly knows what he's about...we hope.

After only a few moments he stops beside a large pond. Expecting all manner of beasts to emerge, we scan the surface apprehensively. 'This', Anthony tells us, 'is the cess pit for the village. You don't want to go falling in there.'

A few minutes later he stops and spotlights a huge frog on

a tree, about the size of a rat. 'This is a poison dart tree frog,' Anthony tells us. 'It's a good idea not to touch it. Its entire skin is poisonous. The Aboriginal natives who lived in this area used to rub the spear tips on the back of the frog, collecting enough toxin to kill small prey outright and stun some of the larger ones.'

Whether it truly was a poison dart frog, normally resident in South America, I can't remember; I wasn't taking notes at the time; just keeping my hands away from things that might kill me. So, we all give the frog a healthy berth, only to find Anthony squatting on the floor. 'And this,' he says, tapping lightly on what looks like a small piece of moss at the base of a tree, 'is where the trap door spider lives.' To prove the point, he uses the point of his knife to ease the trap door open. But if the spider is at home, she's not coming out, about which one of us, at least, is mightily relieved.

We wander on further into the forest, surrounded by strange and malevolent sounds. But Anthony seems unconcerned. Suddenly, he stops dead in his tracks, and I feel an uneasy movement in my nether regions. 'Aw, cute,' he says lightly, his torch beam cutting through the dangling vines and highlighting a black and white bird on a branch. 'That's a pied monarch', he tells us, 'and he's fast asleep. The trouble is that he's directly above our path, and if we just press on we'll wake him up and he'll fly off into the dark and collide with the nearest branch, and might be injured. So, I'm just going forward to highlight a higher branch, and then I'll wake him up and he'll fly up out of harm's way. You lot wait here......'. Er, just a mo-: too late, he's gone. In the darkness we see his beam illuminate a branch and a moment later spot the monarch fly up to it. Amazing, truly amazing. I wouldn't be surprised if this guy could talk to the animals.

There's a certain amount of indecent haste as we press on to re-establish contact with our guide. 'Look at this,' he says, pointing to a tree with large heart-shaped leaves. 'This is Gympie Gympie, the stinging tree. You get a seriously nasty sting...' – there's that understated word again – '...from this tree. The leaves are covered in minute stiff, hollow hairs composed of a tough silica substance, the swollen base of which contains an extremely potent irritant made up of acetic and formic acids, histamine and...' – and he says this ever so nonchalantly – '...at least one other pain-producing chemical that has yet to be identified.'

He pauses for a moment for us to take this in, and there's a soft gurgling sound as twelve people all swallow in unison. 'The hairs are like slivers of glass, and if you brush against them they enter your skin and break off, injecting some of the irritant. At first all you feel is an itchy feeling, but this soon turns to blisters followed by an intense stabbing pain. Splashing water on only makes matters worse because the water enters the hollow hairs and causes further pain and swelling. If you're lucky, the pain would ease by itself in a few weeks, but you'll still be feeling something unpleasant for at least another three months, maybe longer.'

Someone asks if he's ever been stung. 'Yeah, once on the back of my hand. Once is enough. The pain lasted for four months; meanwhile that hand is effectively out of action, and, in a rainforest, keeping it dry can be a nightmare.' Someone else asks how intense the pain is. I'm sure he's smiling when he says 'From one to ten, around thirty'.

He continues: 'There's a story I've no reason to believe untrue about some lumberjack working up in the forest, hot day, wearing only his shorts. The tree he's felling suddenly drops the wrong way and he has to scuttle out of the way rather sharpish. Unfortunately, he stumbles and falls backwards full length into a Gympie Gympie. The pain nearly drives him mad. By the time his mates hear his screams, he's suffering from anaphylactic shock, and by the time they get him to a hospital, he's dead. All in just thirty minutes.'

Apparently even old, dried hairs retain the capacity to sting, anything up to forty years later. And no immediate cure exists. I resolve that in the morning I'm going out of my way to be sure I can recognise this tree anywhere, anytime.

This, I think to myself, is not a tree beneath which young love is ever likely to blossom, or on whose branches entwined hearts will ever be carved. Although it could make a nice birthday present for your mother-in-law...or maybe not.

We're all a bit quiet after that. So Anthony decides to cheer us up by asking us to switch our torches off, just so we can appreciate how truly dark it is in the rainforest at night. We go along with him, but I can tell everyone's listening in case he decides to take his leave. There's audible relief when we hear his voice again. 'If you look down at your feet, you'll see the glow of a fungus, a faint luminescence on the forest floor. That's a bioluminescent fungus, which only grows here. There's so much flora in this forest,' Anthony says. 'The scientists think they haven't even identified as much as ten per cent of what's here.'

Five minutes later, he stops by a huge earthen mound, at least ten feet in diameter and four or five feet high. 'Anyone know what this is?' he asks. There's a non-committal silence, which I decide to break.

'It's a nest.'

'Correct,' he says, 'now just eleven more correct answers and I'll guide you all out of the forest.'

Of course, he's only joking. At least I think he's only joking, but, hey, I don't care, I got the answer right.

'Yes, it's the nest of the Native bush hen. You may hear it calling in the night. It builds this huge pile of decaying matter and lays its eggs in there to incubate.'

Further on we pass a pool in which we can make out eels swimming lazily by.

'They wouldn't kill you, but you'll get a nasty shock from one of those,' Anthony cheerfully tells us.

I'm amazed, and suddenly very keenly aware of how dependent I am on this young man to get me out of here. I decide to stay close by him so that he'll remember me as the guy who got the answer right about the nest. But I needn't have troubled. We were standing only ten metres from the edge of the village, and no-one had noticed. You could hear the tension easing when he concluded his tour, thanking us in turn and hoping we'd enjoyed the experience.

Indeed, we had.

Captain Cook was responsible for discovering this part of Australia when his ship, the *Endeavour* ran aground on the reef about 40 kilometres offshore. All was nearly lost, but after some imaginative running repairs and a deal of good luck, the good captain was under way once more. He named the cape where he experienced so much anxiety, Tribulation.

Given the importance of this, I decided I wanted to visit Cape Tribulation for myself; it's as far north from Cairns as I can get by road in a regular vehicle – after that I'm an intrepid explorer in need of a four-wheel drive. I can't help feeling thankful that I haven't come prepared for intrepid exploration – no comb or toothbrush, and no four-wheel drive.

The area I'm in forms part of the Wet Tropics of Queensland, or Wet Tropics, stretching along the north-east coast of Australia for 450 kilometres and embracing almost 900,000 hectares of tropical rainforest. It's hardly surprising that this became a World Heritage Site, it is stunningly beautiful area and hugely important for its biodiversity. It also presents an unparalleled record of the ecological and evolutionary processes that shaped the flora and fauna of Australia, containing the relicts of the great Gondwanan forest that covered Australia and part of Antarctica 50 to 100 million years ago. It may be scary on one level; you so have to be alert to where you are placing your feet, where you're heading, what you are walking into or under or over, but it is truly magnificent, truly, truly stunning.

Of course, you never get dry here. Apart from the humidity, the average annual rainfall for Cape Tribulation is 3,900mm. In 2006, rainfall was over 6.5 metres and in 2010 it is said to have reached 8 metres; that's almost double the height of a London Routemaster bus. For that reason, the unsealed road north from Cape Tribulation to Cooktown, known as the Bloomfield Track, is often closed during the wet season (February to April), which I gather is a euphemism for it not being there at all.

I spent a couple of nights at Cape Trib, wandered out to Kulki and the knobbly bit that is the cape point, gazed out over the sea to the Great Barrier Reef, and wondered about a hiring a four-wheel drive to go further, but the rainy season was knocking on the door and I was persuaded not to when the local shopkeeper said: 'Well, if you don't mind being stuck in Cooktown for a few months, you go for it, mate, but you'll be out of yer bloody mind by the time you get back'.

I got the impression that there was a concealed message in this hearty recommendation. So, I opted for a retreat to Crocodylus and another session with the tree snakes, golden orb spiders and melomys.

CHAPTER ELEVEN

The Red Centre

Alice Springs – the Telegraph Station – the Desert Park (in the desert) – John Flynn and the Royal Flying Doctor Service

I'm standing in Alice Springs; not the town but the actual spring after which the town was named. It isn't really a spring, just a depression in the riverbed where water gets trapped on a layer of impervious granite. But I feel remarkably smug and self-satisfied just standing here, watching yellow-bellied honeyeaters, zebra finches and ringnecks flit about the gum trees as wedge-tailed eagles and Australian hobbies patrol the skies...and just a bit weird. I can't put my finger on it, but as I walk out into the bed of the waterhole something inspires a melancholic urge to spend the rest of the day sitting beside the spring letting the heat of the sandy streambed seep into my body, eavesdropping on the cosmopolitan conversations that come and go around me, and contentedly centred on my own being.

When William Whitfield Mills, one of the surveyors planning the route of the Overland Telegraph Line, came across this waterhole on the 11th March 1871 and named it after Mrs Alice Todd, wife of the Superintendent of Telegraphs, Sir Charles Todd, there had clearly been rain and the pools were full. But today, apart from a modest puddle, it's bone dry and sandy. Even so, I'm glad I made the short journey out of town to be here. It's a spirit place, a tiny but important dot on my life line.

One thing Alice Springs certainly impresses on you, if you take a moment to dwell on it, is just how in the middle of nowhere you really are. The nearest city is Darwin, a mere 1,513 kilometres (945 miles) or two days driving away; Adelaide is a slightly quicker drive, but another 30 kilometres distant. Cairns is 2,414 kilometres (1,508 miles) away; Melbourne, 2,278 kilometres (1424 miles); Sydney, 2,954 kilometres (1,846 miles), and Perth, a mere four-and-a-half days' driving at 3,628 kilometres (2,267 miles), and the greater part of that across some of the most intolerant and unforgiving terrain imaginable.

Within minutes of leaving town you are nowhere and anywhere. Travelling by road you soon get the message if you're heading in the wrong direction, but try to emulate the Aboriginal people by going walkabout and you could be in serious trouble if you get it wrong.

Close by the riverbed stands the original telegraph station, a fascinating place to explore, around which the town of Alice Springs spread. The Alice Springs Telegraph Station was midway along the overland line from Darwin to Adelaide, a development that played a key role (I'm not sure the pun was intended) in Australia's economic and international growth. Opened in 1872, the line suddenly reduced the isolation of Australians generally from the rest of the world. What this meant in practical terms, particularly in today's age of instant communication across the world, is hard to imagine, but it reduced the exchange of business and personal messages to hours instead of the months it previously took by sea.

By 1900, this very isolated Station was home to a cook, a blacksmith-stockman, a governess, four linesmen-telegraph operators, along with the Station Master and his family. There is no evidence that Mrs Todd ever bothered to visit the station or the town.

Almost in the exact centre of Australia, Alice Springs, usually just called 'Alice', is some 1,200 kilometres (750 miles) from the nearest ocean and 1,500 kilometres (938 miles) from the nearest major cities, Darwin and Adelaide. Alice Springs is the midpoint of the Adelaide-Darwin Railway, along which runs the famous Ghan.

To the south are the striking McDonnell Ranges, with all transport links to the south using 'Heavitree Gap', a pronounced narrow gap in the range where the railway, highway and Todd River run through. The Gap was something else named by William Whitfield Mills, in honour of his former School in Devon (England).

The landscape around Alice Springs is rich with mountain ranges, waterholes, and gorges, many of which are sacred sites to the local indigenous people. The Arrernte (pronounced Arren-de) Aboriginal people have inhabited the Central Australian desert in and around Alice Springs for more than 50,000 years; their name for Alice Springs is Mparntwe. According to the Arrernte traditional stories, in the desert surrounding Alice Springs, the landscape was shaped by caterpillars, wild dogs, travelling boys, sisters, euros (Kangaroo-like creatures) and other ancestral figures. Many sites are of traditional importance in and around Alice Springs, such as Anthwerrke (Emily Gap), Akeyulerre (Billy Goat Hill), Ntaripe (Heavitree Gap), Atnelkentyarliweke (Anzac Hill), and Alhekulyele (Mount Gillen).

Close by the town runs the course of the Todd River, for prolonged periods completely bone dry. In 1962, members of the Rotary Club of Alice Springs met for a picnic at 16 Mile Creek, where once a few beers had flowed they discussed ways of raising money for charity. One of their number, former meteorologist Reg Smith, came up with the idea of a unique, mad-cap event, a waterless 'Regatta' on the dry bed of the Todd River. The idea caught on, and so the Henley-on-Todd Regatta, poking fun at the Henley-on-Thames Regatta in England, is still held each year. Teams cut the bottoms out of boats, step inside and carry them along the bed of the river. The regatta is today officially recognised by the Northern Territories Government as an iconic event. Sadly, Reg died in 2004, but his spirit lives on in Alice.

Todd River is known as an ephemeral river, one that comes and goes, and has its source in the MacDonnell Ranges, where it flows past the Telegraph Station, almost through the centre of Alice Springs, through Heavitree Gap and continues through the western part of the Simpson Desert, where it becomes a tributary of the Hale River, before eventually flowing into Lake Eyre in South Australia.

Far from anywhere, and, as visiting tourists discover, scorchingly hot in summer, averaging 300 sunny days each year, it should come as no surprise to find that Alice Springs in recent times has seen new trials in the harnessing of solar power. The Australian news website (www.news.com.au) reported in December 2013 that between 2008 and mid-2013, this desert community of 25,000 souls was one of seven cities taking part in the federal government's Solar Cities Program, and in so doing solved many of its energy problems.

Sam Latz, general manager of the Alice Solar City program said in a report on the project, released in December 2013: 'Alice Springs receives an abundance of sunshine, but also has high energy needs because of its extreme climate' – it is bitterly cold in winter in spite of its location. Almost all houses have air conditioning units as well as electric, gas or wood heating for winter nights, and about a third of homes have a pool.

The program sought to increase the uptake of solar and energy efficiency technologies and support the community in reducing local greenhouse gas emissions. From just two solar power installations in 2008, by the end of 2013 the town had 700 homes connected, while the town's airport was the first in Australia to be powered by a large-scale solar power station.

Alice Springs now has more than four megawatts of solar

capacity, enough to power 860 average homes, and to meet up to 10 per cent of daytime demand. Solar water heating has accounted for greenhouse gas emissions savings of 28 per cent.

Rex Mooney, Chief Executive of the Alice Springs Town Council commented: 'At a time of great turbulence and uncertainty within energy policy in Australia, Alice Springs serves as a salient reminder of what can be achieved through active cooperation and partnerships between industry, government and the community.' He said the town set an example in the way it has engaged with its community to help them become smarter with their energy use, with a third of households and more than 200 commercial businesses participating in energy audits.

No doubt part of that power goes daily into Kellers Restaurant on Gregory Terrace, just off Todd Street. The chef, a burly man who rejoices in the name of Beat Keller, is Swiss-born. I turned up early at his restaurant in the centre of Alice, to find him and his one assistant waltzing precariously around one another in the tiniest of professional kitchens. What brought him from Switzerland to the centre of Australia, I asked. His response was as laconic as the man himself: 'Dark night; bad map reading'.

Once ensconced in the town, he decided to buy an existing Indian restaurant, which he wanted to call the Yodelling Maharajah, but since (I guess) that his father was stumping up much of the purchase money, it was subdued into a more eponymous Kellers, serving Australian-Indian-Swiss cuisine. I have to say he makes one of the finest fish curries I've tasted, using fish flown in daily from the coast, and my wife can vouch for the quality of his martinis. Billy Connolly said it was the finest restaurant in Australia… allegedly.

More recently, in a downturn in the central Australian restaurant industry, Beat has branched out into selling household and industrial products, not least, of all things, mouse traps following an outbreak of mice in late 2011. But the restaurant goes on, and is a place I visit every time I pass through Alice Springs... which is surprisingly often considering how far away I live.

Sadly, the restaurant is now closed.

Today we might ask: If reality is so good, why do we need an imagination? But in the mid-19th century, the reality of what lay in the very centre of Australia was limited and largely unknown. All anyone had to go on was imagination and self-belief, and it was this – and the prospect of a huge wad of commercial and economic benefits – that prompted the South Australian government in 1879 to agree to build a 3,178-kilometre overland telegraph line connecting Darwin with Port Augusta, conditional on the British-Australian Telegraph Company laying a submarine cable from Java to Darwin. The resultant Overland Telegraph Line, completed astonishingly in just two years, was one of the greatest achievements in Australia's history. It was to put Australia in touch with the rest of the world, and free them from a diet of stale news, often months old.

It is a monumental understatement to say that the task of constructing the line proved immense, not least because it involved crossing mercilessly brutal country about which little was known. The task of construction fell to London-born Sir Charles Todd, son of a tea merchant and grocer, and at the time Superintendent of Post and Telegraphs. Transport of the required 30,000 poles, insulators and batteries plus tons of wire, had been one of his greatest problems. Yet this formidable task, across a scorched landscape of pitiless heat, red sand dunes, little or no water and unending mosquitoes and flies was completed with the loss of only six men. Todd was given the honour of sending the first message along the completed link:

TERRY MARSH

+++WE HAVE THIS DAY, WITHIN TWO YEARS, COMPLETED A LINE OF COMMUNICATIONS TWO THOUSAND MILES LONG THROUGH THE VERY CENTRE OF AUSTRALIA, UNTIL A FEW YEARS AGO A TERRA INCOGNITA BELIEVED TO BE A DESERT +++

In addition to linking Australia with the rest of the world, the Overland Telegraph opened up the Northern Territory, speeded up settlement, and the growth of a pastoral culture. It also led to the discovery of gold deposits at Yam Creek, Sandy Creek, Pine Creek and many other sites, which in turn spawned a gold rush, gold fever, speculation and the formation of hundreds of Gold Mining Companies, during the early 1870s in particular.

In this day and age of modern communications, accessible at the click of a mouse or by pressing a button, it is difficult to get a real grasp of the difficulties of constructing the Overland Telegraph, and of the value difference it was to make to the people of Australia. But it has to be on a par with finding a little old lady with four arms and a pink dress making cheese on a planet orbiting a star a few thousand light years away.

It's a bright morning: not a cloud in the sky, and the temperature is already twenty-five and starting to flex its muscles. I'm keen to explore along the West McDonnell Ranges, an experience that has eluded me in the past. So, I leave Alice along Laparinta Drive and head for Simpson's Gap.

Simpson's Gap (tyunpe in the Aboriginal tongue, pronounced Choo-n-pah) is important to Aboriginal people, but it's also monumentally stunning. As I arrived, groups of people were gathering for a wedding ceremony that was to be performed there, right in the gap. I was too early for the wine, but early enough to catch sight of the black-footed rock wallabies, an endangered species, that bounce gracefully around the red rocks that have fallen from the sheer cliffs that flank the gap. I wandered into the gap, kicking up sand along the dry bed of the waterhole, taking pictures of ghost gums, and walking as far as the pool that remains. It has a powerful aura, one I'm not sure should be demeaned by the spurious thinking that brings people out here to be married. Why impose a Christian service on an Aboriginal sacred site? But then isn't that what Christians worldwide did with Pagan festivals? And, I suppose, that choosing to be married at a sacred Aboriginal site is in a way demonstrating respect for Aboriginal beliefs and talismans.

Tnenkarre (pronounced Art-nung-garra) is the framework for western Arrernte society. It is the traditional law that explains existence and guides daily life, providing rules on how to care for the land and each other. Often called the Dreamtime by non-Aboriginal people, Tnenkarre is extremely important in the lives of Aboriginal people. At the beginning of Tnenkarre, ancestral beings travelled across the land, creating the landscape, the people and all living things. The activities and travels have been passed on over many generations through songs, stories and ceremonies. Many features are regarded as special and sometimes sacred places, still cared for by the Arrernte people today.

Should I ever be challenged to build an attraction that explained to tourists how a desert worked – an unlikely event, but you never know – I'm not sure I would feel the urge to do so in an actual desert. I would probably figure that just by looking around you, the evidence would speak for itself.

So, it was with some scepticism that I approached the Alice Spring Desert Park on Larapinta Drive. A quick 30-minute whizz round, and I'd be on my way. At least that was the plan. More than three hours later, I'm still there, wholly absorbed in wonder.

I can see from searching on the internet that this surprising creation, only recently opened when I first visited, has moved on, and expanded its focus to one that more widely presents and interprets the Australian desert environment and its inhabitants, and contributes to the conservation of Australia's desert flora and fauna. Fundamentally, it presents a series of desert environments, including nocturnal, in a way that not only fascinates and holds your attention, but allows you to get close to Nature. It presents its story in a monosyllabic and logical performance that admirably suits dumbos like me, without insulting anyone's intelligence. I've been back twice since that first visit, when I was so engrossed that I had to adjourn to the on-site restaurant for pie and pea floater sustenance and then return for another hour. And for someone with a lifetime's aversion to displays of this kind and museums in general, that is some admission.

The Park site is of significant cultural importance to the local Arrernte people and includes parts of the Akngwelye Artnwere and Yeperenye Altyerre (Wild Dog and Caterpillar dreaming stories). As such, the Desert Park provides a sensitive and realistic insight into Aboriginal culture by demonstrating and interpreting the traditional use of plants and animals in liaison with local indigenous groups.

In late 2009, I had a coronary heart bypass graft operation, four bypasses to be precise. It wasn't something I had planned, but once diagnosed as potentially close to Death's door I gave myself up to the ministrations of the British National Health Service and let them get on with it. It was a positive, re-assuring and wholly professional experience for which I will ever be grateful, even though they declined to give me the video recording of the actual operation.

A couple of years later as I once more flew over the scorched heartlands of Australia, I wondered how things might have gone had the initiating heart attack occurred out there, in the vast middle of nowhere. That isn't meant to malign the Australia health service, merely a pondering on the practicalities of dealing with a heart attack remote from medical help.

Enter the Australian Royal Flying Doctor Service.

On the way to Simpson's Gap, along Larapinta Drive, stands a monument beneath which lie the ashes of John Flynn. Not exactly a household name, John Flynn was ordained as a Presbyterian minister in 1912, at the age of 31, and sent to investigate the needs of bushmen and women living in the Northern Territory. He found an almost complete lack of services that city people even then took for granted – just two doctors providing the only medical care for an area of almost 2 million square kilometres – and his report challenged the church to improve the lot of outback people. This led to the establishment of the Australian Inland Mission Aerial Medical Service, with Flynn as its first superintendent. Before long Flynn and his Mission had set up the first flying doctor base, in 1928, in Conclurry in Western Queensland. Subsequently, the service changed its name to the more Aussiely prosaic 'Flying Doctor Service' in 1942, and the Royal Flying Doctor Service in 1955.

The present-day statistics for this remarkable service are astounding. Each year, the aircraft fly in excess of 26 million kilometres (over 16 million miles), making over 75,000 landings and effect around 55,000 primary evacuations, inter-hospital transfers, patients transported from a clinic and repatriations, and road transports, and have a daily contact rate of nearly 800. And those hard-working two doctors have expanded into more than 1,000 employees, not literally, of course.

Shortly after Flynn's death in 1951, the RFDS was acknowledged by Prime Minister Sir Robert Menzies as '...perhaps the single greatest contribution to the effective settlement of the far distant country that we have witnessed in our time.'

Until the 1960s, the Service didn't even have their own aircraft; they used contractors to provide aircraft, pilots and servicing. Today, the service has a fleet of over 60 fully instrumented aircraft with the very latest in navigation technology. They operate 21 bases across Australia with their pilots annually flying the equivalent of 25 round trips to the moon!

Following his death, Flynn was buried where the monument now stands on Larapinta Drive, below the red crags of Mount Gillen. A large stone, as a marker for his grave, was transported from the highly sacred women's site Karlu Karlu (or the Devil's Marbles, as they are known today), and for over forty years the Warumungu and Kaytej people pressed for the return of the stone, which is tied to many stories, personal names and cultural beliefs. During the protracted negotiations, a replacement stone was procured from a sacred Caterpillar site and the two stones exchanged in September 1999. In 1994, John Flynn's efforts were acknowledged when his portrait appeared on the $20 banknote.

The drive to Ayers Rock Resort; Uluru (Ayers Rock) – the Dingo Baby Case – an unusual dinner – Kata Tjuta (the Olgas)

No-one visits the Red Centre without the intention of at least seeing Uluru, as Ayers Rock is known; but many come with the express hope of climbing it. Illogically, Japanese tourists have been known to ask for their money back if the park rangers forbid them from climbing Uluru because the heat is such that to do so would at best induce heat exhaustion, at worst death. And herein lies a problem.

The area around Uluru was settled thousands of years ago, and only 'discovered' by the white man in the 1870s. For the Aboriginal people, Uluru was created at the beginning of time by ten ancestors, spirit people, during what they know as the Dreamtime. Dreamtime is the essence of Aboriginal society, culture, traditions and spirituality, a time when ancestors, gods and living mortals come together to learn about the customs and cultural heritage of the Aboriginal people. Dreamtime is the crux of everything, and, of the many sacred sites in Australia, few are as important as Uluru.

DOWN UNDER DREAMING

The lands of the Uluru-Kata Tjuta National Park are the ancestral home of the Pitjantjatjara and Yankunytjatjara people, or Anangu as they are collectively known. According to Uluru Dreamtime, the world was an undistinguished place until the ancestors of the Anangu travelled across the land, creating features like Uluru. Ayers Rock represents the physical evidence of their time on the earth and is one of their most dramatic and inspiring creations.

Sadly, Uluru is the victim of its own reputation. Stac Pollaidh in the Sutherland Highlands of north-west Scotland is every bit as dramatic, awe-inspiring, remote and demanding, and it's higher, but there are no throngs at its base queuing to make the ascent. Much closer, Kata Tjuta, for my money, is infinitely more impressive, and just as sacred a place. So, what is it about Uluru that pulls the crowds?

To begin with it is truly awesome. It defies all expectations, and inspires the level of disbelief you'll encounter back home when your next credit card bill arrives. The Rock, which has the status of a national icon, was named by William Gosse in 1873, after Sir Henry Ayers, Chief Secretary of South Australia five times between 1863 and 1873. The Aboriginal, and official, name is Uluru (with a small accent under the 'r'). The rock was formed over at least 600 million years, and the area around it inhabited by Aboriginal people for the last 10,000 years. Originally the Rock would have lain at the bottom of a sea, but now stands 348 metres (1,142 feet) above ground. Even today, something like 2.5 kilometres (1.6 miles) of its bulk lies underground, although a tiny portion of me wants to question how they know that. But then, if scientists can use a mountain in Scotland - Schiehallion - to determine the weight of the earth, I'm not going to quibble about a few hundred metres of Ayers Rock.

The Rock is about 3.6kms (2¼ miles) in length and 1.9 kilometres (1.2 miles) at its widest, with a circumference of 9.4 kilometres (just under 6 miles). The climb to the top is 1.6

kilometres (1 mile), much of which is at a steep angle, while the summit is generally flat. The surface is made up of valleys, ridges and caves created by erosion over aeons of time.

By all accounts, it is an impressive mountain, and arguably its splendid isolation best appreciated in its entirety on the flight from Alice Springs to Perth, which often passes directly above the Rock. It's much the same going from Perth to Alice Springs. Unfortunately, from this angle it does look rather like a large rectal discharge from an animal I have no wish to meet, hopefully extinct.

On the drive from Alice Springs I set the car to cruise and let the kilometres slip by as I contemplate the bush, the kites and wedge-tailed eagles, the wandering lines of camels and the endless symmetry. It's enough to drive people mad; but I love it. I embrace it with the wholehearted intensity of an utterly new experience. The sameness is mesmeric, the sheer infinity of it mind-blowing: you can't take your eyes off it. I can see how it might drive some people crazy. The chances of seeing something spectacular - like a snake, a camel or a wallaby or two - are pretty slim, but you still look. For over 200 kilometres, as near as makes no difference, the road is straight.

At Erldunda Roadhouse, turn right, and continue for another 240 kilometres or so. Simple; yet at Yulara I overheard someone asking for a road map to get to Alice Springs! I was tempted to give them a piece of paper on which I'd drawn two lines meeting in a T-junction right angle. But the assistant smiles sweetly and explains how it isn't really necessary - but I've an awful suspicion I found them in Kings Canyon a few days later looking for the way out. Kings Canyon is a bit like that, but they shouldn't have been here in the first place; they wanted Alice Springs.

On the way, a huge red, flat-topped upthrust of rock with vertical sides claws at the sky. This is Atila, or Mount Connor, as stunning as any of the world's great rock formations, bigger than but yet so overshadowed by the attraction of Uluru that you may be forgiven for wondering why you've never heard of it. It is, not surprisingly given that by this time the mind is becoming addled with fatigue, often mistaken for Uluru. But when the real thing appears on the horizon, the difference is something that stays forever in your mind. Uluru is dramatic.

I drive on, but the scale doesn't seem to change. I don't seem to be getting any nearer. But four hours after leaving Alice Springs I finally pull into Yulara, Ayers Rock Resort, a desert oasis, a whole self-contained town neatly concealed among the sand dunes with but one purpose in mind – to service the needs of those who come to see Uluru. There's even its own electricity power station tucked away out of sight and earshot, where, one year, I went, beyond the light pollution to take pictures of star trails.

Before dawn I join the train of vehicles heading for Ayers Rock, pay the entrance fee and heading for the sunrise viewing area. Go by mistake to the sunset viewing area and you may have to wait a while for anything impressive to happen. In the pre-dawn light you can't miss the viewing area. Cars and mobile homes down one side of the road, tour coaches down the other, disgorging trestle tables, chairs, flask of tea, coffee, hot water, champagne, caviar, smoked salmon, plates of freshly laundered sandwiches, toast and cereals.

I park at an appropriate spot and start rigging up my camera and tripod as a brightening horizon fanfares the coming moment. I'm part of a firing squad of digital hypnotechno, solar-powered, nano-cumdiddlyo Mark 5, Series 6 camcorders and hulking SLRs with 20-metre zoom lenses: the economic value of the photographic assemblage must have run into millions. Oddly, I'm the only one using a tripod and cable release.

Then the moment of dawn when a dull landscape is transformed into one of heart-warming intensity, vibrant, yet subtle, too, growing quickly from a dull brown-orange to a vivid orange-red. All around a machine gun cacophony of shutters and video drives drowns the reveille calls of crickets, as sedulous flies instantly lace the air in well-rehearsed unison, probing any orifice not protected by insect netting.

And, in moments, it's over; a sudden and mass disappearing trick. The buses have gone, bound for Kata Tjuta, Watarkka, Alice Springs...wherever is next. Another quick tick on the list of lifetime's ambition. I'm left facing the rock alone, shooting pictures at one-minute intervals, and later moving off to the invisible borderline between those parts of Uluru that may be photographed and those that may not. The sky fills with cotton wool balls chasing their own shadows across the intensely red rock, and I'm lost in the power of beautiful and peaceful enthusiasms.

PS. I lied about the lenses.

PPS. The most awesome view of Ayers Rock is from the Kata Tjuta Viewpoint station over 30 miles away along the Lasseter Highway.

The ascent onto Uluru, which I confess I did twice in 1998, and once more since, is the traditional route taken by ancestral Mala men on their arrival at Uluru. As a result, the path is of great spiritual significance, and the Anangu prefer visitors to respect the cultural significance and not to climb. Alas, when cultures clash and sizeable investments have been made simply to stand here in fly-embraced sweatiness, human nature will have its way.

There's only one way to the top of Uluru, and it begins at a sign that announces the closure of the climb if the forecast temperature for the day exceeds 35 degrees – which is most days for much of the year. In practical terms, this means starting your ascent as soon as possible after sunrise, while it is still relatively cool. But, be warned: setting aside the cultural issues of whether to climb, this is no easy undertaking.

It begins with a highly polished slope at the angle of friction; not so bad going up, but an intimidating prospect coming down. A nearby chain is more hindrance than assistance, not least because it is festooned with 'descenders' of a nervous disposition, most seeking purchase on the rock with their hind quarters. Above the chain, heavily breathing wannabe summiteers gather to collect their thoughts and debate the wisdom of what they've started. When I first climbed the Rock, there was a small, circular pool of water here containing a few small crab-like creatures. On the way down, less than an hour later, the pool had dried up and the creatures disappeared into the silt.

A brief rock wall with polished steps deters a few, who then face the descent. For the rest, a short skirmish gets you above the wall, and, no doubt to everyone's surprise, a way to the highest point that is waymarked by white, painted markings identical to those found down the centre of a highway. Evidently something of a compromise that has the effect, like every public right-of-way in Britain, of offering not so much the freedom to roam as a constraint on freedom. Walk this way, but nowhere else.

The summit, marginally higher than the surrounding rock, is non-descript, and, while the view is a predictably far-reaching panorama of endless scrub, there is little real sense of achievement. So, unless you are threaded with a burning ambition to climb Ayers Rock, my advice is to go to the nearby Uluru-Kata Tjuta Aboriginal Cultural Centre, and learn about the Aboriginal way of life.

But I'm still having difficulty rationalising some of the climb/don't climb issues. The Aboriginals don't want you to climb the Rock, it's sacred to them. But they have painted a path trail on the summit for those that do, hoping to influence the route visitors to take, and although nothing prevents a wider exploration of the summit area, descending by other than the upward route is perilous. In 2015, a Taiwanese tourist was trapped on the rock for over 24 hours, having become caught in a crevice while attempting a shortcut, and had to be rescued.

Might it not be simpler to say that climbing on Uluru is

forbidden? But then, how much tourist revenue would be lost to the local economy? It's a long way to come just to stare at a lump of rock. Or is it? Most of those who visit Uluru, especially for the sunrise, are not there long enough to climb it. The issue was debated in 2009 when a dispute arose when the National Park proposed a ban for cultural and environmental reasons, supported by the local Aboriginal community, but the government in the Northern Territory set itself against the ban because it would hurt tourism. There's no denying the fact that the Rock is one of the world's most instantly recognisable icons, along with the Eiffel Tower in France. That alone is a huge draw for anyone.

But is it necessary to climb it?

There are arguably three reasons why people climb Uluru. One, because it's there. Two, because they have paid a lot of money and travelled no mean distance to see it. Three, to do so represents a sense of personal achievement. No doubt, for some, the ascent is a spontaneous response to the sheer magnificence of the Rock; it was for me. I had no prior intentions of climbing it. I just wanted to see it, to walk around it (which I also did, a few times), to try to understand its significance to the Anangu.

Well, two out of three isn't bad. I do understand that it is significant to the Anangu culture. I also can follow the storylines associated with that cultural dimension. But I'm not confident that my identification with the spirituality attached to the Rock by the Anangu is complete. I also wonder whether the ascent of the Rock might for some be a form of pilgrimage, a journey to a place of special or spiritual importance, similar to the many routes across Western Europe that lead to Santiago de Compostela. And who would deny a pilgrim?

By the time of my third ascent, I went because it was a special place, and much more than the top of a mountain...plus I was taking my son on his first and only ascent. Perhaps some of the elusive and evanescent spirituality had rubbed off on me.

DOWN UNDER DREAMING

You don't appreciate quite how big Ayers Rock is until you walk round it, a journey that can take anything up to three hours, or more if you dawdle to absorb the significance of the rock to the Aboriginal culture. For the Aboriginal people, the threads of their being, their society, culture, traditions and spirituality are drawn from Dreamtime, a time when ancestors, gods and living mortals came together to evolve the heritage and customs of the Aboriginal people. Dreamtime is the foundation of everything, and of many sacred sites in Australia, but few are as important as Uluru. The rock is said to have been created at the beginning of time by ten spirit people, ancestors of the Aboriginal people.

According to Uluru dreamtime, the world was a featureless place until the ancestors of the Anangu emerged and travelled the land, creating features like Uluru. The rock archives physical evidence of their time on the earth, one of their most dramatic and inspiring creations. That bit, whatever your beliefs, is astonishingly true; it is dramatic and inspiring and a host of other similar-themed adjectives. Numerous caves, cliffs, fissures and weathered scars contain countless petroglyphs that relay the story of the ancestors across the millennia. Rock outcroppings represent ancestral spirits, and the Anangu believe that by simply touching the rocks they can communicate with dreamtime and receive blessings from their ancestors. It may seem a far-fetched notion, and it probably is, taking an atheistic view of the world, but I still embrace whatever prehistoric monoliths I encounter on my travels, from Carnac to Callanish and beyond.

Uluru remains sacred to local Aboriginal tribes who still perform rituals in the caves and make new rock paintings. Each side of the rock has a different creation story associated with it, and these form the basis of Aboriginal culture in this central and very isolated part of Australia.

In search of enlightenment, albeit not of the spiritual kind, I called into the National Park Administration Centre and sought out Tony English, a bright-faced young man then with the unenviable job of managing the park. 'The original landowners receive twenty-five per cent of the money taken at the park entrance. At the moment, we're getting between three and four hundred thousand paying visitors a year.'

I do a quick calculation: that's a lot of money.

'What do they do with it?' I ask. 'They must be quite wealthy.'

'Not at all. The money is paid to the Central Lands Council, and each November or December is divided up between the seventy or eighty families who have original title to the land. It doesn't work out that much.'

The life of the Aboriginal people in Central Australia is as harsh and unremitting as the desolate and scorching environment in which they live. Setting aside the political dimension for these people, the Anangu, self-determination is proving critical. For over 30,000 years they have walked these desert plains, crossing and re-crossing their traditional homelands around Uluru and Kata Tjuta. Today, many of the community are found at Mutitjulu, a small settlement not far from the Uluru Cultural Centre, and the original site for the motels that served the early tourists. Poor nutrition, lack of exercise and poverty means that one in three Mutitjulu Anangu over the age of twenty suffers from diabetes. Almost 20% suffer from asthma, compared to an average of 11% in Australia generally. Virtually all the children of school age have ear infections of some kind, perforated eardrums or reduced hearing. When I came to pay my bill on leaving the resort a few days later, I noticed that two dollars (less than one pound) had been added to go to the Mutitjulu Foundation, an organisation set up to relieve poverty, improve education and health among the Anangu people. It was a small and in the scale of things fairly meaningless gesture, but my two dollars would be match by the company that owns Yulara on a dollar-for-dollar basis.

Azaria Chantel Loren Chamberlain was a two-month old Australian baby girl killed by a dingo on the night of 17 August 1980 on a family camping trip to Ayers Rock. Her body was never found, and her parents, Lindy and Michael Chamberlain, both reported that she had been taken from their tent by a dingo. However, Lindy was later tried for murder and spent over three years in prison. She was released when a piece of Azaria's clothing was found near a dingo lair: a new inquest was opened. In 2012, 32 years after Azaria's death, the Chamberlains' version of events was finally officially confirmed by a coroner.

An initial inquest held in Alice Springs supported the parents' claim and was critical of the police investigation. The findings of the inquest were broadcast live on television – a first in Australia. Subsequently, Lindy Chamberlain was tried for murder, convicted in October 1982 and sentenced to life imprisonment. Azaria's father, Michael Chamberlain, was convicted as an accessory after the fact and given a suspended sentence. The media focus for the trial was unusually intense and aroused accusations of sensationalism. The Chamberlains made several unsuccessful appeals, including to the High Court appeal, the highest appeal court in Australia.

After all legal options had been exhausted, the chance discovery in 1986 of a piece of Azaria's clothing in an area full of dingo lairs led to Lindy Chamberlain's release from prison. In September 1988, the Northern Territory Court of Criminal Appeals unanimously overturned all convictions against Lindy and Michael Chamberlain. A third inquest was conducted in 1995, which resulted in an open verdict. At a fourth inquest held in June 2012, Coroner Elizabeth Morris delivered her findings that Azaria Chamberlain had been taken and killed by a dingo, and an amended death certificate was issued immediately.

Numerous books have been written about the case. The story has been made into a TV movie, the feature film *Evil Angels* (released outside of Australia and New Zealand as *A Cry in the Dark*), a TV mini-series, a play by Brooke Pierce, a concept album by Australian band The Paradise Motel and an opera, Lindy, by Moya Henderson.

I'm not normally given to joining groups: I prefer my independence when it comes to travel, but at Yulara (better known as the Ayers Rock Resort) I make an exception and buy a place at the attractively billed but inordinately expensive 'Sounds of Silence' dinner. There isn't much silence about it given that a group of jabbering tourists sit at the adjoining table on the left – everyone talking, no-one listening – and a slightly smaller group of giggling and excitable 30-40-50-somethings rather the worse for too much free champagne, on the right.

But the experience is memorable nonetheless.

Dressed in such finery as I can muster seven weeks into a hectic trip, I join the throng for the drive out into the desert along an unsealed corrugated road that shakes my teeth to the point where I wonder if I might spend the evening sucking my steak rather than chewing it. Mercifully, the boneshaker ride, about which I've made far too much, is short-lived, and within minutes we disembark to be shepherded along a path to the top of a sand dune with distant dull-red views of Uluru and Kata Tjuta. Free-flowing champagne and endless canapés fill the time to sunset as everyone chats amiably to the company of throbbing ululations emanating from a didgeridoo played by Ken, who looks decidedly unhappy and keeps stopping to re-adjust the beeswax mouthpiece of his didge, which was melting in the heat. As the sun goes down we all 'Oooh' and 'Aaah' in orchestrated unison before being escorted to our 'dining room', a neat group of tables gathered in front of an al fresco cooking range; our walls are sand dunes, spinifex and desert oak, our ceiling the star-filled night sky. Al fresco dining brings you closer to Nature in more ways than one, as I discover immediately after the chilli pumpkin soup: alongside char-grilled chicken and steamed barramundi we help ourselves to dishes of emu, crocodile salad and the protein-rich kangaroo steaks with the undignified frenzy that hallmarks those who have paid for as much as they can eat and have every intention of getting their money's worth.

Before dessert, the table candles and the kitchen lights are suddenly extinguished, throwing the starlit sky into sharp relief. It is magnificent, it truly is, a spectacle that would have been sullied had the organisers tried to take the credit. But they didn't. Instead, along comes Liah, a resident astronomer to explain the sky to us. We are lucky; the absence of the moon's bright light means that we can easily pick out the great sweep of the Milky Way; the two Magellanic clouds; the Southern Cross - emblem of the Australian flag; Alpha Centauri - the nearest star to Earth (apart from the sun, that is); a few passing shooting stars, and four planets - Venus, Mars, Jupiter and Saturn. Liah does her best to convince us that by a process of imaginative dot-to-dottery the stars can be grouped into identifiable human or animal forms, but hits the nail on the head when she confides that many of them were first described around the time that red wine was invented.

Showtime over, and it really was a commendable show, Liah invites us to her nearby telescopes through which we manage more intimate views of the planets. As I approach, a Lancashire voice is heard to exclaim 'Well, bugger me, I've never seen anything like that afore. 'Ave ye seen this, Gladys? I can see Saturn's rings. It's bloody marvellous. By 'eck. Champion.' You can always count on a Lancastrian to pitch the tone of the moment.

Pudding and port complete the evening before we are bussed back to our hotels. It wasn't the best meal I've had by a long way; it probably wasn't worth what I paid for it. But it was unquestionably one of the finest restaurants, and I did go back a few years later.

Back in my room I'm field-testing another bottle of Rawsons Retreat Merlot as I write up my notes, and I turn to thinking about the experience; not so much the atmosphere, the food and the good company, but the sheer logistical practicality of it all. For a start, for the 800 staff and 400 residents who live and work at Ayers Rock Resort it must be like living on an island, but surrounded by sand not water. There's a whole town here, concealed in the desert. Most of it you can't even see, so well designed is it to blend in with the landscape. At peak capacity, during October and November, when there can be as many as 6,000 people at the resort, this is the third largest town in the Northern Territory, only being surpassed by Darwin and Alice Springs. The nearest source of food and drink is almost 1,300 kilometres (812 miles) away, down the Stuart Highway at Adelaide. The trucks that bring everyone out to the resort don't go back empty; they take all the waste, for recycling. Drinking water comes from the Dunes Plains aquifer and has to be desalinated and purified for human consumption.

Now Kata Tjuta is a whole new experience, and, but for the power of the distinctive shape of Uluru, which gives the Rock the edge, a much more evocative place to visit; one that doesn't involve any hand-wringing over whether to climb or not.

Also known as Mount Olga (or colloquially as The Olgas), Kata Tjuta takes the form of a group of large domed rock formations, or bornhardts, located about 365 kilometres (227 miles) south-west of Alice Springs. With Uluru to the east, Kata Tjuta forms one of the two major landmarks within the Uluru-Kata Tjuta National Park. There is a viewpoint station along the Lasseter Highway from which to take in the knobbly spread of Kata Tjuta. Ironically this actually gives a better view of distant Uluru, which appears as a low, black silhouette against the morning sun.

The 36 domes that make up Kata Tjuta cover an area of 21.68 square kilometres (8.37 square miles), and are composed of conglomerate, a sedimentary rock consisting of cobbles and boulders of varying rock types including granite and basalt, cemented by a matrix of sandstone. The highest point, Mount Olga, is 1,066 metres (3,497 feet) above sea level, 198 metres (650 feet) higher than Uluru. It was named in 1872 by Ernest Giles, in honour of Queen Olga of Württemberg (born Grand Duchess Olga of Russia, daughter of Tsar Nicholas I). She and her husband King Charles I of Wurttemberg had marked their 25th wedding anniversary the previous year by, amongst other things, naming Mueller a Freiherr (baron), making him Ferdinand von Mueller; this was his way of repaying the compliment. You scratch my back and I'll scratch yours.

To the Pitjantjatjara people, however, the name Kata Tjuta simply means 'many heads'; you'll see why when you get there.

At Uluru, the way to explore is by a circular walk around the rock. At Kata Tjuta there is the Valley of the Winds. There used to be twelve different walking routes here, winding through the valleys and gorges between the rocky domes. Today only two remain. The others have been closed, in part to protect the fragile environment, but mostly to allow the Aboriginal owners of the land to conduct their ancient ceremonies. But the area is not only closed to white people, it is also off limits even for Aboriginal people if they have not been inducted to the necessary level as specified by the cultural law, Tjukurpa.

I first visited Kata Tjuta in 1998, and it was this experience that has stayed with me ever since. Unlike Uluru, there was an almost tangible sense of place. Call it the influence of Dreamtime spirits of the forces of Nature, call it what you like, there is a power about Kata Tjuta that invokes awe and reverence.

As I entered the Valley of the Winds I felt compelled, as if by some unseen force, to move as silently as I could. There was no wind that day, just a heavy brooding silence, the heat radiating intensely from the red rock walls that soared all around me, and seemed to change in vibrancy as I moved onward. Somewhere ahead I heard the call of a bird, though I had no idea what it might have been; something primeval and prehistoric, no doubt; nor would I have been surprised. Behind me a piece of the rock wall, disturbed by a group of rock wallabies I'd seen earlier, finally lost its grip and bounced to the ground with a melodic ping that echoed five times. In some other place the sensations I felt might be described as eerie, but in the heart of Kata Tjuta the sense was one of privilege and humility, as if I was being permitted to witness the silent secrets of the valley. And if that sounds as though I'd been out in the sun for too long and that my brains were starting to fry, well, so be it.

There is danger here, and not just from wildlife, but from the very heat of the place, which can dehydrate you in minutes. Somewhat oddly, if mercifully, as I came to the end of the Valley of the Winds walk I found, of all things, a standpipe and tap from which issued a cooling stream of fresh water. It seemed so incongruous, just a solitary tap in the middle of nowhere, but I can well imagine that for some it could have been a life saver.

The man who killed a cow – Kings Canyon – a didgeridoo concert – a trip on The Ghan, across the Never Never

The drive to Watarrka National Park and Kings Canyon passes uneventfully, which is rather more than can be said for the visit planned by Ron Edgar, a Heritage Consultant from Sydney whom I met with his wife, Mary, at my Sounds of Silence dinner. A couple of days later we meet up again, and he tells me how his intended day trip to Kings Canyon ended somewhere around Curtain Springs when a cow, clearly demented by the heat, ran into the road in front of him. He collided with it at 110 kilometres an hour, sent it rocketing into the air only to watch it drop very heavily and with horrifying freeze-frame predictability onto the bonnet of his car. The cow died, the car was a write-off, and Ron and Mary were not a little shaken by the experience. The cow owners, the car rental people and the police were all very jovial about the event; it happens often enough here. But I guess Ron was thinking that next time someone else could savour the experience.

If there are 6,000 thousand souls at the Ayers Rock Resort during peak season, at Watarrka there's only ten per cent of that number. It is considerably lower key, and I for one hope it stays that way. Watarrka is mind-bogglingly precious, stark and primitive in a way that sets it apart from Uluru and Kata Tjuta. When I last visited Watarrka in 2004, it was the final place I explored before heading home, and I experienced a powerful spiritual urge to stay longer, to trek across the desert to that distance crag, to wander along that creek bed, to walk the Giles Track to Kathleen Springs. But more than anything I wanted to find a time of day when I could selfishly have the place to myself, to wander alone around the Canyon, to sit again peacefully beyond the waterhole at Canyon Head and marvel at the wonders and mysteries of Nature for a few lonely, private hours with just flitting yellow-cheeked miners and hovering brown falcons for company.

European visits began with Ernest Giles, the first white man to explore the country to the west of the Overland Telegraph Line. During his first expedition in 1872 he explored and named the George Gill Range, naming its highest and most prominent peak Carmichael's Crag, after his companion Samuel Carmichael. Reaching around 900 metres, the crag is in Aboriginal folklore a sacred woman's site, meant to represent a dingo mother lying down with her pups suckling. The Luritja people are the traditional custodians of the region, and have been present here for in excess of 20,000 years. Luritja is a generic name applied to people who speak the several dialects of the Indigenous Australian Western Desert Language, and thereby also to the dialects themselves.

Ernest Giles (1835-1897) was born in Bristol, England. In 1850, at the age of 15, he emigrated to Australia, joining his parents, and took up residence in Adelaide. In 1852, he went to the Victorian goldfields, became a clerk at the Post Office in Melbourne, and later at the County Court. But he soon tired of town life and went to the back country to gain experience as a bushman that would serve him in good stead during the five major expeditions he led into central Australia. In 1865, he explored north-west of the Darling River in the Yancannia Range looking for pastoral country and land capable of cultivating hemp, as it was valuable for rope at the time.

Giles keenly wanted to take up a pastoral claim at King's Creek, but for want of funds he forfeited the claim to the Tempe Downs Pastoral Association, which had brought in over 6,000 head of cattle by 1889. But tourism didn't get a hold until the 1960s; before then, travel in the outback was for the hardy or the foolish. The first facilities began to appear in the east at Angus Downs. There Jack Cotterill created Wallara Ranch and with his son, Jim, hand built over 100 kilometres of road. Today's Watarrka National Park covers over 71,000 hectares, largely the old pastoral lease area. Kings Canyon Resort is a product of modern times, coming into being only in 1991.

The George Gill Ranges spread like the ramparts of some ancient fortress along an east-west line through the red arid landscape 300 kilometres south-west of Alice Springs. The unending redness is punctuated by the dark trunks of desert oak and mulga which rise from the powder puff balls of straw-coloured spinifex grass. Between 440 and 360 million years ago, the Range was deposited in a shallow inland sea which covered much of Central Australia. 350 million years ago, earth movements squeezed and cracked the sandstone. These cracks criss-cross the Range at right angles, producing a neat pattern of tight-fitting blocks that are later eroded around the edges by wind and rain to form domes and widening the joint lines. Some of the joint lines have been eroded so extensively that they form deep crevices, metres wide, of which Kings Canyon is the largest.

I arrive at Kings Canyon Resort just after mid-day, and hastily check in at my hotel, before dashing off to the entrance to the canyon. It's too late in the day, and far too hot (the thermometer is on 45°C, that's 110°F) to contemplate doing the Rim Walk. So, I wander along the path that follows Kings Creek into the valley bottom, passing twisted river red gums, cycads, ferns and cypress pines. They've built a new viewing platform at the head of the canyon since I was here in '98, and anyone who takes the long diversion from the Lassiter Highway to visit Kings Canyon must be mightily disappointed if they think this is it.

Back in my room I manage an extended spa bath with an accompanying bottle of Lindemans Bin 50 Shiraz 2001, and then settle into bed reading Manning Clark's *A Short History of Australia*. When I awake in the morning the book is on my chest, and I don't appear to have turned any pages. Some would say it was the Shiraz, others that it was the history; maybe it's just the tremendous sense of relaxation this place induces, or the torpor associated with the heavy heat that lies across you like a restraining blanket.

I'll try a Chardonnay next time and a Stephen King novel to see if it makes any difference.

The next year, I did.

It didn't.

It's still dark, but I prepare for the walk, stuffing more than enough bottles of water into my sack. As I leave the Resort, the rocky profile of the George Gill Range sits squat on the skyline, its swooping sandstone flanks carved into great buttresses that have joined in battle with the elements for millions of years.

The walk around the rim begins easily enough, following yesterday's track along Kings Creek, but soon it diverts and ascends onto the plateau above. The climb is steep, and sufficient to deter those who should never contemplate doing the walk, which is no bad thing; fatigue and exhaustion are not conditions that are easily dealt with in the baking heat of the rocky terrain above.

Once above the ascent, a path leads round low bluffs, and past a display of sandstone cross-bedding that would have a geologist drooling with delight. These ancient sand dunes gradually subsided under the weight of yet more sand, compressing and compacting the bottom layers. At some later date, silica-rich water inundated the sand and cemented the grains together; the result is what we see today.

Ahead, beyond a stand of ghost gums (*Eucalyptus papuana*), a narrow defile is the dramatic entrance to a bizarre landscape, the Lost City as it has become known. It leaves you speechless. Piled everywhere on a baked surface of sandstone are domes of crusty red rock, like the primeval dwellings of some ancient civilisation. Here and there are gatherings of cycads, one of the seventeen species of plant that has survived here since the time of the dinosaurs. Elsewhere, fossilised jellyfish are embedded in the rock, and, incredibly, many of the tiny fissures are occupied by flowering plants, like the Minnie daisy (*Minuria leptophylla*), one of 600 plant species identified in the Watarrka National Park. But my attention is caught by a large section of flat rock cast into ripples, such as might be found along a seashore as the tide recedes. In fact, that's what it is, sand ripple rock, a compressed, hardened remnant of the beach of an inland lake or sea that existed here 400 million years ago.

What makes the rock special for me is the realisation not only of what it is, but the even greater comprehension that more than the signature of events that happened aeons ago, this is the last entry in the diary of one single day, 400 million years ago: the day the tide went out and never came back! It may have been a Tuesday or a Thursday, it may even have been Market Day, but on this one day, the waters receded, never to return.

I was astonished, mute with amazement, lost in the wonderment of my own discovery. I was even more bewildered to find, a few metres away, an information panel telling me everything I have just conjectured. And that makes me feel smug. Incredibly, whole troops of guided tourists stomp by without their leader so much as mentioning the significance of what they were passing through; it was the Rim Walk or bust, and to Hell with geology and heritage and prehistoric wonder.

The series of waterholes that have become dubbed the Garden of Eden lie in a narrow ravine lush with feathery cycads and ghost gums, and invariably filled with water. In 1998, I could push past the final waterhole and reach the Canyon Head and a view that would take your breath away if you fell into it, all too painfully if not fatally. Today I can't, and retreat from the gathering of fifty nubile bodies enjoying the chilly water and cool shade between the cliffs.

Back above the canyon, I wander off and find a secluded spot away from the main trail to have a drink and a bite to eat. I don't quite fall asleep, but it's so peaceful, so spiritual, so much the essence of outback Australia that even though in reality I am only a matter of minutes from civilisation and can in no sense comprehend the apprehension, trepidation and enthusiasms of those first explorers, I do feel at one with the landscape, and privileged to be here - not that I could survive unaided for more than a few days on my own.

Back at the Resort, I mooch around taking pictures of desert peas and wander along a boardwalk to look out across to Carmichael's Crag. This is one Hell of a wonderful place.

I was coming to the end of my time in Alice Springs, and decided to overcome my resistance to buying a didgeridoo. One of the problems was that so many of the didges I see on sale are vividly painted tourist souvenirs, not the sort of thing a serious didge player would be seen dead with. But then I'm not a serious player, I can get out of breath doing a crossword puzzle. Even so, I wanted something nearer to the authentic, but short of snatching one from the lips of an Arnhem Land Aboriginal, I was going to have to compromise.

In Todd Mall, I found my compromise solution. It came in the form of the sound of energetic and clearly talented didge playing coming from inside a shop tucked away behind rows of tourist didges. I went in to investigate and found the tall frame of long-haired Andrew Langford bent over a didge, setting the whole shop throbbing with his rhythms. Except that this wasn't just a shop; there was a theatre, too, and that evening Andrew told me there was to be a concert of didge playing to the accompaniment of keyboards and percussion.

The didgeridoo, or 'yumaki' as they are known locally, is just one of 400 names for the instrument. The name didgeridoo only being coined in the 1960s...Yidaki is the type of didgeridoo used by the Yongu people of north-east Arnhem Land, while those from the west of Arnhem Land know it as the Mago.

Cave and rock paintings, many thousands of years old, indicate that the didgeridoo has been used by Aboriginal people for over 40,000 years, and a number of Dreamtime stories mention the instrument. Today, didges, usually 4-6 feet long but occasionally much longer, can be made from many materials, but traditional instruments are constructed from a piece of eucalyptus tree that has been hollowed out by termites.

Aboriginal people, and accomplished others like Andrew Langford, play the didgeridoo by using a technique known as circular breathing, in which you simultaneously breath in through your nose and out through your mouth. This involves trapping air in your mouth and pushing it out with your tongue while you breathe in through your nose. I bought my didgeridoo from Andrew in 2000, an unadorned, simple instrument in the key of E flat, or D sharp as Andrew preferred to call it. I have yet to master circular breathing. It's a classic case of 'Those who can, do;

those who can't, write about it', but I keep practising, much to the annoyance of the dog.

Later that first evening in Alice, I settle into a comfy chair and wait eagerly for the show to start. About twenty didgeridoos of differing shapes and sizes and ornamentation are stacked on the stage, keyboards off to one side and Stage Left being occupied by the sort of percussive armoury that would send an orchestral percussionist into ecstasy. There were drums of all shapes and sizes, from Africa, Australia and central Europe, chimes, gongs, rainsticks from Mexico, clapsticks and an assortment of ancillary noise makers so obscure and diverse I wouldn't be surprised to find that half of them haven't been invented yet, or to learn that they were on some esoteric endangered species list.

It was a truly memorable experience, and one that I've repeated a number of times; even now, whenever I plan visits to Alice Springs, I make sure I stay overnight, and arrange dates around the evening didge concerts.

Across the Never Never: Darwin's railway station is about 20 kilometres out of town, and receives only two trains a week, which must be a huge disappointment to the city's train spotters.

Still, it's a massive improvement on what they had before 3 February 2004, when the inaugural journey northwards from Adelaide and Alice Springs completed the north-south rail link. That first entire journey was a momentous occasion justifying numerous dignatorial bums on seats and quite a few more mooning beside the track in welcome.

As rail journeys go this is something of an epic, 2,979 kilometres (1,861 miles) of a trek - not exactly commuting, then. In fact, this train journey is not about getting from A to B, any more than visiting a Michelin-starred restaurant is about having a meal; it is a travelling experience that hints at a lost era and the elegance of classic rail travel, and one that brings you into contact with the vast hinterland of Australia at somewhat closer quarters than a Qantas Airbus 320. True, you can learn a lot about Australia from the air; its size, the vast emptiness, the unchanging, seemingly unwelcoming land, a massive red parchment networked by dusty roads that appear to lead nowhere, and the cracked lines of river courses that rarely carry water. But The Ghan offers that and much besides, not least greater immediacy and intimacy. The lush tropical vegetation of the north, the red-ochre desert of the centre, and the rolling farmland north of Adelaide are counterpoints that challenge the myth that the heart of Australia is an arid wasteland of repetitive bareness.

The original Ghan, named after the Afghan cameleers who once crossed the desert, departed Adelaide for Alice Springs on 4 August 1929, but plans to extend the line northwards were soon abandoned, air travel and the unpredictability of the weather in the tropical north saw to that. It was described, somewhat dismissively as 'a train line from nowhere to nowhere'; but work on the northern section did begin, in April 2001, and completed ahead of schedule and under budget, the last transcontinental railway to be built anywhere in the world, a train that conquers the Never-Never, and defies the tyranny of distance.

In spite of its newness, there is something delightfully 'old-worlde' about the Ghan: the carriages date from the art deco era of the 1950s and have those memorable 'other time' qualities like wood veneer, stainless steel and hand-cranked Venetian blinds, all encased in long and shiny corrugated carriages that shimmer in the setting sun. It all looks a bit tinnish and outmoded so you expect a bumpy ride, but apart from a few creaks and the odd mysterious bump in the night as the engine deals with sleeping roos on the line, it is a remarkably gentle and dignified journey. That's the key, I suppose, it's a dignified way to travel, something that smacks of lost elegance, refinement and courtesy.

I'd been on the Alice Springs to Adelaide section on a previous trip, leaving Alice Springs during one of the most spectacular thunderstorms it had witnessed for years; apparently six Aboriginal people who had been sleeping off their liquidated gyro in the dried-up bed of the Todd River were washed away to their deaths when the river flooded.

More recently I have driven from Darwin to Alice beside good lengths of the gleaming new line, so I had some idea what to expect both from the scenic and comfort points of view. But The Ghan has a happy knack of exceeding everything you could ask for, ploughing steadfastly on at a nonchalant 40-50mph, and with those small but important touches, like friendly service, a wake-up cup of tea or coffee, newspapers, magazines, on-board commentaries, and a small but prized memento in the form of a lapel pin and certificate.

The Gold Kangaroo double cabins have their own facilities and are more than adequate and comfortable for two. The single cabin is less generous and encourages regular trips to the bar and lounge; nor does it have the use of exclusive facilities, other than a wash-hand basin. When the bed is lowered – while you're enjoying kangaroo steak or teriyaki king fish – available space is severely restricted. But, if you're happy to be closeted in splendid isolation then the single cabins are a great escape, and fit where they touch... sleep walking is not an option.

The beauty of the Gold Kangaroo accommodation is the ability to shut yourself away or join in, to come and go as you please. In recent years, they have introduced an even higher standard of service, Platinum. When you travel Platinum you experience the very best The Ghan has to offer: spacious private lounge style cabins; Premium en suite cabin with twin or double bed; panoramic views to each side; personalised cabin steward service, and much more.

Between Darwin and Katherine, where a scheduled four-hour stop allows off-train excursions (at additional cost, but not if you're travelling Platinum apparently), the landscape is spread with trees and shrubs – red gums, eucalypts, ghost gums, cycads – scattered homesteads and wide spreads of cathedral and magnetic termite mounds, the latter predominant in Litchfield National Park through which The Ghan slips. This is a place of raw and unrelenting beauty, and passing through it on The Ghan allows an appreciation of the austere landscape, and the pioneers who heroically believed they could cross it.

Pine Creek, 240 kilometres south of Darwin and named with typical Australian matter-of-factness because the creek there was lined with pines, brings a brief interlude of marginally more 'civilised' landscape, with fruit orchards flanking the track. But these belie Pine Creek's place in history as the site of a major Northern Territory gold rush when telegraph construction workers discovered alluvial gold.

The lonely outpost of Tennant Creek and the splendour of the Devil's Marbles are scenes passed in the night as The Ghan pushes on towards Alice Springs. Somewhere during the night we also pass the lonely outpost of Barrow Creek, an overnight halt for motorists. The Ghan staff joke that Barrow Creek is a township with a population of just eleven people, all of whom work in the local bar. Which rather begs the question that if there are only eleven people in town and they all work in the bar, who are they serving? The fact is that they serve motorists who want to break their journey between Tennant Creek and Alice. Even so, it's a lonely spot that only comes to life once a year in August when they hold the Barrow Creek Races.

At Alice Springs, more off-train excursions are available, but even with only a few hours available, it's worth opting instead to take a stroll around this remarkable outback town made famous by Neville Shute in his novel A Town like Alice. At the very heart of Australia, Alice Springs is not exactly a drop-in centre, but it has a tantalising and irresistible attraction that draws you back.

Back on board there's no stopping now, other than nominally, until the train reaches Adelaide. On the way, we cross the invariably dry Finke River, which extends for over 1,000 kilometres from the MacDonnell Ranges in the north into Lake Eyre, and is said to be one of the oldest rivers in the world, although these days it flows for its entire length only once or twice each century. The river is a popular meeting place for Aboriginal people, who call it 'Larapinta', meaning serpent. Many of the river's numerous waterholes hold cultural significance for Aboriginal people.

Shortly after crossing Finke River, The Ghan passes the Iron Man, a weird assembly of rail track impedimenta constructed (with a certain amount of alcoholic imagination) into the form of a man. It marks the site of the one millionth sleeper laid on the stretch of line of line between Tarcoola and Alice Springs.

The original line of The Ghan south of Alice Springs followed the route of the explorer John MacDouall Stuart, along a light, narrow gauge track well to the east of the present line. The old line suffered from flash floods, fire and damage by termites that, inconveniently, persisted in eating it. Travel was rather more haphazard in those days and legend has it that The Ghan was once stranded by floods for two weeks, and the engine driver shot wild goats to feed his passengers, which probably explains why goats appear reluctant to graze anywhere near the track these days.

Alas, much of the stretch from Alice southwards is passed unseen at night, unless you are one of those who can't sleep on a moving train. Dawn breaks around Port Augusta, and, if there haven't been any night time hold-ups (to let freight trains pass – they do own the line after all) or break downs (to tinker with the 4,000-horse power engines that pull the train), then it's a steady pull now down through the wheatlands north of Adelaide, flanking the Flinders Range of mountains.

This is a very relaxing moment. I'm not fully awake, but I've been in the lounge car since before dawn, watching the changing landscape slip quietly by, spotting groups of emus making the most of the field stubble, or black kites circling in search of something suitable for their breakfast menu. There are still camels here, descendants of those early beasts that played such an important part in Australia's history. But, like the goats, they keep their distance in case The Ghan breaks down again and suddenly everyone gets a taste for camel steak.

Somewhat too soon for my liking we're pulling into Keswick Station on the outskirts of Adelaide; pity, I was just getting into the sort of romantically fuelled state of mind necessary to get the most out of the history, culture and achievement of this great rail journey.

Maybe I should just have stayed on board and gone back to Darwin.

The Ghan, however, is not the only long-distance train in Australia. In 2007, I boarded the Indian-Pacific, which, as the name suggests, Links the Indian Ocean (Perth) with the Pacific Ocean (Sydney). This monumental train first ran in February 1970, and travels a distance of 4,352 kilometres (2,720 miles) in around 65 hours.

What makes the Indian-Pacific special, apart from its creaking journey through the Blue Mountains out of Sydney, is that the route includes the world's longest straight stretch of railway track, a 478-kilometre (297 mi) stretch across the Nullarbor Plain. I stood directly in front of the engine at one of the halts – a curious place with (then) just two inhabitants, who carried out a weekly fire drill – and gazed ahead at the arrow-straight track disappearing into heat haze. I was joyously bewildered.

That little town was Cook, and essentially a ghost town, in 2009 with a population of four. It is the only scheduled stop across the Nullarbor Plain, but has little other than curiosity for passengers, and is named after the sixth Prime Minister of Australia, Joseph Cook.

DOWN UNDER DREAMING

You've got to love a country where a 25-carriage, one kilometre-long cross-country train stops along its staggeringly long journey at a town with a population of just four.

CHAPTER TWELVE

THE NORTH

Darwin and the Top End – Along the Stuart Highway to Kakadu National Park – early morning trip on the Yellow River – encounters with crocs, a tawny frogmouth and thick-knees – unbearable mosquitoes and a midnight escape – On being a hero

Established in 1869, and having survived Japanese bombing during World War II and the breezy attentions of Cyclone Tracy in 1974, Darwin today, so the blurb tells me, is a '...modern tropical city with a relaxed personality'. What the blurb doesn't say is that it's rather prone to high temperatures – which shouldn't come as much of a surprise given its proximity to the equator – and around 150% humidity, which might.

Okay, I exaggerate about the humidity; it's only around 95%. But what this means in day-to-day terms is that you get condensation on the outside of hotel windows rather than inside, and trying to dry anything you may have washed (including your face) is pretty near a thankless task. More to the point, anything even remotely energetic, like breathing, raising eyelids, or thinking about getting out of bed, will have you trolling about in your personal soup of sweat, steam and bodily gunge. Don't even think about copulation; you would dissolve into a slimy, protoplasmic primordial globule in an instant...probably not the sort of climax you had in mind.

On the plus side, Darwin is the place to come and relax – notice I didn't say 'chill out' – to embrace the frontier ethic that still prevails in those Aussie towns and cities where there is a strong mix of white and aboriginal people. Throw in an Asian influence, and suddenly Darwin has the makings of quite a cosmopolitan little place, a multicultural centre long before multi-culturism became the vogue 'down south'. It just gets on with things, too distant from the mayhem of daily action in this vast country to care overmuch, and somewhat prone to a superb tropical ambience and a litany of rather inspiring lightning effects. Visit just as the wet seasons is brinking, and you'll get pyrotechnic displays to rival any, courtesy of Mother Nature. And all for free.

And, of course, you'll get rain, lots of it, but apparently not enough in the right places to meet the country's needs. Still, let's face it, anywhere that allows car registrations like BOLLOKS, FANNYS, FISHING, WATT 4, ONTHERUN, DAFFY and COZIKAN can't be all bad.

In the evening, scantily clad female backpackers, young, fit-looking and beautifully tanned, gather overlooking the harbour to watch the sun go down; scruffily clad male backpackers scan the assembled females like they're choosing a beer. I'd like to think they were in pursuit of universal happiness, harmony and understanding, but somehow I don't think this, or for that matter beer, is on their collective minds. With a herd instinct for survival all the young ladies gather together and move in close formation back into town to be picked off, one-by-one by the predatory sharks, or not, according to their own game plan.

In the town centre, rainbow lorikeets are roosting by the thousand and setting up an almighty racket. Aboriginal people are sitting on the walkway playing a didge and clapsticks (good), or just thumping the ground with a stick and yowling at the moon (not so good). Actually they play or yowl only as a potential hand-out approaches, not until – stand across the street for a while and watch, if you don't believe me; economy of effort, I guess. I give them a few coins – I like a good yowl from time to time – and move on wondering whether it was the right thing to do; not because they're Aboriginal, but because they're begging.

On the way out, passing through Singapore's Changi Airport, I notice the weather forecast for Darwin looked pretty malevolent, so I was expecting a bumpy ride; something, happily that didn't arrive. Storms come, storms go. But I did get chatting with Jim and Kathy Morgan, on their way back from England 'Thank goodness', by which I take them to mean that they were happy to be coming home rather than, necessarily, because they were leaving England; although they did say they'd spent a lot of time in Wales. Anyway, we chat about the recent demise of Steve Irwin, the zoological icon of Australia, and his bizarre death off the Queensland coast, and that takes us on to talking about snakes.

In my visits to Australia I've had a few close encounters with snakes: a tiger snake, that slithered right between my legs when I was walking through the rain forest around Lake Sinclair in Tasmania, the green tree snake and Amethystine python in Daintree and a small but apparently very nasty red-bellied black snake (Pseudechis porphyriacus) encountered at close quarters in a Sydney suburb. And then there was the huge snake in the backpackers' hostel in Perth, but that turned out to be a Danish penis.

Jim is banging on about taipans. Nasty and highly toxic, they were a problem where they live, above Port Douglas. Moreover, they can strike over more than double their own length, and don't content themselves with just one nip; they bite two or three times in rapid succession, just to be sure. He tells me he's been on a course on how to treat taipan bites, and noticed they only talked about bandaging arms and legs. 'What happens if one bites me on the arse?' he wanted to know. 'Well', the doctor replied, 'you have a nice tree outside your house and a fridge inside, so get yourself a cool stubby and die quietly in the shade of your tree.' Let's face it; you really do have to hand it to the Aussie health service industry for practical, no nonsense, down-to-earth advice.

DOWN UNDER DREAMING

Somewhere high above Bali, Jim tells me about a ringer, a cattle hand, who turned up rather the worse for alcoholic wear at one of the small airports. It seems this was his first flight, and Jim recalls how, once airborne, the ringer dropped on to the fact that every time he pushed the overhead call button, a beautiful young woman would appear and ply him with yet more alcohol. Inevitably he became more and more demanding, and started causing a general disturbance. Towards the end of the flight, a meal was served, and Jim and the air stewardess watched in silent amusement as the ringer tussled with the sealed packet containing the knife and fork he needed in order to eat his meal. The stewardess waited and waited, checked her watch, and then finally relented and unwrapped the plastic packet, and placed knife and fork firmly beside the ringer's plate. As he took his second mouthful she reappeared and whipped everything away. 'Too late', she smiled, 'we're landing now.'

Somewhere in the outback, every time a plane goes over, a grumpy ringer makes a rude gesture to the skies. If you meet him, don't let on you know why.

Drink was causing a problem elsewhere the day I reached Darwin. Still jetlagged I wander along Mitchell Street and stop at Café Uno for a Corona Extra (La Cerveza mas fina), which has considerately come all the way from Mexico to be with me now. But it isn't really a Corona I want; it's a Cooper's Pale Ale. But I've seen the ad by the door for Corona, and get confused. The guy on my right, from Holland, is having trouble, too, in his case getting a beer big enough. His starter, a bottle of Foster's isn't worth taking the top off for. He wants something bigger. Out comes a bottle of Grolsch; well, it is a little bigger, and 'It won't hurt you'. But this guy wants something huge with a great froth on top, which for some reason the Germans, Danes, Dutch and Austrians think is the only way to drink beer. 'Well', advises the bartender with droll insincerity, 'if you go up the street to Coles supermarket you can get a one-gallon stubby up there. Tastes like shit, but it's big.'

On my left, another guy orders a small glass of Chardonnay, but wants it watering down as he's on a strict medical diet, and must have no more than a half glass of weak wine a day. Once that is out of the way and his dietary strictures complied with, he's happy to take on a couple of Foster's and, as he's seen the Dutch guy with one, a bottle of Grolsch, too, before finishing off with a small brandy...purely for medicinal purposes, of course.

It's all mildly amusing, rather like the young couple who set up a stall across the street and are proudly advertising organic mangoes, straight from the orchard, although it doesn't say whose orchard. They're both wearing 'Top End' three-piece suits – shorts, singlet and flip-flops – normal attire here, although you do get a few two-piece Rambos who go around barefoot. While they wait for the droves to arrive, they have a fag each, and sit there letting cigarette smoke drift over the mangoes, which strikes me as profoundly odd. Sure, you don't eat the mango skin, but, well, I mean...

Darwin has always had the aura of a frontier town, isolated as it is at the 'Top End' of Australia; a steamy, tropical, far-flung outpost, separated from the rest of the country by days of lonely highway, or expensive domestic flights. Men (and a few women) came here to seek their fortune on the back of the mining industry, or in pearls. It was, by all accounts, rough and ready.

But things are changing, and although there are numerous empty shops in the central arcades, development is going on at a rate of knots. Soon, so I read, the 'excitement and mystery of Chinatown' will descend, as a large area is being rapidly transformed. Elsewhere, down around the harbour, whole scale redevelopment is going on, but it's too soon to say what's going to appear at the end of it all.

Drink is important to Top Enders, according to local statistics, which suggest that the people of Darwin pro rata drink more booze than the rest of the country, but then they do need rather more liquid intake. Food, too, plays an important part; the best restaurant in town (2006) is Lewinsky's on Mitchell Street, where, so the local wags would have it, 'the food sucks'...well, so long as it doesn't bite.

Kakadu is the largest National Park in Australia; at 20,000 square kilometres, it's almost as large as Wales (20,799 sq km) – hopefully Wales doesn't mind being used as a unit of measurement, but, just in case they do, then it's also almost half the size of Switzerland.

The traditional owners, the Bininj Mungguy, have lived on and cared for this country for over 50,000 years. Today, more than half the park is Aboriginal land, and all of Kakadu is special to its traditional owners, who manage the park in partnership with Parks Australia. The park is home to almost 300 species of bird, about one-third of the total species in Australia. There are also 117 species of reptile, and it's reassuring to know that only four of the 36 snake species present – the taipan, the death adder, the king brown and the western brown – are considered potentially lethal to humans. Amazingly, the Oenpelli python, long known to Aboriginal man, was only discovered by Western scientists in 1976, although that's not meant to imply that there is only one of them. Elsewhere, there are more than 2,000 different types of plants that vary dramatically as you drive from one part of Kakadu to another, and provide an ever-changing backdrop to time spent here. The coastal mangrove areas blend into expansive flood plains and lowland hills flanked to the east by sandstone escarpments, all interwoven between open woodland and forest habitats.

This is a timeless place that even now, many years after my first visit, thrills me, frightens me and brings back a few painful memories. Kakadu is a cultural landscape, and awarded World Heritage Status for its outstanding cultural and natural values, with one of the finest collections of rock art in the world.

I first visited Kakadu in 1998, driving out from Darwin

optimistically and with an air of adventure along the Arnhem Highway. About 100 kilometres out from Darwin, having stopped a few times en route to check out the towering cathedral termite mounds, some more than six metres high, I reach the famed Bark Hut Inn just in time for a connoisseur's lunch - a pie and pea floater and a beer. Not too far away, I decide to investigate the Annaburroo Billabong. In retrospect, I'm not sure it was one of my better ideas, not least because there are over 10,000 crocodiles in Kakadu (an average of one for every 2 sq km), and they do like to lurk in billabongs, as the plentiful warning signs seem to delight in telling you. On the plus side, there a countless barramundi, one of the finest fishes you'll taste anywhere.

There are two species of crocodile in Kakadu: the freshwater crocodile (*Crocodylus johnstonii*), aka 'Freshie', and the estuarine, or saltwater, crocodile (*C. porosus*), aka 'Saltie'. If you have the time or inclination to think about such things, freshwater crocodiles are identified by their narrow snout and a single row of four large dermal plates (known as scutes) immediately behind the head. Estuarine crocodiles do not have these scutes and their snout is broader. These salties are most common in tidal rivers, floodplain billabongs and coastal waters, but are also found in freshwater billabongs and waterways as far inland as the base of the Arnhem Land escarpment. This information is useful to have so that, in the event of your being snapped by a croc, and surviving, then you can be confident of describing your attacker to the park authorities, after all, it's unfair to blame a freshie for something a saltie did.

Alert to the possibility of crocodilian ambush, I move as silently as I can through the scrub and speargrass fringing the billabong, and find myself in a dense woodland. I stop to relieve myself, and when I look up see a pair of barking owls directly above my head, snoozing through the day until night falls. One is half awake, and woofs at me softly, like a disgruntled puppy, watching me as I move on.

About an hour into the woodland, I come to a clearing containing a ramshackle shack and two gents of the hill-billy persuasion loading up a truck. They greet me affably, and the thought never enters my head that I might be entering the final moments of my life; no-one knows I'm here, and my only defence against attack is my camera, an expensive Nikon. But I had no need to fear; squabbling like a pair of old women, they offered me a lift back to Annaburroo, seated somewhat bizarrely on a three-seater sofa lashed to a trailer at the back of their truck. It was all rather magisterial in an hallucinogenic kind of way.

I drive further into Kakadu, making for the small centre of Ubirr and the famed Nourlangie Rock, today known as Burrunggui. In the event, Ubirr is inaccessible because of flooding, and so it is that I find myself in Jabiru. It is here that I encounter the Kakadu state bird, otherwise known as the mosquito. These little monsters are everywhere, with a pneumatic proboscis that penetrates any and all forms of clothing. If you can list all the adjectives that describe evil, then the Kakadu mossie ticks all of them. Stay well away from the water areas where they breed, and you may never notice them, but the Jabiru campsite, as it is in 1998, is close to the Yellow River, and that is not good. I don't have a tent, but I go to the campsite anyway in the hope of getting into one of their cabin rooms, best described as a skip with a roof and air conditioning. But they are fully booked until tomorrow. So, it comes to the last thing I want, an uncomfortable – I am yet to learn just how uncomfortable – night in the car, in temperatures well above 30°C.

No matter what I do, the mosquitoes have an answer. If I close the windows, it is to find that I have contrived to confine a few dozen inside. They are the advance guard, marking out the most tender parts of my anatomy for the troops that are to follow. With towels and jackets over my head in the hope of protection, I swelter to the point of expiry, all to no avail. So, in a moment of burgeoning madness, I decide to try to sleep underneath the car. Just getting there admits a few trillion mossies into the car, which means it is never going to be safe to return, while the little blighters send out night patrols in search of anyone sleeping under cars. Then a light bulb moment...mossies don't like the cold, and the campsite shower rooms have air conditioning. So, off I trot, only to find the shower rooms filled with mossies cooling off from the heat outside, not that I could have slept with the air conditioning on anyway. As I return to the car, a barking owl on a rotary washing line woofs at me, mockingly. I'm just not cut out for mossie wars, and stumble about on the point of tears. They say these mossies can make a grown man cry; it's true.

Finally, somewhere around two in the morning, with campers in mossie coil-protected tents snoozing away, I hit on the idea of opening all the windows on the car, and the tailgate, and driving off the campsite at speed to waft the mossies out. And it works; I get rid of all of them within two minutes of leaving the campsite. On the way, I swerve round a thick knees patrolling the road, and screech to a halt just before running over a tawny frogmouth sitting in the middle of the road. Safely parked down some side road, miles from anywhere, I finally close the car down and get some sleep, cursing that I hadn't thought of this ploy hours earlier.

With the dawn, I am already bound for Burrunggui, one of the most astonishing locations depicting rock art anywhere in the world. All the art deals with Aboriginal mythology, and the setting, an outlying formation of the Arnhem Land Escarpment, is mesmeric. The paintings represent one of the longest historical records of any group of people in the world, a remarkable record of human interaction with the environment over many thousands of years. Some 5,000 art sites have been recorded, and a further 10,000 sites are believed to exist. Concentrated along the escarpment, in gorges, and on rock outliers, the art sites display a range of styles including naturalistic paintings of animals and traditional x-ray art. There are some recent depictions, notably those that capture the first contact of Westerners with the Aboriginal people, and, so our guide tells us, many of the paintings are 'touched up' and revived with new colour as they fade.

Itching from head to toe and beyond mossie bites, I nevertheless feel privileged to be here, and make the most of the opportunity to wander the surrounding countryside that has since become cloistered into walkways and corrals of Aboriginal interpretation. It was here that I met Tansi Baker. It wasn't an auspicious meeting, since she had driven into the shade of a grove of trees and not noticed the spongy ground ahead. As a result, her car was well and truly bogged down, a circumstance not improved by the sixty large bottles of water she carried in the boot of the car. Fortunately, for her, I had just met an English couple touring in a powerful 4-wheel drive Aussie Land Rover whom I was able to bring to the rescue. Later that day, boarding for a cruise on the Yellow River, I meet Tansi again, and am introduced to her family as some kind of hero. Well, there has to be a first time for everything.

On reflection, unless you are tolerant of mossie bites or well dosed to the point of over-dose with antihistamine, then a visit to Kakadu is not a good idea at the start of a visit to Australia. Go as you are about to bid farewell to the country, and after an irritating flight home, at least you can savour counting the spots in the comfort of your own home...I gave up counting at 500, and I could still feel them a week later. But, in spite of the discomfort, I would not use that as a reason to forego a return visit...nor did I.

North to south, the drive from Darwin to Adelaide, calling in at Katherine Gorge, the Devil's Marbles and Tennant Creek

I think it must have been the third bottle of chardonnay that persuaded me that to drive from Darwin to Adelaide would be a giggle, a mere 2,616 kilometres (1,625 miles). The other thing that was in retrospect a trifle bizarre was that although my wife was with me, I have no recollection of her presence in Darwin. She didn't appear in my overloaded memory until we reach the Devil's Marbles, and that was two days into the drive. I wonder where she got to.

We – my invisible wife and I – took time out to take a half-day boat safari into Katherine Gorge, known locally as Nitmiluk National Park. The fact that I shot five rolls of film seemed to amuse the driver, or whatever you call them. Of course, he didn't know what a lousy photographer I am, and that I figured that even I had to get a least a couple of half-way decent pictures from over 150.

I didn't, and had to go back the next year, when I didn't take my wife just in case I lost her for real.

This 292,800-hectare National Park is owned by the Jawoyn Aboriginal people and jointly managed with the Parks and Wildlife Commission of the Northern Territory. In the language of the Jawoyn, Nitmiluk means 'place of the cicada dreaming'. It is a magnificent deep gorge carved through ancient sandstone that is both 'tourist pretty' and 'geologist magnificent', admittedly qualities it shares with an awful lot of Australia.

Although many parts of the gorge are described as ideal for canoeing and swimming, the fact remains that freshwater crocodiles are widely distributed along the river year-round. During the wet season, rises in water levels may allow saltwater crocodiles to enter the gorge, where they are captured and returned to lower levels when the dry season begins. 'Freshies', as they call the freshwater crocs, are allegedly harmless to humans, but if you see one swimming towards you, are you going to ask for ID before deciding whether to head back to the riverbank?

But for me, the interest lay in the birdlife. Every time I've been to Australia I've had to buy a new 'Birds of Australia' guide because I forget, and leave the ones I have at home. So, I figure that birdwatching has to feature somewhere in each day if only to justify the expense. In this respect, there is nothing to beat northern Queensland, but Katherine Gorge is home to a number of endangered species including the elusive Gouldian finch. Elsewhere I noticed osprey, red-tailed black cockatoo, bowerbird, white-gaped Honeyeaters and red-winged parrots plus a couple of thousand flying fox hanging from the branches of trees directly above the boat jetty and depositing free-range guano on all and sundry that pass below. Just one of the perks of a Katherine Gorge visit.

I had promised myself a visit to the so-called Devil's Marbles when I first saw a picture of them on the wall of my local gymnasium. Quite why it should feature in the gym no-one seemed to know; it was just a lovely picture I guess. But it hatched a plan to visit. Alas, a few years were to pass before it happened, but, heading south on the Stuart Highway from an overnight halt in Tennant Creek the Marbles – Karlu Karlu in local-speak – are unavoidable.

The Marbles are of great cultural and spiritual significance to the Aboriginal owners of the land, and the Karlu Karlu/Devil's Marbles Conservation Reserve protects one of the oldest religious sites in the world. The English name comes from John Ross, part of the Australian Overland Telegraph Line expedition in 1870, who wrote: 'This is the Devil's country; he's even emptied his bag of marbles around the place!'

Geologically, the Marbles are large granitic boulders that form the exposed top layer of an extensive and largely subterranean granite formation. The natural processes of weathering and erosion have created weird shapes with some of the boulders naturally but precariously balanced on top of one another or on larger rock formations, while others have been split cleanly down the middle by natural forces.

The natural geological formations of Australia, all of them significant in Aboriginal history, will amaze and dumbfound anyone with even a modicum of curiosity. Karlu Karlu are no exception, and most of the reserve is a Registered Sacred Site, protected under the Northern Territory Aboriginal Sacred Sites Act. Aboriginal mythology holds that the Karlu Karlu boulders are the eggs of the Rainbow Serpent. One of the boulders was taken to Alice Springs in 1952 to form a memorial to John Flynn, the founder of the Royal Flying Doctor Service. The boulder, chosen as a symbol of Flynn's link to the outback, however, became the source of controversy having been unwittingly removed from a site sacred to the Aboriginal women of the area. It took 45 years of negotiation before a boulder swap was arranged and the sacred boulder returned to its original place in early September 1999. The grave is now marked with a similar but non-sacred boulder donated by the Arrernte people.

What is so telling about this is that it reflects not so much the Aboriginal people scoring cultural points, or the modern population of Australia acknowledging the injustices of the past, but of both peoples underpinning a very deep-rooted cultural heritage that to outsiders like me is stunningly and endlessly fascinating.

For reasons that have no validity whatsoever, I had somehow come to look upon Tennant Creek, 1,000 kilometres south of Darwin and 500 kilometres north of Alice Springs, as the archetypal Walkabout Creek in the 'Crocodile Dundee' films.

This remote township of just over 3,000 souls, is nothing like Walkabout Creek. The locals of Tennant Creek enjoy modern facilities including an airport, The Ghan railway halt, sporting venues, art galleries, a civic hall, a primary and a high school and library. It's also home to Australia's premier go-karting event, held on a street circuit through the town.

European history of the area began in 1860 when explorer John McDouall Stuart passed by on an unsuccessful first attempt to cross the continent from south to north. He named a creek to the north of town after John Tennant, a financier of his expedition and a pastoralist from Port Lincoln, South Australia, in gratitude for the financial help provided for Stuart's expeditions across Australia.

Aboriginal people have lived in this region (Barkly) for over 40,000 years, a place steeped in the ancient traditions and beliefs of its traditional custodians, and nine or so Aboriginal groups call the area home, including the Warumungu, Warlpiri, Kaytetye and Alyawarre people.

Perhaps surprisingly, given its comparative isolation, Tennant Creek has a rich and colourful musical community, and the Winanjjikari Music Centre is home to emerging singers, songwriters and musicians. In 2003, the award-winning Nyinkka Nyunyu Cultural Centre was opened, a purpose-built centre housing exhibitions on local history from an Aboriginal point of view, cultural displays and local artwork.

Tennant Creek was the site of Australia's last gold rush – during the 1930s, when the town became the third-largest gold producer in Australia. Gold was discovered three miles north of the town in 1926. The following year, Charles Windley, a telegraph operator, found gold on what would become Tennant Creek's first mine, the Great Northern. Australia's last great Gold Rush did not commence, however, until after Frank Juppurla, a local indigenous man, took gold to telegraph operator Woody Woodruffe in December 1932.

In the event, I miscalculated the daily distances I had to drive after leaving Tennant Creek in order to get to Adelaide in time to catch the west-going Indian Pacific train service to Perth. So, to cover my embarrassment, we decided to fly direct from Alice Springs, and I treated my wife, who had somehow miraculously re-appeared, to a night in one of Adelaide's finest hotels.

Sometimes you just have to eat 5-star humble pie.

APPENDIX

A Few Words of Aussie Slang

If it's sometimes difficult to get your tongue around many of the Aboriginal place names, it can be equally mystifying to follow, without the aid of alcohol, many of the Aussie slang words that are in frequent use. Australian slang, known as 'Strine', is a way of using certain words and phrases that have become iconic to Australians. Here is a small selection:

Aerial ping-pong: Australian Rules football
Amber fluid: beer
Ankle-biter: child
Arvo: afternoon
Aussie salute: brushing away flies with the hand
Barbie: barbeque
Bastard: term of endearment
Bitzer: mongrel dog (bits of this and bits of that)
Black Stump, beyond the: a long way away, the back of nowhere
Bush oyster: nasal mucus
Bush telly: campfire
BYO stands for 'Bring your own', and means that you can take your own drinks to a restaurant. It makes eating out more affordable.
Chook: a chicken
Dunny: toilet
Esky: ice box
Figjam: "F*ck I'm good; just ask me". Nickname for people who have a high opinion of themselves.

Idiot box: television
Kangaroos loose in the top paddock: Intellectually inadequate ("he's got kangaroos loose in the top paddock")
Liquid laugh: vomit
Never Never: The Outback, centre of Australia
Rug up: dress warmly
Shark biscuit: somebody new to surfing
Slab: pack of 24 cans of beer
Swamp donkey: unattractive woman
Technicolor yawn: vomit
Thongs: flip flops, cheap rubber backless sandles
Tittybong: the act of the female appendage leaping from its cotton, underwired prison, assisted or otherwise.
Trough lolly: the solid piece of perfumed disinfectant in a men's urinal
White pointers: topless (female) sunbathers
Wuss: a coward
XXXX: pronounced Four X, brand of beer made in Queensland
Yobbo: a rowdy/loud/disruptive person